Sartorial Japonisme and the Experience of Kimonos in Britain, 1865–1914

Using interdisciplinary research and critical analysis, this book examines experiences through (or with) kimonos in Britain during the late Victorian and Edwardian periods.

Bringing new perspectives to challenge the existing model of 'Japonisme in fashion' and introducing overlooked contacts between kimonos and people, this book explores not only fine arts and department stores but also a variety of theatres and cheap postcards. Putting a particular focus on the responses and reactions elicited by kimonos in visual, textual and material forms, this book initiates an entirely new discussion on the British adoption of Japanese kimonos beyond the monolithic view of the relationship between the East and West.

This book will be of interest to scholars working in fashion studies, British studies, Japanese studies, design history and art history.

Arisa Yamaguchi is Assistant Professor at the University of Tsukuba, Japan.

Routledge Research in Design History

Routledge Research in Design History is a new series focusing on the history of designed objects, including architecture, fashion, crafts, interiors, textiles and graphic design. Proposals for monographs and edited collections on this topic are welcomed.

Art, Design and Capital Since the 1980s
Production by Design
Bill Roberts

Nordic Design Cultures in Transformation, 1960–1980
Revolt and Resilience
Edited by Kjetil Fallan, Christina Zetterlund and Anders V. Munch

Design Theory, Language and Architectural Space in Lewis Carroll
Caroline Dionne

Design, Displacement, Migration
Spatial and Material Histories
Edited by Sarah A. Lichtman and Jilly Traganou

Sartorial Japonisme and the Experience of Kimonos in Britain, 1865–1914
Arisa Yamaguchi

For more information about this series, please visit: https://www.routledge.com/Routledge-Research-in-Design-History/book-series/RRDH

Sartorial Japonisme and the Experience of Kimonos in Britain, 1865–1914

Arisa Yamaguchi

Designed cover image: Philip Wilson Steer. *The Japanese Gown*, 1896. Oil on canvas. 127.5 x 102.2cm. National Gallery of Victoria, Melbourne. 264-2

First published 2024
by Routledge
605 Third Avenue, New York, NY 10158

and by Routledge
4 Park Square, Milton Park, Abingdon, Oxon, OX14 4RN

Routledge is an imprint of the Taylor & Francis Group, an informa business

© 2024 Arisa Yamaguchi

The right of Arisa Yamaguchi to be identified as author of this work has been asserted in accordance with sections 77 and 78 of the Copyright, Designs and Patents Act 1988.

All rights reserved. No part of this book may be reprinted or reproduced or utilised in any form or by any electronic, mechanical, or other means, now known or hereafter invented, including photocopying and recording, or in any information storage or retrieval system, without permission in writing from the publishers.

Trademark notice: Product or corporate names may be trademarks or registered trademarks, and are used only for identification and explanation without intent to infringe.

ISBN: 978-1-032-36871-9 (hbk)
ISBN: 978-1-032-36872-6 (pbk)
ISBN: 978-1-003-33425-5 (ebk)

DOI: 10.4324/9781003334255

Typeset in Sabon
by codeMantra

To my mother, Mayumi

Contents

List of Figures	*ix*
Acknowledgements	xv

Introduction   1
Dress History 2
Japonisme and Orientalism 3
From Fashion to Experience 5
'Kimono' in Britain 8
The Framework 8

1   Translating Bodies   15
Fine Art, 1865–1900 15
West End, 1885–1905 36

2   Creating Fashion   59
Aestheticism to Department Stores: Luxury Kimonos, 1879–1914 60
New Japonisme of the New Century, 1900–1914 74

3   Making it 'Picturesque'   93
Fancy Dressed Described, 1887, 1896 93
The Devonshire's House Ball, 1897 100
Grand Japanese Bazaar, 1882 103
Amateur Theatricals, 1900–1914 105

4   Educating People   111
The Japanese Native Village, 1885 111
The Japanese Exhibition at the Whitechapel Art Gallery, 1902 117
The Japan-British Exhibition, 1910 121
Variety Theatres, 1867–1914 125

viii *Contents*

5 Circulating Beyond 138
Postcards and the Visual Culture of Edwardian Britain 138
Kimonos in Edwardian Postcards, 1900–1914 142
Kimonos for Cross-Dressing, 1905 149

Conclusion 162

Index 165

Figures

1.1 James-Jacques-Joseph Tissot. *Japonaise au Bain, huile sur toile* (Japanese Girl Bathing), 1864.Oil on canvas. 208 × 124 cm. Musée des beaux-arts de Dijon. Inv. 2831 and J167.© Musée des Beaux-Arts de Dijon/François Jay   17

1.2 Jacques Joseph Tissot. *Young Lady Holding Japanese Objects*, 1865. Oil on panel. 46 × 36.5 cm. © Peter Nahum at The Leicester Galleries, London   18

1.3 Jacques-Joseph James Tissot (1836–1902), *Young Women Looking at Japanese Articles*, 1869. Oil on canvas. 70.5 × 50.2 cm. Cincinnati Art Museum, Ohio, USA. CIN408385. © Cincinnati Art Museum /Gift of Henry M. Goodyear, M.D./Bridgeman Images   19

1.4 Dante Gabriel Rossetti. *The Beloved ('The Bride')*, 1865–1866. Oil on canvas. 82.5 × 76.2 cm. Tate, London. 3053. © Tate, Photo: Tate   20

1.5 James Abbott McNeil Whistler. *The Princess from the Land of Porcelain*, 1863–1864. Oil on canvas. 201.5 × 116.1 cm. Freer Gallery of Art, Smithsonian Institution, Washington, D.C. F1903.91a-b   22

1.6 James Abbott McNeil Whistler. *Variations in Flesh Colour and Green – The Balcony*, 1864–1870. Oil on wood panel. 61.4 × 48.5 cm. Freer Gallery of Art, Smithsonian Institution, Washington, D.C. F1892.23a-b   23

1.7 Torii Kiyonaga. *Minami Juni-ko*, circa 1780. Woodblock print. 50.7 × 68.5 cm. The British Museum, London. Museum Number 1949.0409.0.66.1-2. © The Trustees of the British Museum   24

1.8 James Abbott McNeil Whistler. *Caprice in Purple and Gold—The Golden Screen*, 1864. Oil on wood panel. 50.1 × 68.5 cm. Freer Gallery of Art, Smithsonian Institution, Washington, D.C. F1904.75a   25

1.9 Samuel Alex Walker. *Ellen Terry*, circa 1874. Guy Little Collection, Victoria and Albert Museum. S.133:418-2007 © Victoria and Albert Museum, London   27

1.10 Théodore Roussel. *The Reading Girl*, 1886–1887. Oil on canvas. 152.4 × 161.3 cm. Tate, London. 4361. © Tate, Photo: Tate   28

1.11 William Rothenstein. *The Browning Readers*, 1900. Oil on canvas. 76 × 96.5 cm. Bradford Art Galleries and Museums, West Yorkshire, UK© Bradford Museums &Galleries/Bridgeman Images   29

1.12 Philip Wilson Steer. *The Japanese Gown*, 1896. Oil on canvas. 127.5 × 102.2 cm. National Gallery of Victoria, Melbourne. 264-2   31

x *Figures*

1.13 Aubrey Beardsley. *Cinesias Entreating Myrrhina to Coition*, 1896. Print. 23.4 × 16.2 cm. Victoria and Albert Museum. E.345-1972. ©Victoria & Albert Museum, London 32

1.14 Aubrey Beardsley. *Two Athenian Women in Distress*, 1896. Print. 26 × 18 cm. Victoria and Albert Museum. E.298-1972. © Victoria & Albert Museum, London 34

1.15 Aubrey Beardsley. *The Toilette of Salome I*, 1894. Line block print on Japanese vellum. 22.4 × 16.1 cm. Victoria and Albert Museum. E.434-1972. ©Victoria & Albert Museum, London 35

1.16 'The Three Little Maids from School' in *The Sketch*, 15 January 1896, p. 615. ©Illustrated London News/Mary Evans Picture Library, London 39

1.17 'Miss Rosina Brandram as Katisha' in *The Sketch*, 8 January 1896, p. 565. ©Illustrated London News/Mary Evans Picture Library, London 40

1.18 'Mr. Walter Passmore as Ko-Ko' in *The Sketch*, 15 January 1896, p. 617. ©Illustrated London News/Mary Evans Picture Library, London 41

1.19 'Mr. Rutland Barrington as Pooh-Bah' in *The Sketch*, 15 January 1896, p. 613. ©Illustrated London News/Mary Evans Picture Library, London 42

1.20 Marie Tempest riding a bike in the role of O Mimosa San in 'The Geisha' at Daly's Theatre in 1896 in *The Sketch*, 20 May 1896, p. 139. ©Illustrated London News/Mary Evans Picture Library, London 43

1.21 'I can dance to any measure that is gay'. Letty Lind in The Geisha at Dalys Theatre in 1896 in *The Sketch*, 13 May 1896, p. 99. ©Illustrated London News/Mary Evans Picture Library, London 44

1.22 'Just look at me, what a pretty thing I've done.' Letty Lind in 'The Geisha' at Daly's Theatre in 1896 in *The Sketch*, 13 May 1896, p. 99. ©Illustrated London News/Mary Evans Picture Library, London 45

1.23 'A Parasol, and Last of All, a White Chrysanthemum' in *The Play Pictorial*, 1905, p. 140. © British Library Board, London, P.P.5224.db 39, Vol. VI, 1905, p. 140 48

1.24 "A Little Bit of Fun while the Admiral's away' in *The Play Pictorial*, 1905, p. 152. © British Library Board, London, P.P.5224.db 39, Vol. VI, 1905, p. 152 49

1.25 'Sybil, anticipating Reggie's return, dresses up as O'San, The White Chrysanthemum' in *The Play Pictorial*, 1905, p. 142. © British Library Board, London, P.P.5224.db 39, Vol. VI, 1905, p. 142 50

2.1 '"Kimino" Tea Gown' in *The Queen*, 2 January 1892, p. 12. Newspaper image © The British Library Board. All rights reserved. With thanks to The British Newspaper Archive (www.britishnewspaperarchive.co.uk) 63

2.2 Tea Gown, c. 1895. © The Kyoto Costume Institute, photo by Richard Haughton 64

2.3 Crayon Drawing by Albert Moore in *Aglaia: The Journal of the Healthy and Artistic Dress Union*, 1894, p. 26. By permission of University of Southampton 67

2.4 'Japanese Silk Dressing Gowns and Jackets' in *'Liberty' Yule-Tide Gifts*, 1896, p. 17. By permission of University of Brighton Library Services 68

Figures xi

2.5 Shiino Shobey Silk Store. At-Home Gown, c. 1875. © The Kyoto Costume Institute, photo by Richard Haughton 69

2.6 Liberty & Co. Ltd. Dress, 1894. Victoria and Albert Museum. T.56-1976. ©Victoria and Albert Museum, London 70

2.7 'Japanese Kimono (or Native Dress)' in *'Liberty' Yule-Tide Gifts*, 1896, p. 15. By permission of University of Brighton Library Services 71

2.8 'Kimono (or Japanese Robe)' in *'Liberty' Yule-Tide Gifts*, 1900, p. 25. By permission of University of Brighton Library Services 72

2.9 Mariano Fortuny. Kimono Coat, 1910s. © The Kyoto Costume Institute, photo by Richard Haughton 75

2.10 Iida Takashimaya. At-Home Gown, c. 1906. © The Kyoto Costume Institute 77

2.11 Takashimaya. *Novelties in Japanese Articles*, 1911, pp. 28–29. With kind permission of Takashimaya Historical Archive, Osaka 78

2.12 Takashimaya. The photographs of kimonos made for the West in *Takashimaya Photo Album of Export Goods*, circa 1910–1929. Takashimaya Historical Archive, ツ 45. With kind permission of Takashimaya Historical Archive, Osaka 79

2.13 Satin Kimono, 1900. Worthing Museum and Art Gallery. 1961/706. Personal photograph by the author, with kind permission of Worthing Museum and Art Gallery 81

2.14 Dressing Gown, 20th century. Chertsey Museum. M. 1986.15. Image courtesy of the Olive Matthews Collection, Chertsey Museum. Photo by John Chase Photography 82

2.15 Kimono, 1833–1866. Tunbridge Wells Museum & Art Gallery. Museum Number TUNWM: 1993.149. © Tunbridge Wells Borough Council t/a The Amelia. Personal photograph by the author 83

2.16 Kimono. Bexhill Museum. Personal photograph by the author, with kind permission of Bexhill Museum, Bexhill-on-Sea 84

2.17 Kimono. Bexhill Museum. Personal photograph by the author, with kind permission of Bexhill Museum, Bexhill-on-Sea 85

2.18 Kimono, 1890–1910. Tunbridge Wells Museum & Art Gallery. Museum Number TUNWM: 1993.239. © Tunbridge Wells Borough Council t/a The Amelia. Personal photograph by the author 86

3.1 Charles Frederick Worth, House of Worth. Fancy dress costume, ca. 1870. 2009.300.1363a, b. Brooklyn Museum Costume Collection at The Metropolitan Museum of Art, Gift of the Brooklyn Museum, 2009; Designated Purchase Fund, 1983 96

3.2 Eduard Uhlenhuth. *Princess Alexandra of Edinburgh* in *Portraits of Royal Children Vol. 38 1889–1890*, 1889. Albumen print mounted on album page. 13.7 × 8.8 cm. Royal Collection Trust. RCIN 2904829. © His Majesty King Charles III 2023 97

3.3 Miss Lilian Young, *Springtime in Japan* in *Fancy Dresses Described: What to Wear at Fancy Balls* 6th edition, 1896, p. 141. By permission of University of Brighton Library Services 99

3.4 Esmé Collings. *Miss Sassoon as a Japanese Lady*, 1897. Photogravure. 17.9 × 11.3 cm. National Portrait Gallery. NPG Ax41224. © National Portrait Gallery, London 101

xii *Figures*

3.5 Bennett & Sons, Worcester, Japanese Entertainment at Worcester. 'Amateur Theatricals' in *The Ladies' Field*, 19 January 1901, p. 252. By permission of University of Brighton Library Services — 106

3.6 T. Bennett and Sons, Worcester and Malvern, Part of Chorus in Japanese Musical Scenes at Malvern Wells. 'Amateur Theatricals' in *The Ladies' Field*, 14 December 1901, p. 51. By permission of University of Brighton Library Services — 107

4.1 'The Japanese Village, Knightsbridge' in The Illustrated Sporting and Dramatic News, 14 March 1885, p. 648. ©Illustrated London News/Mary Evans Picture Library, London — 115

4.2 'The Tea-House' in The Illustrated London News, 21 February 1885, p. 203. ©Illustrated London News/Mary Evans Picture Library, London — 116

4.3 Unknown. Hina-Matsuri Stage, 1800–1900. The Victoria and Albert Museum. 354-1903. ©Victoria and Albert Museum, London — 120

4.4 'Visitors from the Land of Cherry Blossoms: Some of Japan's Fair Daughters at the White City' in The Graphic, 23 July 1910, p. 137. ©Illustrated London News/Mary Evans Picture Library, London — 123

4.5 'Miss Marie San-toi' in The Leeds Mercury, 4 March 1907, p. 8. Newspaper image © The British Library Board. All rights reserved. With thanks to The British Newspaper Archive (www.britishnewspaperarchive.co.uk) — 127

4.6 'The Imperial Japanese Troupe at Lyceum Theatre' in The Illustrated London News, 2 May 1868, p. 433. ©Illustrated London News/Mary Evans Picture Library, London — 129

4.7 Still from *Japanese Acrobats (1913)*. The BFI National Archive. 18813. Courtesy of the BFI National Archive — 130

4.8 Still from *Japanese Acrobats (1913)*. The BFI National Archive. 18813. Courtesy of the BFI National Archive — 131

4.9 Raphael Tuck & Sons. 'Japanese Acrobats' of Japanese at Home series, 1910. Photographic postcard. Tuck DB Postcards. 6465. https://tuckdbpostcards.org/items/81000/pictures/108895. Accessed 18 March 2023 — 132

5.1 Raphael Tuck & Sons. 'L'entente Cordiale' of Young Japan and Friends series. Photographic postcard. Tuck DB Postcards. 6546. https://tuckdbpostcards.org/items/133601. Accessed 12 August 2021 — 141

5.2 Raphael Tuck & Sons. 'Geisha Mother with Baby on her Back Holds Hands with Girl beside Large Tree Trunk' of Life in Japan series, 1904. Photographic postcard. Tuck DB Postcards. 1728. https://tuckdbpostcards.org/items/50441. Accessed 12 August 2021 — 143

5.3 Raphael Tuck & Sons. 'Geisha Standing in front of Open Gate' of Life in Japan series, 1906. Photographic postcard. Tuck DB Postcards. 1727. https://tuckdbpostcards.org/items/50435. Accessed 12 August 2021 — 144

5.4 Raphael Tuck & Sons. 'Geisha & Young Man in Western Dress' of Life in Japan series, 1905. Photographic postcard. Tuck DB Postcards. 1729. https://tuckdbpostcards.org/items/50442. Accessed 12 August 2021 — 145

Figures xiii

5.5 Raphael Tuck & Sons. Back of 'Geisha & Young Man in Western Dress' of Life in Japan series, 1905. Photographic postcard. Tuck DB Postcards. 1729. https://tuckdbpostcards.org/items/50442. Accessed 12 August 2021   146

5.6 Raphael Tuck & Sons. 'Two little Geishas', 1904. Photographic postcard. Tuck DB Postcards. 571. https://tuckdbpostcards.org/items/49876. Accessed 12 August 2021   147

5.7 'Two Young Men in Drag Wearing Japanese Costumes', 1905. Photographic postcard. 13.7 × 8.6 cm. Wellcome Collection. 2043410i76. ©Wellcome Collection, London   151

5.8 'A Man in Drag', 1905. Photographic postcard. 14.2 × 8.8 cm. Wellcome Collection. 2044540i. ©Wellcome Collection, London   152

5.9 'Malcom Scott in character as a "Gibson Girl"', the 1910s. Photographic postcard. 13.7 × 8.5 cm. Wellcome Collection. 2044785i. ©Wellcome Collection, London   153

Acknowledgements

'Let's see where the study will take you'.

That was the first advice that an amazing dress historian, Lou Taylor, Professor Emeritus at the University of Brighton, gave me when I entered the graduate school in 2013. Indeed, this project, after all, took me to all kinds of places in the past ten years. The project began in the graduate school at the University of Brighton. I conducted numerous amounts of research at archives and museums in Britain, France and Japan with the great help of Professor Taylor. I am grateful for her continued support and encouragement. This project would not have even started without her.

In Brighton, I learnt the significance of material objects, visual imagery as well as written documents in helping reinterpret the history. The education at the graduate school and the experience of volunteering at Worthing Museum & Art Gallery taught me how to handle and analyse the objects, especially the historical garments. I would like to thank the lecturers and professors of MA History of Design and Material Culture at the University of Brighton and Gerry Connolly of Worthing Museum & Art Gallery for having me and teaching me everything I need to know when I research the surviving objects.

Back in Japan, I continued my study at the University of Tsukuba, where I further learnt 'what I can say about the objects' as referencing critical theories. My tutor and an amazing mentor, Professor Eriko Yamaguchi, provided me with years of support and insightful feedback, continually challenging me to improve my research, writing and thinking. Also, Professor Motoko Nakada, Professor Michiko Hayashi, Professor Michiko Tsushima and Professor Ryota Kanayama helped my research tremendously. I also want to thank all staff members at the University of Tsukuba for the technical support and assistance I have received throughout the writing of my PhD thesis.

I, fortunately, met so many wonderful scholars in the last ten years. Their advices and comments benefitted my research greatly. I thank Professor Yusuke Tanaka at Aoyama Gakuin University, Dr. Elizabeth Kramer at Northumbria University, Dr. Sarah Chang at Royal College of Art, Professor Christopher Reed at Pennsylvania State University, Professor Toshio Watanabe at Sainsbury Institute for the Study of Japanese Arts and Cultures and Professor Keiko Suzuki at Ritsumeikan University.

This research could have not been undertaken without the kind help and support of the institutions that facilitated vital access to garments, documents and images connected with the research theme: Gerry Connolly at Worthing Museum & Art Gallery, Grace Evans at Chertsey Museum, Julian Porter and Georgina Bradley at Bexhill Museum, Kiichiro Tanaka at Takashimaya Historical Archive, Peter Nahum at The Leicester Galleries, Musée des Beaux-Arts de Dijon, Tunbridge Wells Museum & Art Gallery, Kyoto Costume Institute, the Victoria and Albert Museum, the British Library, St Peters House Library team at the University of Brighton, Mary Evans Picture Library, the

xvi *Acknowledgements*

British Newspaper Archive, the Whitechapel Gallery, the British Film Institute and the Wellcome Collection.

A special thank you to my wonderful friends, Caroline Sumner and Alexandra Hamer, for their support and advice that continue to this day. Their knowledge and ideas on history, fashion and culture are always insightful and inspiring. I can proudly say that the countless amazing discussions we had in the past ten years helped pave the way for my work. My research has also benefitted from the support and feedback of friends and colleagues including Tricia and Martin Bach, Syed Ahmad, Yui Hayakawa, Noguchi Arthur Takanobu, Casey Allen-Murray and Matthew Bach.

Last, huge thanks are due to my family for the love and support they have provided over the past years. I am especially grateful to my mother, Mayumi, and my grandfather, Kazuo, for supporting me in every way throughout the journey. I also thank Takuya Miyagi for always encouraging me. Finally, I offer my most heartfelt thanks to my puppy, Chutney, for putting up with me always working. This book would never have been completed without them.

Introduction

This book, *Sartorial Japonisme and the Experience of Kimonos*, explores the adoption of kimonos in Britain in the period from 1865 to 1914. It demonstrates how the 'experience of kimonos' influenced British art, fashion, popular culture and day-to-day communication. In previous studies, kimonos were either victimised as being appropriated or described using positive expressions as being embraced as exotic curiosities that inspired new design trends in western culture. However, this study takes neither of these positions. It instead sees sartorial Japonisme interactively, examining how kimonos affected culture, society and lives as well as how kimonos were modified in Britain. Therefore, it focuses on Victorian and Edwardian people's emotional and sensory responses to their everyday encounters with kimonos, as well as the ways in which kimonos were altered and appropriated in the process of being adopted in Britain. This research aims to focus on 'what kimonos did' and 'to what extent the effects of kimonos affected Britain' in more inclusive terms than simply looking at luxury fashion or cultures, which could further widen the scope of sartorial Japonisme in Britain by including the people, spaces and cultures that have often been overlooked in previous academic studies of Japonisme.

In Britain, kimonos have acquired several different meanings and roles in various places from the late Victorian to early Edwardian period. They were first embedded with some artistic and social movements when it first appeared around the mid-1860s but then slowly slid down the social class to circulate across the country by being associated with mass production, popular culture and everyday communication. Kimono's formless characteristic—it is variable enough to create several different silhouettes—allowed people to have a sartorial experience that must have been unique to most contemporary British citizens. Furthermore, kimonos as imagery were also given several meanings in Britain, most of which had nothing to do with the actual kimonos in Japan of the period that was covered in this book. Because kimonos were related to many different aspects in Britain—erotic, feminine, peculiar, fashionable, graceful, exotic, aesthetic, submissive—they could fit in various situations, periods and spaces. Hence, their shifting presence could affect and disturb in various cases within society and culture in Britain.

This study includes the influence of kimonos on the everyday experiences of British contemporaries, as well as their representations in fine arts and Couture fashion. In 1934, American philosopher John Dewey defined 'experience' as 'the everyday events, doings, and sufferings', which should be studied and analysed to facilitate the holistic comprehension of these objects (3). Dewey challenged the classical assumptions and theories of fine arts, reiterating the importance of studying 'experience'. He stated, 'In order to understand the meaning of artistic products, we have to [...] have recourse to the ordinary forces and conditions of experience that we do not usually regard as esthetic' (4).

DOI: 10.4324/9781003334255-1

2 Introduction

In contrast, emphasising the importance of 'everyday aesthetics', Yuriko Saito suggested that 'non-art objects and practices exist and are experienced in their [people's] everyday context and usage' (*Everyday Aesthetics* 28). The following statement demonstrates why the experience of the 'non-art objects and practices' is also significant:

> They are free from those expectations and conventions governing the institutional artworld, and in turn can be a source of aesthetic appreciation that incorporates qualities not shared by paradigmatic art, such as their functionality and effects on bodily senses (28).

In her book, *Aesthetics of the Familiar*, Saito argued that 'everyday' experiences are carried out in two kinds of spaces. She suggested that everyday aesthetics includes routine and occasional events such as parties, weddings and funerals. She wrote, 'Some aspects of our everyday life are more art-like in the sense of intentional attention to aesthetics, while other aspects are primarily experienced without conscious aesthetic attention'. She stated that 'the core of everyday aesthetics resides in the latter'; however, she added that 'there is no reason to exclude the former' (*Aesthetics of the Familiar* 9–11). Thus, *Sartorial Japonisme and the Experience of Kimonos* focuses on the influence of kimonos on the 'everyday experiences' of individuals in fine arts as well as ordinary life. It presents and analyses examples to capture mundane bodily acts performed even in the extraordinary contexts of fine arts and theatre performances; it also examines the ways in which kimonos were 'experienced without conscious aesthetic attention' in the context of non-art practices such as exchanging postcards.

Dress History

It is imperative to define the terms used in this book clearly. The term 'dress' has been used instead of 'fashion' when describing the focus of this study. This choice conforms to the existing methodology of 'dress history', which was established and developed in Britain. In her two publications, *The Study of Dress History* (2002) and *Establishing Dress History* (2004), dress history was established as an academic discipline by the British dress historian, Lou Taylor. She continues to influence generations of scholars. Dress history as an academic discipline distinguishes between 'costume', 'fashion' and 'dress' by citing the approaches proposed by anthropologists Joanne Eicher and Susan Kaiser. 'Costume' refers to clothing worn by a particular group of people on account of specific events or during a specific historical period (Nicklas and Pollen 2). Kaiser continued, 'Fashion' refers to 'change in dress over time' and the 'dynamic social *process*' by which this change occurs (qtd. in Nicklas and Pollen 2). The usage of the term 'dress' in this context is distinct from its conventional usage, which typically refers to a woman's one-piece garment. It rather encompasses 'all adornment and modification of the body' (2). Consequently, 'dress history' covers every kind of decoration that comes in contact—both physically and culturally—with the human body; it also involves the outcomes resulting from this contact. In other words, 'dress history' covers the relationships between humans and these adornments.

Because clothing has 'multi-faceted' functions 'within any society and any culture', 'clothing provides a powerful analytical tool across many disciplines' (Taylor 1). According to Taylor, dress history was first acknowledged as an academic discipline in the 1990s. Since many dress historians have conducted interdisciplinary studies on a broad range of topics worldwide, significant gaps persist among the approaches employed for studying dress and textiles. These gaps include a lack of cultural 'meaning' in object-based studies and a lack of information on the materials required to study the economic history of dress (Taylor 2). Thus, scholarship on dress history must bridge the various approaches; furthermore, such scholarship must integrate different methodologies to achieve a broader exploration and interpretation of dress history. For these reasons, I would like to declare that this study falls into the category of 'dress history' instead of 'fashion history' to stress inclusivity and interdisciplinarity.

Japonisme and Orientalism

According to Toshio Watanabe, the term 'Japonisme' was used for the first time by Philippe Burty (1830–1890), a French critic and collector of Japanese art, in his publication written during the period 1872–1873. Commenting on Burty's definition of Japonisme, Watanabe writes that 'the aim of such a study was not so much to pursue academic research but to promote Japan and to disseminate more information about it'. Therefore, Watanabe borrowed Burty's words to define this term as 'a pro-Japan attitude and its manifestation in the West'. Thus, 'Japonisme' is distinguished from 'Japonaiserie', which, Watanabe explained, was 'mostly used in connection with actual Japanese objects, motifs and works of art' (13–15). In the world outside of both fine and decorative art, however, both 'Japonisme' and 'Japonaiserie' attitudes were closely intertwined. In this book, therefore, the term 'Japonisme' mostly indicates the general popularity of Japan and Japanese goods in Britain throughout the late nineteenth and the early twentieth century, except for cases that specifically refer to the art movement of the Victorian period.

The academic study of 'Japonisme', the western interest in Japanese arts and culture in the second half of the nineteenth century, developed within history and art history in both Euro-American countries and Japan. Many initial studies focused more on the development of Japonisme in France, where Japanese influence on fine and decorative arts was conspicuous. In the late 1980s, the development of Japonisme exclusively in Britain began to be researched. Toshio Yokoyama's 1987 work, *Japan in the Victorian Mind: a Study of Stereotyped Images of a Nation*, was one of the most significant studies to review the British reception of Japanese culture. Yokoyama analysed numerous textual references to Japan in Victorian Britain and argued that 'the gap between Japanese reality and British perception' could provide 'an important clue to understanding the role of subjectivity [...] in generating images of others' (23).

Another remarkable study of Japonisme in Victorian Britain was followed by Toshio Watanabe's *High Victorian Japonisme*, published in 1991. It further developed a discussion on both theoretical and artistic reactions to Japanese art in Victorian Britain. Watanabe's work extended to the British reception of Japanese art in the early twentieth century and led to the opening of the exhibition *Japan and Britain: An Aesthetic Dialogue 1850–1930*, held in both Japan and Britain in 1992. Japanese historian Ayako Ono also conducted in-depth research on Japonisme in fine and decorative arts developed in association with British artistic movements in her study *Japonisme in Britain: Whistler, Menpes, Henry, Hornel and Nineteenth-Century Japan* published in 2003. Kazusa Kume's 2016 study of Japonisme and its female consumers brought a new interpretation to bear on Japonisme in Britain. Her study concentrated on the upper-middle-class women who used and enjoyed Japonisme in their everyday lives rather than on the male artists, designers and promoters. These key studies revealed details of Japonisme that

4 *Introduction*

developed exclusively in artistic circles in Britain and argued that this trend was appreciated much more widely in the Victorian culture of the middle classes.

Although the main focus was on Japonisme in France, Elizabeth Emery conducted an outstanding approach towards Japonisme in her book titled *Reframing Japonisme: Women and the Asian Art Market in Nineteenth-Century France, 1853–1914* that was published in 2020. Emery pursued women's role in the development of Japonisme in France from the mid-nineteenth to the early twentieth century, most of which has long been neglected in the academic studies. Her attitude to include rather than to specialise the phenomenon as something exclusive that was generated by certain groups of people is what the study of history desperately needs today. Emery proves that these women also shaped the trajectory of the massive markets of Asian art in France that now form the collections of the museums worldwide.

In his book *Orientalism* (1978), Edward Said defined the Orient as 'an idea that has a history and a tradition of thought, imagery, and vocabulary that have given it reality and presence in and for the West'. The Orient has often been victimised and placed in a subservient position to the Occident (5). Said declared that Orientalism referred to 'a Western style for dominating, restructuring and having authority over the Orient'. In addition, the term has various academic and imaginative implications (3). Indeed, when studying Orientalism-related practices, it is imperative to consider the history of the West's hegemonic control over Eastern culture and tradition. However, it is also important to be aware that these phenomena are *always* interrelated and influence one another.

Although Said did not discuss the Far East at length in his argument, John M. MacKenzie analysed Japonisme in his study titled *Orientalism: History, Theory and the Arts* published in 1995. Here, he incorporated more positive terms to describe Orientalism:

> What is clear is that a complete understanding of the 'oriental obsession' can only come from placing the successive fascinations with Muslim, Indian and Japanese traditions together. When regard for eastern arts is viewed in its entirety, its relationship with imperial power becomes less a matter of Said's 'flexible positional superiority' and more a reflection of Victorian doubt and apprehension, suffered with a yearning for trans cultural inspiration (133).

MacKenzie stated that although Orientalism might have been invented in the West, it often represented a creative challenge and an escape from western ideology. He also wrote that:

> even if the products and the visions or aural perceptions of eastern arts were thus devised and prefabricated rather than faithfully reproduced, none the less they represented characteristics, forms, techniques, moods, modes of thinking and feeling which were perceived to be radically divergent from–and therefore capable of transforming–those of Europe (210).

This book generally adopts MacKenzie's approach towards Orientalism, Japonisme and kimonos in Britain. His argument allows us to transcend the monolithic view of the relationship between the East and West and understand how kimonos influenced and inspired the citizens of Britain.

From Fashion to Experience

The academic study of Japonisme and fashion developed within the world of high fashion began with a key exhibition, *Japonisme in Fashion*, organised by the Kyoto Costume Institute in 1994. It opened in Japan and toured Paris, Los Angeles and New York. In his remark, the Institute's chairman, Koichi Tsukamoto, defined *Japonisme in Fashion* as 'the first exhibition that proved Japonisme was one of the factors which deeply influenced the western fashion of the late nineteenth century' (Kyoto Costume Institute 5). Akiko Fukai, who curated this exhibition, published her study on the topic that year. Her work analysed Japonisme in Paris couture and Lyon fashion textile design. It focused on outlining the influence of Japanese art and design in the world of high fashion centred in Paris.

Since the 2010s, academic studies of Japonisme, specifically within British sartorial culture, have started to appear. '"Not So Japan-Easy": the British Reception of Japanese Dress in the Late Nineteenth Century' (2013) by Elizabeth Kramer is an early example of a study that specifically focused on sartorial interaction between Britain and Japan. It was followed by Akiko Savas' discussion of the mass production and consumption of kimono-shaped gowns for the middle classes in the early twentieth century.

In Japan, Yukiko Komeima and Kei Sasai produced a study in 2015 of theatre costumes in Japanese-themed performances in London's West End: *The Mikado* (1885) and *The Geisha* (1896). In her own study of late Victorian fashion, also published in 2015, Sasai referenced high-society journals and fashion magazines of the late nineteenth century and analysed the Japanese influence on luxury fashion designs. These studies outlined the impact of Japonisme on the fashion of upper- and upper-middle-class women from the late nineteenth to the early twentieth century, in association with other significant artistic, social and financial factors.

The exhibition titled *Kimono: Kyoto to Catwalk*, which opened at Victoria and Albert Museum in London in February 2020, was one of the most recent studies that demonstrated the kimono's history in Britain and Japan. It comprehensively covered the story of kimonos from the seventeenth century to the present day. Yet, the analysis of the British adoption of kimonos in the late nineteenth and early twentieth centuries remained limited to the art movement or the fashion among the upper- and upper-middle classes.

Even though some of those studies referenced above do not directly mention the modification and appropriation of kimonos in the West, the main focus was often on how kimonos or the Japanese way of dressing were represented, altered and translated in Britain. While some discussed kimonos in relation to the dress reform movement, they focused on the concept or the hybrid design of the movement rather than the practices or the responses that could have been experienced more personally. Furthermore, most of the previous studies of Japonisme exclusively limited their focus to the culture of upper- and upper-middle-class people; about 85% of the British population were overlooked as if they had no contact with kimonos.

Consequently, two crucial tasks must be performed in this book. The first is to study sartorial Japonisme from both directions: how British culture, society and people experienced kimonos in addition to how kimonos were changed in Britain. The reciprocity of kimonos in Japonisme has not yet been explored in academic studies. This study could bring a new aspect to the understanding of sartorial Japonisme during the Victorian and Edwardian periods. The second is to conduct inclusive research that considers people and spaces ignored or overlooked in academic research. Including 'everyday experiences'

6 *Introduction*

into the analysis of sartorial Japonisme allows studying the working-classes' contact, responses and reactions to kimonos, which widens the scope of Japonisme studies. For these purposes, this book takes the notion of 'material agency' as a critical starting point. It considers how material objects shaped and were shaped by contemporary culture, society and people's everyday lives, putting a particular focus on the intertwined relationship between living human beings and material objects.

The approach of focusing on the 'agency' of images, artefacts and 'things' entails a relatively long history.[1] In 1989, David Freedberg addressed the importance of studying the 'effectiveness and provocativeness of images' in *The Power of Images: Studies in the History and Theory of Response* (26). His approach of focusing on the viewers' responses rather than the painter and the artwork served as the inspiration for the methodology of this book.

It is imperative to further discuss the material agency of visual images that are referred to in this book. The definition of the term 'image' differs depending on the disciplines and the fields of study.[2] An anthropologist, Hans Belting, defines 'image' as (1) 'a product of a given medium' such as 'photography, painting, or video' and (2) 'a product of our selves' such as 'dreams, imaginings, personal perceptions' and continues that it was 'the act of *fabrication* and the act of *perception*' that our living body associates with the images in *An Anthropology of Images: Picture, Medium, Body* (3). He stresses the importance of the relationship between the visual images and human bodies as:

> An 'image' is more than a product of perception. It is created as the result of personal or collective knowledge and intention. We live with images, we comprehend the world in images. And this living repertory of our internal images connects with the physical production of external pictures that we stage in the social realm (9).

While Belting deliberately seeks to bring the living bodies into the discussion of visual images, the tangible interaction that could occur between the images and our living bodies is completely neglected from his discussion of body and image.

According to Belting, it was either 'the act of *fabrication*' or 'the act of *perception*' that the human bodies are in deep relationship with images (3). However, focusing on the materiality of visual images can bring up the possibility of referring to the third significant interaction between visual image and living bodies—i.e. the act of transformation, or perhaps, the act of violation. The material cultural studies should be largely referenced when considering the materiality of visual images that allow human beings to 'work' on the images as Daniel Miller, an anthropologist, discusses in the explanation of 'consumption as work' that:

> If the item is allocated by the state, then all specificity is a result of work done upon the object following its receipt. [...] Work in this sense does not necessarily mean physical labour transforming the object; it may signify the time of possession, a particular context of presentation as ritual gift or memorabilia, or the incorporation of the single object into a stylistic array which is used to express the creator's place in relation to peers engaged in similar activities. The object is transformed by its intimate association with a particular individual or social group, or with the relationship between these (*Material Culture and Mass Consumption* 190–191).

The physical contact between the image and the body as seen in photographs, postcards and so forth in a personal level is one of the most important parts of the experience that was framed by the material agency. This book, therefore, also tries to involve the tangible experience with visual images as much as possible.

Since the 1980s, the generating potential of 'things' has been bidirectionally discussed in cultural studies, anthropology, archaeology and museum studies. In 1986, anthropologist Arjun Appadurai conducted a thorough study on the power of 'commodities'. In his book *The Social Life of Things: Commodities in Cultural Perspective*, he proposed 'a new perspective on the circulation of commodities in social life' (3). He argued that because commodities are circulated and exchanged, they 'have social lives' like people (3). Although Appadurai distinguished commodities from 'products', 'objects', 'goods', 'artefacts' and other 'things', many other studies claimed that these categories also possessed generating potentials and harboured the power to create spaces for responses and reactions regardless of whether they were circulated.

In her book *Museums, Objects and Collections: A Cultural Study*, published in 1992, historian and archaeologist Susan Pearce stated that objects 'are intentional inscriptions on the physical world that embody social meaning'. She suggested that 'social ideas cannot exist without physical content, but physical objects are meaningless without social content' (21). In her innovative essay 'Beyond Words', social and cultural historian Leora Auslander also wrote that 'objects not only are the product of history, they are also active agents in history' (1017) and that '[i]n their communicative, performative, emotive, and expressive capacities, they act, have effects in the world' (1017).

In the 2000s, British dress historians began claiming that objects—particularly, pieces of clothing—have power over bodies, ideas and behaviours. Daniel Miller's notion of 'material culture' is often referenced in dress history studies. Citing the German sociologist Georg Simmel (1858–1918), Miller argued that 'what people do with objects' demonstrated how they 'create a world of practice' ('Why Some Things Matter' 19). This perception of material culture as the key to 'the nature of culture' is a crucial perspective to consider when discussing objects and materials—including dress and accessories—that come in close and intimate contact with human bodies (19). For example, in 2015, dress historians Charlotte Nicklas and Annebella Pollen wrote:

> The particular material qualities and affordances of clothing–sensual, intimate and proximate to the body, while simultaneously public, declarative and performative– place it at centre stage culturally as well as at the heart of lived experience. Materially and metaphorically, dress can variously conceal, embellish, envelop and shape ideas as well as bodies (12).

Many contemporary dress historians have employed an approach that analysed the responses and reactions of individuals towards dresses and accessories. While this approach has firmly established in dress history, the studies of kimonos have not yet taken this kind of approach. Although material objects have been portrayed as powerful, significant analytical tools, the intimate, emotive and sensory responses and reactions elicited by kimonos and kimono-related garments—in the form of visual images as well as material objects in Britain—remain vastly understudied. The power of kimonos created spaces for culture, society and people to respond and react. What occurred in this space is what is defined as the 'experience of kimono' in this book. This experience, therefore, includes not only the clichéd fantasy created 'in and for the West' but also the response, reaction or, perhaps, *change* brought about by the power of kimonos. The approach of looking at the 'material agency' enables a more inclusive discussion of Japonisme in Victorian and Edwardian Britain.

8 Introduction

'Kimono' in Britain

The Japanese term 'kimono' refers to both female and male traditional costumes. It typically entails a T-shaped form and is secured with an *obi*-belt. Although the term 'kimono' in this book refers to the garment as opposed to kimono fabrics and dress textiles, the garment itself has several different forms. The *Oxford English Dictionary* stated that the term 'kimono' was first used in Britain in 1886.[3] However, Isabella Bird (1831–1904), a Victorian traveller who had visited Japan in 1878, used the term in her book *Unbeaten Tracks in Japan*, which was published in 1880. Bird included 'kimono' in the glossary of her book and defined it as '[a] long, sleeved robe, open in front and folding over, worn by both sexes with a girdle' (xxii). Bird provided a physical description of the Japanese kimono, from the width of the fabric to the functions of the sleeves. Moreover, she stated with conviction: 'The kimono has no "fit" and slouches over the shoulders' (37–38). She also referred to the kimono as 'a very scanty dressing-gown' (37), which reflected that Bird was possibly aware of the exotic dressing gown trend back in Britain and that she considered her readers to be wealthy enough to purchase a 'not-so-scanty' dressing gown. Bird also revealed that she slept in a Japanese kimono while staying in Japan. She related that an emergency once caused her to step out on to the street clad in her kimono; she was pleasantly surprised to discover that she 'escaped recognition as a foreigner' (380). In her work, Bird repeatedly described kimonos and Japanese people wearing kimonos; however, Bird's book offers a rather authentic description, as opposed to a stereotyped translation of kimonos developed in Britain.

In Britain, 'kimono' could not only indicate the costume in Japan but also mean the several different styles of garments. As far as this book referenced, it was in 1892 when a luxury fashion journal, *The Queen*, first used the term 'kimino' to describe a kimono-inspired tea gown. Those kimono-inspired tea gowns that started to be favoured by wealthy ladies from the late 1870s, which will be discussed in Chapter 2. These tea gowns look different from the original Japanese kimono in form, pattern and silhouette. They usually have a silhouette of a western female dress but possess some notable Japanese characteristics such as *obi*-belts, hanging-sleeves or crossed-front necklines.

From around 1896, kimono-shaped gowns made both in Japan and in Britain started to be sold across Britain. Kimono-shaped gowns looked like original Japanese kimonos but were often tailored differently. Although they are distinct from the kimonos actually worn in Japan, the kimono-shaped tea gowns sold from 1896 were also recognised as 'kimono' in Britain. These kimonos were mass produced and consumed across Britain at the beginning of the twentieth century, which will also be discussed in Chapter 2. From the late nineteenth century, the term 'kimono' indicated not just one but many kinds of garment in Britain. By the early twentieth century, any gown began to be called a 'kimono' provided it was a Japanese or Asian-related loose gown. In this book, the term 'kimono' encompasses all these definitions, but each specific type will be identified when necessary.

The Framework

As my title suggests, the five chapters of this book aim to present the overview of the experiences of kimonos in Britain. Each chapter engages in interdisciplinary research and critical analysis of experiences through (or with) kimonos in Britain.

Chapter 1, titled '*Translating Bodies*', examines the representations of Japanese kimonos in Victorian fine art and West End theatres, both of which played influential roles in building up the 'impressions of kimonos' that continued to be shared among many British citizens during the period covered in this book. Kimonos imported from Japan were collected by artists in the second half of the nineteenth century and were depicted repeatedly in their artworks. The representations of kimonos in paintings were immensely diverse, each suggesting a unique expression of human bodies. In theatres, kimonos were experienced much more closely to the actors and the audience. This chapter investigates three Japanese-themed theatrical performances—i.e. *The Mikado*, *The Geisha* and *The White Chrysanthemum*—organised in the West End from 1885 to 1905. Hybrid costume designs and the Japanese kimono's cultural and social representations that had developed in Britain were integrated on stage, suggesting that kimonos deeply influenced the wearers' behaviours and feelings as well as others' perceptions of them on stage. Kimonos on stage produced significant and unique meanings both within stories and for audiences while simultaneously adorning and disguising characters. This chapter argues that in representations, the kimono exercised its power to translate western bodies, restructuring an alternative and unfamiliar relationship between body and clothes to its wearers and audiences.

Chapter 2, titled '*Creating Fashion*', outlines the emergence of Japonisme in Aestheticism and the world of luxury Fashion to mass production and consumption of the twentieth century. The 'tea gown' marks the entrance of Japanese-style dress designs in British luxury fashion in Britain. The origin of the tea gown is deeply intertwined with the aesthetic movements of late-nineteenth-century Britain. By associating Japanese dress with Greek dress, which was idealised by contemporary aesthetes, it came to be perceived as an alternative to restrictive western women's attire. This process of kimono's commercialisation is similar to that of the classical body in the eighteenth century which Cora Gilroy-Ware recently studied.[4] In her words, kimono was 're-enchanted' and became 'ripe for the reinterpretation, the embellishment, the feminization' to 'survive and thrive' (9–10). These 're-enchanted' kimonos possessed the power to provide people with an ideal sartorial experience, as suggested by the keen promoters of aesthetic dresses. This chapter reviews the role of kimonos in British sartorial culture and examines the effects of kimonos and kimono-inspired tea gowns on contemporary aesthetes, wealthy ladies with artistic inclinations and their observers in Britain who did not wear kimonos or tea gowns but saw and read about them in newspapers and journals.

This chapter also addresses the adoption of the kimonos within the early twentieth century. In the new century, Victorian westernised kimonos were replaced by the gowns that had a similar silhouette with the original Japanese kimonos. Cheaper kimonos were also produced, and the fabric or material used became a marker of wealth and class. Expensive and cheap kimonos have completely different textures and, therefore, different silhouettes. Object-based analysis of surviving examples reveals that cheap kimonos were usually lighter and softer than expensive ones and could, thus, be draped around the wearer's body. This demonstrates that cheaper kimonos were designed to free the wearer's body, which parallels the early-twentieth-century fashion innovations of Paris couture designers. During the new century, the power of kimonos emancipated bodies and created new bodies within both the world of innovative luxury fashion and the sphere of mass consumption, occupied primarily by the lower-middle classes.

Chapter 3, titled '*Making it "Picturesque"*', reviews kimonos worn as ephemeral costumes presented within more public spaces by the wealthy women in Britain, examining Victorian fancy dresses, costumes worn at the Japanese Bazaar held in Bath in 1882 and the amateur theatricals in the 1900s. The kimonos examined in this chapter are deeply associated with the identification and the self-expression of British women, allowing

10   *Introduction*

them to have an experience that they actively initiated, created and customised instead of receiving what was presented for them. In the early twentieth century, the experience of kimonos for the wealthy ladies was not only limited to their own employment of kimonos at home, but they also offered the experience to others. Some of them organised charity bazaars and amateur theatricals and chose Japan as their theme, recreating 'picturesque version of Japan' on stage or at the venue. The wealthy women have long been considered the main consumers of the Japonisme craze of the late nineteenth and the early twentieth century. But, the events and the examples introduced here show that some British women of upper and upper-middle classes played much more active role in 'creating' experiences of kimonos rather than just accepting them. Kimonos possessed the power to transform each setting as well as each wearer's body respectively 'picturesque', by which each participant's self-expression also helped construct the trajectory of sartorial Japonisme in Britain by being widely presented at the public events. This chapter illustrates what kind of costumes were worn and how they were experienced at each event, showcasing how these special costumes of the ephemeral events also developed the ideas of kimonos and Japan in Britain at the turn of the century.

Chapter 4, titled *'Educating People'*, focuses on kimonos that were presented to be observed by the Victorian and Edwardian audience. It discusses the displays of 'Japanese bodies' at the Japanese Native Village opened in London in 1885, the Japanese Exhibition at the Whitechapel Art Gallery in London in 1902, The Japan-British Exhibition held in London in 1910 and the Japanese acrobats that performed across Europe during the 1900s and 1910s. Displays and exhibitions of Japan allowed numerous numbers of British citizens to delve into the staged 'Japan' and its culture. The visitors from much wider social classes could see, hear and possibly touch Japanese kimonos being worn by the actual Japanese people or by the dolls, however, unlike the wealthy British ladies who actually dressed up as a 'Japanese lady' at fancy dress balls or the Japanese Bazaar, the experience offered at the displays and exhibitions created distance between the one who 'observed' and 'were observed', often playing manipulative role in building biased-impressions of the latter. But here, it aims to capture not only the one-sided representation of Japan but also how the observers and the participants experienced what was presented for them. Thus, it seeks to show the agency of kimonos at the Japanese-themed displays and exhibitions opened in London and beyond.

As an example, the costumes of the Japanese troupes that performed at the variety theatres of the early twentieth century reflected the process of turning the idea of 'Old Japan' into that of 'New Japan' on stage by costuming real Japanese bodies in anglicised kimonos. *Fin de siècle* theatres gradually invited audiences from various social backgrounds instead of dividing them by social class. Although the audiences from different social classes did not literally 'mix' at the new variety theatres, all who were there saw the same act.[5] This was extraordinary progress for the entertainment industry in Britain. Japanese troupes also started performing at the new variety theatres, giving members of the urban and rural working class the opportunity to see real Japanese performers. The kimono-shaped gowns that were originally made for the western market worn by the Japanese troupes had the power to translate Japanese bodies, which created and presented a different kind of 'Japanese' from the 'grotesque' and 'hazardous' imagery resided in the Victorian period. Furthermore, some Japanese troupes of the early twentieth century took their kimono-shaped gowns off on stage, which allowed the clichéd representations of 'Old Japan' as exotic, peculiar and uncivilised to be juxtaposed with the strength and confidence of 'New Japan' by exposing athletic bodies inside of the open-front anglicised

Introduction 11

kimonos. Kimonos displayed at the exhibitions and performances revealed a complex tension within contemporary Britain and Japan, serving as subject that connoted racial, colonial, political and hierarchical relationships and communications.

Chapter 5, titled '*Circulating Beyond*', examines postcards, the most popular form of Japonisme. Postcards were widely used by the working-class people in Britain as cheap and easy modes of communication. From around 1905, various kinds of kimonos began being reproduced on postcards circulated across the country, offering a unique interaction with images of kimonos to the senders and recipients of postcards. Although 'wearing' kimonos—whether kimono-inspired tea gowns or kimono-shaped gowns—was not technically a part of their everyday lives, many working-class people participated in the process of selecting, writing and personalising postcards that reproduced individuals wearing kimonos. The former section of this chapter shows eight postcards that are held by Raphael Tuck & Sons' archive.

Postcards were not only a mass-produced medium but also a form of material culture that carried unique meanings. Purchasing and exchanging postcards, therefore, cannot just be seen as a practice similar to the habit of 'collecting the world' but rather a material cultural practice of personalising objects. The 'Postcard Japonisme' of the British 'masses' connected image, media and people, enabling the image of the kimono to circulate across Britain as a part of everyday communication. According to Said, any representation of the East could be an idea given 'in and for the West' and the power relationship between East and West also certainly exists in this example discussed in this chapter.[6] However, this chapter also tried to show that there was a layered system of power within the West as well. The image of Japan or Japonisme reproduced on Edwardian postcards was something nurtured and developed by 'the others in the West' who lived in different times, positions or situations from those of the actual consumers of postcards. What was experienced by the Edwardian consumers was the reinterpretation and reconstruction of the ideas of 'Japan' and 'Japonisme' developed during the Victorian period instead of directly appropriating the East or the 'Orient'.

The latter section of this chapter deals with two postcards depicting three cross-dressers in kimonos. The images on postcards, in this case, were not a clichéd image of kimono but rather a radically subverted one, showing female impersonation in extraordinary way. Combined with each personal message, these radical images created a unique space that connected the ordinary and extraordinary that was only shared between the sender and the recipient while the images on the card physically travelled. Kimonos circulated across Britain, beyond the role as something to wear or imagery to observe; kimonos on postcards circulated as a diverse, private and intimate everyday communication.

The kimono circulated across Britain in material, visual and textual forms from 1865 to 1914. This book seeks to highlight the responses and reactions induced by the effectiveness and provocativeness of kimonos and show the generating potential of kimonos and kimono-related garments as well as their images of kimonos, which significantly transformed contemporary art, the body and communication.

By not focusing thoroughly on a 'dress' but rather examining the experiences of individuals through (or with) the 'dress', this book initiates an entirely new discussion on Japonisme. While Victorian Japonisme belonged to upper- and upper-middle-class households, its form has evolved in the new century and became a part of the everyday experiences of a wider range of people from various social classes. Therefore, this research challenges the existing model and assumptions of Japonisme and dresses. In addition to the design, consumption and wearing of kimonos, the broader topic of bodily, cultural

12 Introduction

and social experiences must also be investigated. Through interdisciplinary research on kimonos from 1865 to 1914, this study will generate new knowledge that will benefit existing interpretations of Japonisme and dresses.

Notes

1 Agency is a concept that has often been discussed within the field of anthropology and social sciences since Talcott Parsons who translated the works of Max Weber (1864–1920), first introduced the concept to English-speaking countries in the 1990s. The term means the 'possibility of some kind of actions that could affect the people or environment'. See Fabio 2. In 1998, Alfred Gell formulated an anthropological theory of *agency* in objects as well as artefacts. Gell defines the 'agent' and the 'patient' in his book *Art and Agency: An Anthropological Theory*. See Akiyama 146–149. Japanese anthropologist Masakazu Tanaka argues that agency resides not only in the individual but also in mutual communication. He also states that agency has the potential to suggest, create and alter the site of mutual communication, which constitutes most of our everyday lives. Thus, Tanaka suggests focusing on agency in our everyday lives, and he considers human bodies as central to his argument. See Tanaka 17–18. Bruno Latour and Michel Callon, two sociologists endorsing the actor-network theory, also focused on the agency found in everyday lives; however, they maintained that not only humans but also objects have agency. See Latour 63; Callon 5.
2 In art history, iconology was first pursued by a German art historian, Aby Moritz Warburg (1866–1929) but then later established by Erwin Panofsky (1892–1968) in the 1930s. Panofsky's methodology in interpreting artworks was later criticised by the scholars such as Ernst Hans Josef Gombrich (1909–2001) and Georges Didi=Huberman. Didi=Huberman reconstruct the traditional way of extracting 'meanings' within visual arts in his work titled *Devant l'image: Question posée aux fins d'une histoire de l'art* first published in French in 1990. For more on Didi=Huberman's argument, see Didi=Huberman, *Devant l'image*.
3 According to *Oxford English Dictionary*, William Conn's English translation of Maurice DuBard's *Le Japon Pittoresque*, published in French in 1879 and titled *Japanese Life, Love & Legend*, was the first publication to use the term 'kimono' to describe the life of a Japanese person.
4 Gilroy-Ware is an art historian who researched the commercialisation of the classical body in the eighteenth-century Britain. She wrote that '[k]nown collectively as "the antique," Greco-Roman sculptural exemplars were reinterpreted, embellished, and feminized, producing works of contemporary art so divorced from the relics of Greece and Rome that they evolved into something quite different' (10). The commercialisation and popularisation of the kimono also show a similar process. See Gilroy-Ware 9–14.
5 Most of the theatres were designed to use a different entrance for the cheap ticket holders. The front entrance was usually for the audiences who had more expensive tickets.
6 Said wrote that 'the Orient is an idea that has a history and a tradition of thought, imagery, and vocabulary that have given it reality and presence in and for the West'. See Said 5.

Works Cited

Akiyama, Akira 秋山聡. 'Seizou/Guzou no agency wo meguru note' 聖像 / 偶像のエージエンシーをめぐるノート ['Note on Agency of Icon/Idol']. *Studies in Western Art* 西洋美術研究, vol. 20, 2020, pp. 144–164.

Aoyama, Masahiko 青山征彦. 'Ningen to Bushitu no agency wo dou rikai suruka: agency wo megutte (2)' 人間と物質のエージエンシーをどう理解するか：エージエンシーをめぐって(2) ['How Do We Understand the Nature of Human/Material Agency?: On Agency (2)']. *Surugadai University Studies* 駿河台大学論叢, vol. 37, 2008, pp. 125–137.

Appadurai, Arjun. 'Introduction: Commodities and the Politics of Value'. *The Social Life of Things: Commodities in Cultural Perspectives*, edited by Arjun Appadurai, Cambridge UP, 1986, pp. 3–63.

Attfield, Judy. *Wild Things: The Material Culture of Everyday Life*. Berg, 2000.

Auslander, Leora. 'Beyond Words'. *The American Historical Review*, vol. 10, no. 4, 2005, pp. 1015–1045.

Belting, Hans. *An Anthropology of Images: Picture, Medium, Body*. Translated by Thomas Dunlap, Princeton UP, 2011 [first published by Verlag Wilhelm Fink in German in 2001].

Bird, Isabella L. *Unbeaten Tracks in Japan: An Account of Travels in the Interior, Including Visits to the Aborigines of Yezo and the Shrines of Nikko and Ise*. New York, G. P. Putnam's Sons, 1880.

Boer, Inge. 'Just a Fashion?: Cultural Cross-dressing and the Dynamics of Cross-cultural Representations'. *Fashion Theory*, vol. 6, no. 4, 2002, pp. 421–440.

Buckley, Cheryl and Hazel Clark. *Fashion and Everyday Life: London and New York*. Bloomsbury, 2017.

Callon, Michel. 'The Role of Hybrid Communities and Socio-Technical Arrangements in the Participatory Design'. *Journal of the Center for Information Studies*, vol. 5, no. 3, 2004, pp. 3–10.

Dewey, John. *Art as Experience*. 1934. Capricorn Books, 1958.

Didi-Huberman, Georges. *Devant l'image: Question posée aux fins d'une histoire de l'art*. Les Éditions de minuit, 1990.

Emery, Elizabeth. *Reframing Japonisme: Women and the Asian Art Market in Nineteenth-Century France, 1853–1914*. Bloomsbury, 2020.

Fabio, Gigi ファビオ・ギギ. 'kouisya to shite no "mono": agency no gainen no kakutyou nikansuru ichi kousatsu' 行為者としての『モノ』—エージェンシーの概念の拡張に関する一考察— ['Things as actors: some reflections on the extension of the concept of agency']. *Doushisha Review of Sociology*, vol. 15, 2011, pp. 1–12.

Freedberg, David. *The Power of Images: Studies in the History and Theory of Response*. U of Chicago P, 1989.

Fukai, Akiko 深井晃子. *Japonisme in Fashion: umi wo watatta kimono* ジャポニスム・イン・ファッション—海を渡ったキモノ [*Japonisme in Fashion: Kimonos in Overseas*]. Heibonsha, 1994.

———. *Kimono to Japonisme: seiyou no me ga mita nihon no biishiki* きものとジャポニズム：西洋の眼が見た日本の美意識 [*Kimono and Japonisme: Japanese Sense of Beauty Seen by West*]. Heibonsha, 2017.

———. 'Radical Restructure: the Impact of Kimono'. *Kimono: Kyoto to Catwalk*, edited by Anna Jackson, V&A Publishing, 2020, pp. 198–207.

Gagnier, Regenia. *Individualism, Decadence and Globalization: On the Relationship of Part to Whole, 1859–1920*. Palgrave Macmillan, 2010.

Gilbert, Pamela K. *Victorian Skin: Surface, Self, History*. Cornell UP, 2019.

Gilroy-Ware, Cora. *The Classical Body in Romantic Britain*. Paul Mellon Centre for Studies in British Art, 2020.

Jackson, Anna. 'Imaging Japan: The Victorian Perception and Acquision of Japanese Culture'. *The Journal of Design History*, vol. 5, no. 4, 1992, pp. 245–256.

———, eds. *Kimono: Kyoto to Catwalk*. V&A Publishing, 2020.

Johnson, Donald Clay and Helen Bradley Foster, editors. *Dress Sense: Emotional and Sensory Experiences of the Body and Clothes*. Berg, 2007.

Komeima, Yukiko 米今由希子and Kei Sasai 佐々井啓. '19 seiki kouhan no igirisu engeki ni mirunihon no fukusyoku' 19 世紀後半のイギリス演劇にみる日本の服飾 ['Japanese Costumes in British Musical Comedies in the Late 19th Century']. *Nihon Jyoshi Daigaku Daigakuin Kiyou* 日本女子大学大学院紀要 [*Journal of Japan Women's University*], vol. 18, 2012, pp. 161–170.

Kramer, Elizabeth. '"Not so Japan-Easy": The British Reception of Japanese Dress in the Late Nineteenth Century'. *Textile History*, vol. 44, no. 1, 2013, pp. 3–24.

Kume, Kazusa 粂和沙. *Bi to taishu: Japonisme to igirisu no zyosei-tachi* 美と大衆—ジャポニスムとイギリスの女性たち [*Beauty and the Mass: Japonisme and Women in Britain*]. Brucke ブリュッケ, 2016.

14 Introduction

Kyoto Costume Institute 京都服飾文化研究財団. *Mode no Japonisme* モードのジヤポニズム [*Japonisme in Fashion*]. Tokyo Creation Festival 東京クリエイシヨンフエスティバル実行委員会, 1996.

Latour, Bruno. *Reassembling the Social: An Introduction to Actor-Network-Theory*. Oxford UP, 2005.

Lavery, Grace E. *Quaint, Exquisite: Victorian Aesthetics and the Idea of Japan*. Princeton UP, 2019.

MacKenzie, John M. *Orientalism: History, Theory and the Arts*. Manchester UP, 1995.

Miller, Daniel. *Material Culture and Mass Consumption*. Basil Blackwell, 1987.

———. 'Why Some Things Matter'. *Material Cultures: Why Some Things Matter*, edited by Daniel Miller, UCL Press, 1998, pp. 3–21.

Nicklas, Charlotte and Annebella Pollen. 'Introduction; Dress History Now: Terms, Themes and Tools'. *Dress History: New Directions in Theory and Practice*, edited by Charlotte Nicklas and Annebella Pollen, Bloomsbury, 2015, pp. 1–14.

Ono, Ayako. *Japonisme in Britain: Whistler, Menpes, Henry, Hornel and Nineteenth-Century Japan*. Taylor & Francis, 2003.

Pearce, Susan. *Museums, Objects and Collections: A Cultural Study*. 1992. Smithsonian Institution Press, 1993.

Said, Edward W. *Orientalism*. 1978. Penguin Books, 2003.

Saito, Yuriko. *Aesthetics of the Familiar: Everyday Life and World-Making*. Oxford UP, 2017.

———. *Everyday Aesthetics*. Oxford UP, 2007.

Sasso, Elenora. *The Pre-Raphaelites and Orientalism: Language and Cognition in Remediations of the East*. Edinburgh UP, 2018.

Sato, Tomoko and Toshio Watanabe. *Japan and Britain: An Aesthetic Dialogue, 1850–1930*. Lund Humphries, 1991.

Savas, Akiko サワシユ晃子. '20 seiki syotou no eikoku ni okeru nihonsei yusyutsuyou kimono no ryutsu to nichiei gyousha no sougo kousyou ni tsuite 20 世紀初頭の英国における日本製輸出用キモノの流通と日英業者の相互交渉にいて ['Japanese Kimonos for the British Market at the Beginning of the 20th Century']. *Journal of the Japan Society of Design*, vol. 65, 2014, pp. 15–29.

———. '20 seiki syotou no eikoku no taisyu shosetsu ni okeru kimono to kimono Sugata no josei hyoushou no henka' 20 世紀初頭の英国の大衆小説におけるキモノとキモノ姿の女性表象の変化ーキモノブームという視点からー ['Changes in the Representation of Kimono and Kimono-clad Women in British Popular Fiction in the Early Twentieth Century']. *Studies in Japonisme*, vol.35, 2015, pp. 77–95.

———. 'Dilute to Taste: Kimonos for the British Market at the Beginning of the Twentieth Century'. *International Journal of Fashion Studies*, vol. 4, no.2, 2017, pp. 157–181.

Tanaka, Masakazu 田中雅一. 'Micro jinruigaku no kadai' ミクロ人類学の課題 ['The Issue of Micro Anthropology']. *Micro jinruigaku no jittsen* ミクロ人類学の実践 [*The Practice of Micro Anthropology*], edited by Masakazu Tanaka 田中雅一 and Motoji Matsuda 松田素二, Sekaishisousha 世界思想社, 2006, pp. 1–37.

Taylor, Lou. *Establishing Dress History*. Manchester UP, 2004.

———. *The Study of Dress History*. Manchester UP, 2002.

Watanabe, Toshio. *High Victorian Japonisme*. Peter Lang, 1991.

Weisberg, Gabriel P. *Art Nouveau Bing: Paris Style 1900*. Abrams, 1986.

Wentworth, Michael. 'Tissot and Japonisme'. *Japonisme in Art: An International Symposium*, edited by Chisaburo Yamada, Kodansha International, 1980, pp. 127–146.

Wilson, Verity. 'Western Modes and Asian Clothes: Reflections on Borrowing Other People's Dress'. *Costume*, vol. 36, no. 1, 2013, pp. 139–157.

Yokoyama, Toshio. *Japan in the Victorian Mind: A Study of Stereotyped Images of a Nation 1850–80*. Macmillan, 1987.

1 Translating Bodies

This study begins with exploring the earlier representations of kimonos in paintings and theatre performances. Late Victorian paintings that depicted Japanese kimonos and the Japanese-themed theatre performances in London's West End all played significant roles in constructing the initial idea of 'kimono' and 'Japan' in British society. Japonisme, when it was researched within the traditional art history discipline, focuses on the technical reference or the employment of Japanese motifs and objects as Geneviève Lacambre explained the influence of Japanese art in France in the four stages given as follows:

1 Adopting Japanese motifs within the eclectic range of designs. This is a mixture of decorative motifs of different periods and countries
2 Adopting Japanese exotic and natural motifs
3 Imitating sophisticated techniques of Japan
4 The analysis and practice of principle and method of Japanese art

(Lacambre 43)

This process by Lacambre explains the technical development of Japonisme in order to show how the 'production' of Japonisme was executed in the artworld in Europe. Perhaps, both in fine art and in decorative art, Japanese kimonos were often also regarded as one of these 'Japonisme' objects that were to be collected, analysed and taken into another process of production. In Japanese, however, kimono means 'thing to wear', inclusively indicating its relationship with bodies and spaces around. Kimonos, whether they are worn or not worn, cannot be separated from sensory, emotional and tangible experiences with human bodies. This chapter, thus, focuses more on how kimonos are experienced by the living figures that surrounded or interacted with them in paintings and theatre performances. In these initial interpretations, kimonos manipulate bodily images, while their 'exoticness' was also often exploited by the artists and producers. The representations of kimonos expressed in paintings and on stage also suggest (naked or clothed) bodies to be in a different state, restructuring an alternative relationship between body and clothes.

Fine Art, 1865–1900

The story of the development of kimonos in paintings must begin by introducing some key works painted by the French Japonisan painter Jacques Joseph Tissot (1836–1902) during the 1860s. Tissot was known as a Japonist who collected many Japanese things, including kimonos. He lived in Paris during the 1860s and moved to London in 1871,

DOI: 10.4324/9781003334255-2

16   *Translating Bodies*

where he stayed until 1882 (Wood 53, 122). In the 1860s, Paris was home to several shops selling Japanese objects, such as *La Porte Chinoise* and *Au Celeste Empire*, and the shop run by Mme Desoye, which was opened on the Rue de Rivioli in 1862 (Ono 59). It was the world of fine arts that first welcomed and celebrated Japanese art and craft. Mme Desoye's shop was a meeting place for young artists which attracted many famous figures not only from France but also from other countries. Well-known artists such as Tissot, Whistler and the Rossetti brothers were among her customers (Watanabe 95). In 1864, Dante Gabriel Rossetti (1828–1882) wrote to his mother after visiting a Japanese shop in Paris that 'all the costumes were being snapped up' by Tissot (Fredeman ed. vol.3.64.154).

In the same year, Tissot depicted a woman in a kimono in his painting *Japanese Girl Bathing* (Figure 1.1). In 1864, Tissot was in France before he moved to London in 1871. Tissot was educated in a very conservative and traditional way in Paris, which convinces that the body in this painting is depicted according to the traditional canon of academic paintings (Wood 21). As Michael Wentworth used the word 'superficial' for explaining the figure in this work (129), it shows an idealised body that meets the criteria for being considered a 'nude' as defined by Kenneth Clark, in that it is a 'balanced, prosperous and confident body'; although the subject is technically clothed, the painting has been acknowledged as a 'classic nude' (3). Art historian Lynda Nead critically argued Clark's nude/naked model and wrote that '[t]he transformation from the naked to the nude' was 'the shift from the actual to the ideal' (14). In her argument, 'the actual' indicated the naked body that held 'the negative values of the body' that were associated with 'femininity', but 'the ideal' was the nude body that was 'the recognition of unity and constraint, the regulated economy of art' (14). *Japanese Girl Bathing* is the only work by Tissot that depicted a female nude, and the body reminds of a rather superficial ideal 'nude', which is separated from the 'negative values of the body' residing in the actual living world in France in 1864. However, the direct gaze of the model and the relaxed kimono half-falling off from her shoulders give an outstanding impact that is somewhat different from the other idealised 'nudes' nor the other works by Tissot that depicted the fashionable high society. In *Japanese Girl Bathing*, *attraction* and *désir*, as Georges Didi-Huberman rephrased Clark's definition of the naked in *Ouvrir Vénus: Nudité, rêve, cruauté* (1999), are made apparent by her opened kimono, its drapery and the sensual scarlet linings (25).[1]

Kimono, in *Japanese Girl Bathing*, is worn without an *obi* or a sash, leaving the front of the garment open. The linings of bright red adorn the lower half of the model's body. According to Musée des Beaux-Arts de Dijon's record, Tissot painted her as a 'geisha', equating it with a prostitute (La Japonaise au Bain, 1864). Indeed, it is possible that *Japanese Girl Bathing* disguises the actual contemporary mores in Japan and depicts 'geisha' as a prostitute by employing the hair ornaments of the Japanese courtesans as well as depicting her confident naked body. The body framed in the opened kimono is, therefore, located in-between the classical 'nude' and the eroticised white 'geisha'. Furthermore, although Tissot never visited Japan, all of the Oriental objects, including the kimono, are depicted by his close observation of the Japanese objects that were available in Paris. They are thoroughly realistic, creating a gap between this sharp realism and the 'superficial' female nude.[2] In other words, the kimono in this painting has a power to translate the 'nude' by relocating it to the ambiguous schema.

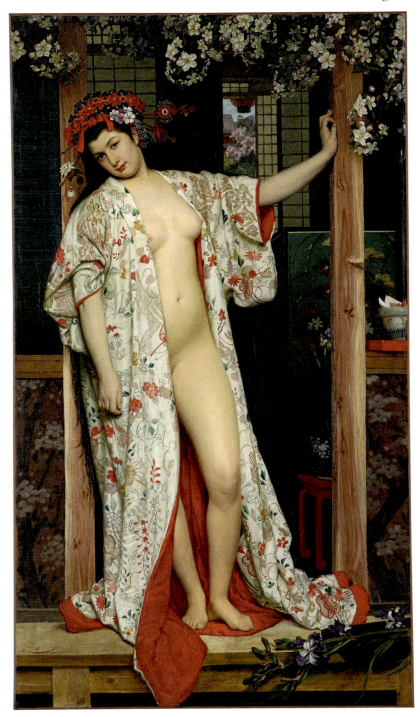

Figure 1.1 James-Jacques-Joseph Tissot. *Japonaise au Bain, huile sur toile* (Japanese Girl Bathing), 1864. Oil on canvas. 208 × 124 cm. Musée des beaux-arts de Dijon. Inv. 2831 and J167. © Musée des Beaux-Arts de Dijon/François Jay.

18   *Translating Bodies*

Figure 1.2 Jacques Joseph Tissot. *Young Lady Holding Japanese Objects*, 1865. Oil on panel. 46 × 36.5 cm. © Peter Nahum at The Leicester Galleries, London.

A year later, also in France, Tissot completed another painting of a woman in a Japanese kimono titled *Young Lady Holding Japanese Objects* (Figure 1.2).[3] In this painting, unlike *Japanese Girl Bathing*, the woman is represented as Japanese. Tissot looked at a Japanese doll for inspiration regarding her facial features (Wood 37). Here, the female figure is depicted as a soulless doll, whose body is fully hidden beneath her kimono. Both *Japanese Girl Bathing* and *Young Lady Holding Japanese Objects* located models in the clutters of Japanese material culture found in the artist's collections. But in *Young Lady*, the Japanese-looking model is thoroughly clothed, being tightly laced by an *obi*. In this example, the model might be again 'superficial' but there seem no other implications than that. The fully clothed kimono further stresses the life-lessness of the body, representing the porcelains, the kimono and the body inside are all part of the Oriental collection equally introduced in the picture.

The third Tissot painting, *Young Women Looking at Japanese Articles* (Figure 1.3), depicts kimonos as an artist's collection that stresses its emptiness in greater clarity. In *Young Women Looking at Japanese Articles*, a kimono is spread on a cabinet like a tablecloth under a ship-like ornament, which two women examine with curious interest. In this painting, the kimono is free not only from the movement of the human body but also from any bodily contact at all. The kimono with its emptiness contrasts with the fashionable dresses worn by the two young women, who are 'alive' with expression and movement. In this example, despite the sharp realism, the kimono's power as a 'thing to

Figure 1.3 Jacques-Joseph James Tissot (1836–1902), *Young Women Looking at Japanese Articles*, 1869. Oil on canvas. 70.5 × 50.2 cm. Cincinnati Art Museum, Ohio, USA. CIN408385. © Cincinnati Art Museum/Gift of Henry M. Goodyear, M.D./Bridgeman Images.

20 *Translating Bodies*

wear' was removed, leaving it as a mere piece of cloth that couldn't be experienced nor be looked at. The hand placed on the kimono connects it with the two women, bearing a strong distinction between the flatness of the kimono and the decorativeness of their fashionable western dresses.

A Victorian painter Dante Gabriel Rossetti completed a work titled *The Beloved ('The Bride')* (Figure 1.4) in 1865–1866 after returning to England from a short visit to Paris. The central figure in the painting is a bride; the scene as a whole was inspired by the biblical *Song of Solomon* ('The Beloved ["The Bride"]'). According to a diary kept by Rossetti's fellow painter George Price Boyce (1826–1897), the green Japanese kimono featured in

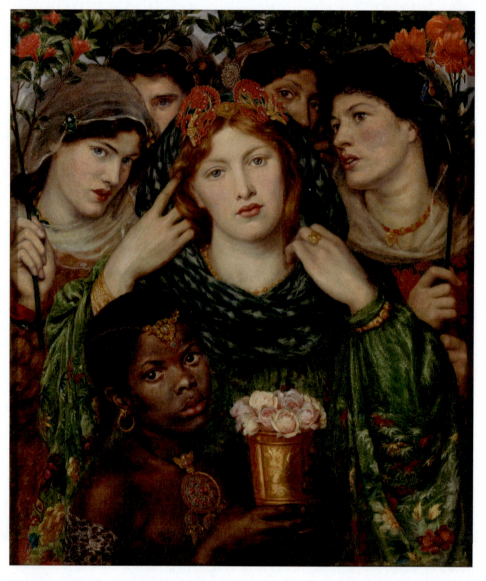

Figure 1.4 Dante Gabriel Rossetti. *The Beloved ('The Bride')*, 1865–1866. Oil on canvas. 82.5 × 76.2 cm. Tate, London. 3053. © Tate, Photo: Tate.

the painting and the jewel on the forehead of the black child were borrowed from Boyce (Suetees, ed. 42). As other studies have already pointed out, the bride in the painting is wearing the green kimono back to front rather than in the originally intended way. Perhaps, the back of the kimono was opened or otherwise altered. The gathered cuffs also imply that the bride's costume was never meant to represent the authentic use of a Japanese kimono, but rather to act as an exotic decoration and a sign of aesthetic taste. As Rossetti himself explained, the colour in this painting was meant 'to be like jewels'; thus, the decorative role of the kimono is stressed (Rossetti 51). Tomoko Sato and Toshio Watanabe confirmed this characteristic of Rossetti's work in their catalogue of a remarkable exhibition on Japonisme in Britain, held at the Barbican Art Gallery and Setagaya Art Museum during 1991/1992. They note that Rossetti's painting depicted 'an exotic world of his own invention' and that 'Rossetti's main interest was in the colour and the decorative quality of Japanese objects' (Sato and Watanabe 22). Therefore, the kimono is displayed along with other 'exotic' artefacts. Even the women around the bride may be included among this collection, as they appear to have darker skin and hair than the bride herself does.[4] The bride's headdress, made of red feather work, meanwhile, is Peruvian (Marillier 132).

In Tissot's works, while kimonos were physically present, touched or worn, the Oriental subjects and objects kept a good distance from both the artist and the western observers. They were still the orientalised representations of Japan and kimono, suggesting them as 'other'. Rossetti's *The Beloved*, on the contrary, was challenging the conservative representation of the 'Orient'. As Elenora Sasso wrote that 'Rossetti aims at avoiding ethnocentric violence and resisting the British practice of domestication' (Sasso 13), there are no geographical or periodical information implied in *The Beloved*, taking both the models and the viewers to a biblical yet mythical space that could have been highly unfamiliar to all of them. This painting is not part of the fad that shows exotic objects and subjects as a fashionable theme.

Furthermore, the painter employed challenging composition which made this work even more exceptional. In her research on Rossetti and other Pre-Raphaelite painters, Eriko Yamaguchi pointed out that Rossetti's works stressed the decorative quality of the paintings by employing a flat expression, ignoring the perspective (Yamaguchi 'The Rossetti Collection of Ukiyoe Prints' 155). Flatness was stressed even more by the kimono in this work, making the whole space in the painting denser by eliminating the depth. Indeed, the Japanese kimono is originally a highly flat garment and the Rossetti's green kimono stressed its flatness even more by showing the smooth back of the garment instead of showing the opened front. Yamaguchi further analysed that Rossetti's 'flat' paintings could violate the distance between what's depicted and the viewer standing in front of it (Yamaguchi 'Primitivism in the Pre-Raphaelite Brotherhood' 144). The women and their exotic accessories in *The Beloved* are so dense that they are almost approaching the viewer. Rossetti's radical technique that distorted the comfortable distance between what's represented in the painting and who observed them is achieved by a single kimono. The blended characteristics of the Orient and the flatness and density of the painting encouraged by the green back-to-front kimono take the bodies of the models and the viewers to an unknown, unfamiliar and unidentified space.

The initial representations of kimonos in paintings in the works by Tissot and Rossetti in the 1860s show that, even though kimono was treated as one of the decorative objects, it cannot be separated from its relationship with bodies. Furthermore, one significant difference between the depictions of the kimonos by Tissot and Rossetti is that the kimono in Rossetti's painting is not necessarily intended to depict genuine Japanese costume. While both representations of kimonos stress the garment's materiality and its use as a decorative object that adorns both the model and the picture, Rossetti's kimono simplifies functions as 'something exotic', not necessarily linked with a particular foreign culture. The kimono, however, even though its origin was not specified, already has some visual and tangible influences on the bodies both within and in front of the paintings.

During the 1860s, kimonos were also depicted in paintings as tactile 'thing to wear' set in much more familiar settings in Britain. Although they have a different style, an American painter who resided in Britain, James Abbot McNeil Whistler (1834–1903), and the British painter from Leeds, John Atkinson Grimshaw (1836–1893), share a similarity in a way that they both depicted kimonos being worn by the western models in their works. Kimonos in both of their works were represented as an exotic indoor gown that expects the growing popularity of kimono-inspired tea gowns that would be widely circulated in Euro-American countries since around the late 1870s, which will be further discussed in the following chapter.

James Whistler studied art in Paris and settled in London in 1859. He spent most of his creative years in London and died there in 1903. *The Princess from the Land of Porcelain* (Figure 1.5), painted during 1863–1864, shows a model standing with a fan in her hand. This painting was first found in Dante Gabriel Rossetti's studio but then purchased by an unidentified collector who held it until 1872 before Frederick Richards Leyland (1832–1892) purchased it to hang in the famous Peacock Room that was decorated by Whistler (Pennell 124–125).[5] It depicts a white woman actually 'wearing' a Japanese kimono as 'clothing'. The model wears two kimonos layered and slouching as seen in

Figure 1.5 James Abbott McNeil Whistler. *The Princess from the Land of Porcelain*, 1863–1864. Oil on canvas. 201.5 × 116.1 cm. Freer Gallery of Art, Smithsonian Institution, Washington, D.C. F1903.91a-b.

some Japanese *ukiyo-e* prints. Her kimonos, which are undoubtably 'worn' by her, bear a strong contrast with an empty cloth (possibly a kimono) hanged over the screen behind.

Another work by Whistler, *Variations in Flesh Colour and Green–The Balcony* (Figure 1.6), was painted during 1864–1870. This work was purchased by George John Cavafy

Figure 1.6 James Abbott McNeil Whistler. *Variations in Flesh Colour and Green – The Balcony*, 1864–1870. Oil on wood panel. 61.4 × 48.5 cm. Freer Gallery of Art, Smithsonian Institution, Washington, D.C. F1892.23a-b.

(1805–1891), a Turkish merchant in London and the collector of the paintings of Whistler, which shows that the oriental-themed works were appreciated and appropriated much more globally than the usual understanding as solely being adopted within the Euro-American community.[6] The kimonos in *The Balcony*, in contrast to those depicted by Tissot and Rossetti, are moulded to the bodies of their wearers, taking on a variety of shapes according to their wearers' activity, whether they are playing Japanese guitar, leaning over the railing or reclining on the ground. These lively representations of white models in Japanese kimonos reminded western viewers that kimonos were 'clothing' that responded to the movements of the human body rather than mere ornaments in which one could only put on a mannequin or be laid down as though on display. Figure 1.7 shows a Japanese *ukiyo-e* print by Torii Kiyonaga (1752–1815) made in circa 1780. This print, one of a series called *Minami Juni-ko*, which shows scenes from Tokyo's red-light districts, was donated to the British Museum, London, by Whistler's sister-in-law, Rosalind Birnie Philip in 1949 (1873–1958). The composition of *The Balcony* is similar to that of *Minami Juni-ko*, except that Whistler excluded the male figure that is presented in the original print and transformed the background scene of Shinagawa Bay into an industrial area by the Thames River in London. It is possible that Whistler saw Japanese *ukiyo-es*, including *Minami Juni-ko*, allowing models in his work to dress kimonos in a similar slouchy way.

Figure 1.7 Torii Kiyonaga. *Minami Juni-ko*, circa 1780. Woodblock print. 50.7 × 68.5 cm. The British Museum, London. Museum Number 1949.0409.0.66.1-2. © The Trustees of the British Museum.

Whistler's *Caprice in Purple and Gold–The Golden Screen* (Figure 1.8), painted in 1864, also captures a kimono flowing with the movement of a human body. It was owned by an aristocratic politician who was also a patron of art, Cyril Flower (1843–1907), until 1904.[7] A female figure is sitting on the floor observing *ukiyo-e* prints with a dark-purple and a cream-coloured kimono wrapped around her body. Her kimono creates crinkles and draperies according to the model's movement, making her a living figure. Art historians and scholars have discussed draperies depicted in fine art for a long time. An English art critic, Alfred Lys Baldry (1858–1939), confirms that drapery was used to deal with 'vital facts' in the works of the Old Masters, while it was neglected in the contemporary art in his paper titled 'The Treatment of Drapery in Painting' that was published in *The Art Journal* in 1909 (234).[8] In a more recent example, an art historian, Anne Hollander defines 'drapery' as holding 'the potential elements of a created fiction' in the chapter of her book that was dedicated solely to the drapery of classical to modern art (2).

Indeed, drapery could be an important marker of a reference to the great art of the past and an essential element for the pictorial schema as Baldry and Hollander concluded. Additionally, some recent studies also look at the sensory side of drapery in paintings. For example, Chihiro Minato references *Le Verrou* (1777–1778) by Jean-Honoré Fragonard (1732–1806) and writes that the folds and drapery appeared on the surface of a fabric indicate the essence of the scene depicted in the work of art (108).[9] Eriko Yamaguchi

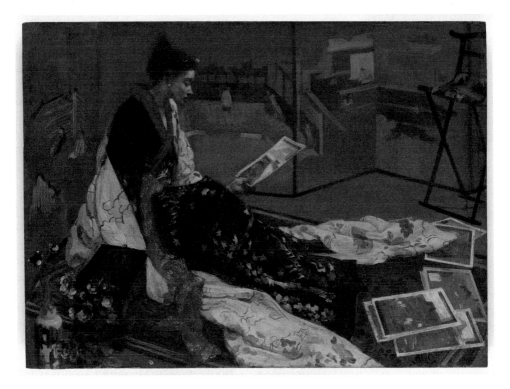

Figure 1.8 James Abbott McNeil Whistler. *Caprice in Purple and Gold—The Golden Screen*, 1864. Oil on wood panel. 50.1 × 68.5 cm. Freer Gallery of Art, Smithsonian Institution, Washington, D.C. F1904.75a.

26 *Translating Bodies*

captures draperies in the works by Albert Moore and describes them as mirroring the 'wriggling' of body and mind ('Beyond Drapery' 153, 157–158).[10] The kimonos depicted in Whistler's works create folds and draperies according to the movements of the models' bodies. In *Caprice in Purple and Gold*, an Irish model, Joanna Hiffernan (1843–1903) dressed in kimonos sits on the floor and browses *ukiyo-e* prints; her white kimono slips down and creates drapery as she moves her arms and shoulders; and the hem of her kimono creates folds along with the pose of her legs...all of which hint that she is a living figure. Freer Gallery of Art explains that Whistler, too, attempted to depict the model as 'a Japanese courtesan', being inspired by Utagawa Hiroshige's *ukiyo-e* prints.[11] However, unlike Tissot's *Japanese Girl Bathing* (Figure 1.1) that also attempted to represent a sexualised female figure in a Japanese kimono, Hiffernan is fully clothed in her dark-purple kimono, being depicted as an actual human being with movements, expressions and thoughts.

The physicality of the kimono is stressed and expressed in Whistler's works. Whistler had little interest in the rational/hygienic aspects of dress reform or the effect of Aesthetic dress, which emphasised mobility and comfort, on the 'natural' female form. Instead, Whistler simply explored 'the ways that Aesthetic dress might be visualised' in some of his paintings (Wahl 36). Because he did not intend to promote Aesthetic dress through his paintings, the kimonos depicted in Figures 1.5, 1.6 and 1.8 do not stress the 'healthy' aspect. Instead, the kimonos reflect the artist's attempts to explore his idea of 'Aesthetic dress' by referencing Japanese *ukiyo-e* prints.[12] The kimonos in Whistler's paintings are 'worn' on his female models' bodies, always being depicted with relaxed postures of these bodies. As the feminisation and eroticisation of Japan and Japanese objects are often discussed in the studies of Japonisme in Britain, the contemporary people may also have detected eroticism or sensuality in these paintings by Whistler (Goldstein-Gidoni 351–370; Sik 107–126). Indeed, a dress historian who studies Japanese dress in Britain and France, Anna Marie Kirk, confirmed that the relaxed way in which kimonos in Victorian paintings were worn emphasised the garment's sensuality (122). Whistler was exceptional because he represented the erotic aspect of a Japanese kimono by actually getting his models fully dressed in them without showing any skins of the models. Referencing Japanese *ukiyo-es*, Whistler depicted kimonos as clothes to be 'worn' in the same way as the Japanese figures in *ukiyo-es*, which made it possible to unite the kimonos and the model's bodies including their postures and gestures.

During the 1870s, kimonos and other garments associated with Japanese culture began to be employed within the artistic circle. Japonists, especially the artists' wives, enjoyed wearing Japanese kimonos in both private and public spaces. Laura Alma-Tadema (1852–1909), the second wife of Victorian painter Sir Laurence Alma-Tadema (1836–1912), appeared at an 1873 Royal Academy reception dressed in 'Japanese embroidered silk', although it is unclear whether her garment was a Japanese kimono or a western-style dress made of Japanese embroidered silk (Gere 96). Appearing at a formal event in a Japanese-themed garment was, at the time, a way of conveying the wearer's artistic and aesthetic taste. Likewise, an English actor Ellen Terry (1848–1928) posed in a Japanese kimono (Figure 1.9) and was known to own several other Japanese kimonos. Terry was in a relationship with the architect and designer Edward William Godwin (1833–1886) who drew most of his inspiration from Japanese art and design (Issac). During the early 1870s, wearing Japanese kimonos symbolised that the wearer belonged to the artistic elite within Victorian society. Japanese-themed dresses slowly gained popularity as luxury indoor gowns but were especially favoured by upper- and upper-middle-class women with artistic taste. These gowns only took western

Figure 1.9 Samuel Alex Walker. *Ellen Terry*, circa 1874. Guy Little Collection, Victoria and Albert Museum. S.133:418-2007 © Victoria and Albert Museum, London.

forms, in which Japanese elements were merely, modestly attached. Wearing a non-modified Japanese kimono, on the contrary, was yet only enjoyed within the artistic circle until about mid-1890s.

A self-taught artist based in Leeds, John Atkinson Grimshaw, seems to take an interest in Japanese cultural artefacts in 1875, for he painted two pictures of women with Japanese objects that year: one titled *In the Pleasaunce*, in which a woman holds a Japanese parasol, and another titled *Spring*, which depicts a model in a white Japanese kimono caring for plants in an artistic and luxurious middle-class household, alongside blue-and-white china and Indian and Chinese fabrics.[13] The kimono in *Spring* is worn without an obi or a sash. The model's body is depicted as if it is drowned in a big kimono, making it impossible for the viewers to see what's inside of her kimono.

Grimshaw apprenticed to James Tissot during the 1870s, so he painted a number of works of women in decorated interiors that clearly show the influence of Tissot's works (Wood 16). While the room is filled with artefacts of the Orient, the woman wearing the kimono is clearly not part of the 'collections'; instead, she appears as the collector and cultivator. The way that the painting only depicts the back of the model, refusing to show whatever she's wearing (or not wearing) underneath, completes a highly conservative representation of both a woman and a Japanese kimono. Because her kimono is hiding her entire body, her neat hairstyle and her graceful attention to the needs of her home (as shown by her act of watering the plants), along with her western-style hat, could suggest that she is likely wearing western-style clothing, possibly including a corset underneath

28 *Translating Bodies*

her kimono. Grimshaw's *Spring* succeeds in protecting her respectability in the middle-class household by allowing the Japanese kimono to conceal her body and all the messages it could deliver to the viewers. It has become fully incorporated into the British sartorial criterion. Thus, kimonos were finally allowed to be worn as clothing within the British households; yet, for this to be possible, kimonos had to hide the wearer's body to conform to Victorian sartorial expectations.

Kimonos were depicted as 'things to wear', while there was also a clichéd representation of them as 'things to undress', which is one of the common representations of Japanese kimonos that continues today. Théodore Roussel (1847–1926), who was born in France but moved to London in 1870, painted a female nude with a kimono in 1886–1887. This painting, *The Reading Girl* (Figure 1.10), depicting a naked model sitting on a folding chair, was exhibited at the New English Art Club in 1887 with 'the clear intention of counteracting the pervasive power of the Academy' (Sato and Watanabe 47). The dominance of the Royal Academy over the Victorian world of fine arts began to be questioned in the second half of the nineteenth century; at the same time, representations of Japanese

Figure 1.10 Théodore Roussel. *The Reading Girl*, 1886–1887. Oil on canvas. 152.4 × 161.3 cm. Tate, London. 4361. © Tate, Photo: Tate.

objects/subjects in paintings also shifted towards a more democratic approach (47). The work was said to have paid tribute to Edouard Manet's *Olympia* (1863), combining modernism with classicism that looked back to Jean-Auguste-Dominique Ingres (1780–1867) (Fowle). The model was Harriet Selina Pettigrew (1867–1953), whose sisters, Rose and Lily, were also popular models for artists. Harriet met Roussel in 1884 and became his mistress and gave birth to his child. While some critics described the model as robust and healthy, the painting was also negatively criticised (Fowle). A critic for the *Spectator* wrote, in April 1887, that 'the artist's eye see[s] only the vulgar outside of his model' ('Art. The New English Art Club'). The fact that the female nude is confined within a dark room gives the viewer an approximation of the experience of peeping at a girl's private moments, which could be interpreted as having erotic overtones. Indeed, the way in which the kimono is discarded on the folding chair suggests that the model had been wearing it a moment ago. The nude model's relaxed posture in the chair may be immediately associated with sensual tension, but her act of reading ensures that she is different from other female nudes who were considered scandalous. The act of reading, for example, is represented as a respectable habit for middle-class women in *The Browning Readers*, painted in 1900 by a British painter William Rothenstein (1872–1945) (Figure 1.11). There is a woman reading and the other selecting a book from the shelf. The title of the work implies that the two are reading the works by an English poet, Robert Browning

Figure 1.11 William Rothenstein. *The Browning Readers*, 1900. Oil on canvas. 76 × 96.5 cm. Bradford Art Galleries and Museums, West Yorkshire, UK© Bradford Museums &Galleries/Bridgeman Images.

30 *Translating Bodies*

(1812–1889), and it also shows the austerely aesthetic tastes with the blue-and-white china wares on the bookshelf and the oriental statue displayed on the mantlepiece, all of which displays an intellectual undertone.

Roussel was a member of Whistler's intimate circle during the 1880s, and a modern critic has noted that *The Reading Girl* has 'a Whistlerian restraint in its limited colour and tone and sense of aesthetic reverie' (Upstone 252). Roussel's main intention in this work is to experiment with the scientific and technological process of matching tones and pigments rather than promoting healthier dress styles. Although it seemed unintentional, the representation of the garment in *The Reading Girl* is somewhat unique in the way that a pink sash or the linings discarded on the chair and the floor is almost as if it is an extension of a flesh oozing out from a kimono, implying a strong connection with the naked body depicted in a similar pinkish nude tone. There is an undeniable connotation of sensuality in this work. Naturally, the depiction of a female nude beside a discarded kimono is challenging. However, *The Reading Girl* suggests a different expression from just presenting the oriental sensuality or the erotic representation of a naked body. *The Reading Girl* shows a rather subtle representation of orientalism. While Tissot's and Whistler's works introduced earlier were all surrounded by all kinds of oriental goods, Roussel's work only shows a kimono, a chair and a woman. This simplicity evokes that the kimono on the chair belongs to the woman, implying that she has just taken it off. Nothing is 'superficial' in this work, but it is rather a lively expression of a contemporary artistic woman. Furthermore, the fact that the naked figure is 'reading' makes it a whole different kind of representation from the other works that depict female naked bodies. Although the girl in Roussel's *The Reading Girl* is completely naked, it is obvious that she is a literate woman capable of losing herself in what she is reading.

The next example located a kimono in a much more familiar scope for the western viewers, depicting the habit of 'changing' the clothes. *The Japanese Gown* (Figure 1.12), completed in 1896 by Philip Wilson Steer (1860–1942), shows a woman in a Japanese kimono that was probably made for export. The model for this work was one of the sisters of the model for Roussel's *The Reading Girl*, Rose Amy Pettigrew (1872–1905), a professional and a popular model in London.[14] Steer was not only educated at the art schools in England but also studied in Paris between 1882 and 1884 after he was rejected by the Royal Academy (Laughton 3). The garment she is wearing underneath her kimono is visible in this work; she is wearing a loose nightdress. The scene shows her either just having changed out of a dress into the kimono or just about to remove her kimono to change into her dress. Either way, the act of 'changing' her clothes, i.e., dressing and undressing, is implied in the picture. Although the Japanese kimono had been established since the 1860s as a 'thing to wear' in paintings by artists such as Whistler and Grimshaw, the act of taking off the kimono began to be more and more commonly and blatantly depicted in later years.

Roussel and Steer, like Whistler and Grimshaw, allow western models to wear kimonos and depict them as indoor gowns. Roussel, on the contrary, drew an empty kimono next to the naked body, emphasising that it belongs to her and she herself took it off. Not only is there an erotic overtone but also it shows a unique representation of a naked body by depicting an exotic and foreign garment and by allowing her to read. Thus, Roussel did not paint a naked body with a kimono as an extension of a mere erotic Orient, but *The Reading Girl* rather suggests an alternative expression of a naked body by suggesting a slight independence by allowing 'her' to take the kimono off and to read, which was rarely employed in the other contemporary western paintings of a naked female body.

Figure 1.12 Philip Wilson Steer. *The Japanese Gown*, 1896. Oil on canvas. 127.5 × 102.2 cm. National Gallery of Victoria, Melbourne. 264-2.

Steer, on the contrary, linked a kimono with much more familiar behaviour and a space, allowing it to be represented as an indoor gown that could easily be worn and taken off. Steer invited the kimono into an everyday scene of a British model by showing her nightdress worn underneath. The kimono in Roussel and Steer's works thereby are worn but also taken off, and both of those bodily movements were completely up to the wearers,

32 *Translating Bodies*

since the models need no help to put on or to take off their kimonos, which brings female independence in the paintings.

By contrast, capturing the scene of taking a kimono off could naturally be used to express and stress the overt erotic tension. Oriental themes or subjects had often been linked with the conceptual metaphors that were defined by various representations of the Orient in Victorian Britain. A lot of these metaphors came from the *Arabian Nights* (*One Thousand and One Nights*), which was translated into English and published widely across Britain in 1885.[15] Sasso defined these metaphors as 'EAST IS CRIME', 'EAST IS SEX' and 'EAST IS MAGIC' and argued that the Pre-Raphaelite artists projected them in their works (12). While the representation and interpretation of Islamic and Japanese culture were technically different, it cannot be fully denied that kimonos were, too, another 'Oriental' object and were also often linked to some of those pre-set metaphors of the Orient. Because kimonos were considered feminine in western culture, people often sought Oriental eroticism in kimonos. An example by an English illustrator, Aubrey Beardsley (1872–1898), shows the expression of overt eroticism through the depiction of a Japanese kimono. His illustration, named *Cinesias Entreating Myrrhina to Coition* (Figure 1.13), was drawn in 1896 as one of the illustrations for the ancient Greek comedy, *The Lysistrata*.[16] In this illustration, a woman is pursued by a man with a sizable phallus. Her robe, which is being pulled by the man, looks like a kimono with wide hanging sleeves. *The Lysistrata* is an ancient Greek comedy. It tells the story of Athenian and Spartan women who ended the Peloponnesian War by withholding sex from men.

Figure 1.13 Aubrey Beardsley. *Cinesias Entreating Myrrhina to Coition*, 1896. Print. 23.4 × 16.2 cm. Victoria and Albert Museum. E.345-1972. ©Victoria & Albert Museum, London.

The scene portrayed in *Cinesias Entreating Myrrhina to Coition* depicts Myrrhina being persuaded and seduced by her husband, Cinesias. Myrrhina manages to keep her oath at the end of the scene by running away from him. The actual scene in the play is more comical than what is depicted in Beardsley's illustration.

The publisher of this book, Leonard Smithers, was said to be deeply associated with the Decadent movement of the late nineteenth century and was not afraid to deal with 'indecent' subjects. Thus, *The Lysistrata of Aristophanes*, published in 1896, was only made available to some people privately (Tate 'Curiosa'). In the Victorian society, Beardsley's work often came under scrutiny for its 'indecent' subjects and themes and were even described as 'vulgar, ill-tempered caricatures, garrulous with flippant morbidities' in one such contemporary criticism (Zatlin 92; 'Aubrey Beardsley from a Japanese Standpoint' 23). His work was particularly noteworthy following Oscar Wilde's arrest and trial in the spring of 1895. Beardsley, who had worked with Wilde on *Salomé* in 1894, was regarded in the same light (Sturgis 24). This connection reinforced the widespread recognition of Beardsley as an artist of vulgarity and indecency.

'Grotesque' and 'erotic' were the two themes that Beardsley actively worked on, and it was Japanese *shunga* [Japanese erotic *ukiyo-e* prints] as well as other *ukiyo-e* that inspired him to pursue these themes. Beardsley's artwork often contains methodological similarities inspired by ancient Greece and Japan, which are seen in Beardsley's famous black-and-white starkly linear style that is said to be 'inspired by his knowledge of Ancient Greek vase painting and Japanese erotic prints' (Tate Britain 'Curiosa'). Beardsley owned a book of *shunga* that was given to him by his fellow painter, William Rothenstein, in 1893.[17] The end of the nineteenth century saw British society face the strain of middle-class standards of decorum with visual culture being greatly affected by these changing attitudes. Some supported this contemporary shift by advocating morality, but 'Beardsley used the grotesque for the purpose of ironic critique' of contemporary society (Zatlin 92). Linda Gertner Zatlin continues these 'grotesque' means through the physical exaggeration and the deformation and distortion of normal structures (91). In *Cinesias Entreating Myrrhina to Coition*, those characteristics of 'grotesque' are all present in the illustration. The phallus of Cinesias is obviously exaggerated (Beardsley often uses this technique). The bodies and faces of the two people depicted are distorted and deformed in order to create a bizarre atmosphere.

The kimono of Myrrhina is pulled by Cinesias, falling off from Myrrhina's shoulder. Along with the two characters, kimono is also distorted, reminding the formlessness of a Japanese kimono. Myrrhina's kimono flows from the centre of the illustration to the bottom left and contrasts her fitted stockings and the clothing worn by Cinesias, which seem a little hard to remove. As discussed earlier, the kimono is usually good at hiding. But simultaneously, it can also be taken off rather easily. Because a Japanese kimono is not constructed to fit but is made to drape around the body, this makes it easier to expose it as well. In *Cinesias Entreating Myrrhina to Coition*, Beardsley depicted a kimono as a 'thing to be taken off' by allowing it to exaggerate the erotic aspect of the garment. Distortion of the kimono that is achieved by Cinesias is also the part of Bearsley's 'grotesque' expression.

Other illustrations in *The Lysistrata of Aristophanes*, on the contrary, depict women in western-style dresses. One of them shows two women who broke their oath and fled to their homes (which in this play means that they were going to have sex) (Figure 1.14). The woman to the left is wearing a diaphanous cape that is somewhat similar to the style of a *robe à l'anglaise* from the eighteenth century. This kind of robe usually requires a

34 *Translating Bodies*

Figure 1.14 Aubrey Beardsley. *Two Athenian Women in Distress*, 1896. Print. 26 × 18 cm. Victoria and Albert Museum. E.298-1972. ©Victoria & Albert Museum, London.

petticoat under it to cover the lower half of the body. The woman in the illustration, however, is standing without a petticoat and her naked genital area is exposed. Her dress implies her willing attitude towards what is going to happen. While Myrrhina was running away from seduction, this woman was running away from her oath of denying the act of sex. Myrrihina's kimono could conceal her whole body, but the cape of one of the women in *Two Athenian Women in Distress* only exaggerates and exposes the lower half of her body. In this way, costumes depicted in Beardsley's illustrations play a key role in visualising the different degrees of erotic desire exchanged within the play. The kimono in Beardsley's work, which utilised 'grotesque' and 'erotic' expressions and techniques from Japanese *ukiyo-e* and *shunga*, was represented as the dividing line between the naked body and the act of sex. In *Cinesias Entreating Myrrhina to Coition*, a kimono was the only thing that segregated Cinesias's desire from Myrrhina's defenceless naked body.

One of Beardsley's most famous works, illustrations for *Salomé* by Oscar Wilde, which was published three years prior to the completion of *The Lysistrata of Aristophanes*, also depicts kimonos in some of the illustrations. The work titled *The Toilette of Salomé (first version)* shows Salomé in her boudoir (Figure 1.15). A kimono-like gown is rested on her shoulder revealing her naked body. This first version was rejected by the publishers because it was too 'risqué', so it was replaced by a different version.[18] This illustration was not only scandalous because Salomé was depicted naked but also problematic because Salomé in Wilde's play was depicted as a sensual figure who 'unveils' her own body during the Dance of the Seven Veils. The sensuality is overtly exaggerated in this illustration.

Translating Bodies 35

Figure 1.15 Aubrey Beardsley. *The Toilette of Salome I*, 1894. Line block print on Japanese vellum. 22.4 × 16.1 cm. Victoria and Albert Museum. E.434-1972. ©Victoria & Albert Museum, London.

Unlike the Roussel's *The Reading Girl*, the woman depicted with a kimono in the rejected version of *The Toilette of Salomé* is not a respectable English woman reading but the femme fatale who manipulates King Herod to obtain the head of John the Baptist. Kimono was there to eroticise Salomé's naked body by implying the act of 'unveiling'. Furthermore, the location of this illustration is a boudoir where changing is usually taken place, which also shows one of the roles of kimonos in Victorian Britain as a garment to remove by being associated with the act of 'changing'.

Both kimonos depicted in Beardsley's works were placed within narratives that had nothing to do with Japan. *The Lysistrata of Aristophanes* is an ancient Greek comedy and *Salomé* is set in ancient Israel. However, what Beardsley attempted was to juxtapose or blend geographically different things to bring out the certain atmospheres he wanted for his works. His experiment succeeded in locating traditional topics within the complex layers of cultures; in Elenora Sasso's words, Beardsley 'over-Orientalises' different topics by bringing ancient Greek, ancient Israel and Japan together (6). Beardsley uses Japanese kimonos for exaggerating sensuality by projecting kimonos within the process of taking or being taken off.

All the works analysed in this section reflect the artists' keen interests in Japanese or oriental subjects and objects, but each of them showed a different expression of a garment. Depicted as a decorative piece of cloth in one artwork, the kimono was represented as an aesthetic dress in another. Furthermore, a lot of the works depicted kimonos with

36 *Translating Bodies*

erotic and sensual overtones, among which Beardsley stands out the most in his use of kimonos to express sensuality. But kimono's power in paintings was not only in bringing exotic or sensual atmosphere but also in allowing to suggest a unique expression of bodies. Steer's *The Japanese Gown*, for example, displays a body dressed yet being undressed at the same time by locating a kimono in an acquainted space of a western boudoir. Kimonos in paintings hold a power to suggest, reconstruct, manipulate and interpret bodies in and around them.

West End, 1885–1905

This chapter also explores the kimonos that were used as costumes in Japanese-themed productions in the West End theatre district of London, from 1885 to 1905, with a particular focus on *The Mikado* (1885 and 1895), *The Geisha* (1896) and *The White Chrysanthemum* (1905). An analysis of the costumes used in these performances reveals the different transformations evoked by kimonos. The kimono on stage was not just presented as an object or a costume to be looked at, but it also functioned as an experience that could transform western bodies and minds. Furthermore, in West End, this experience changed highly depending on the degree to which kimonos were adopted into contemporary British fashion.

Japanese-themed performances are often discussed within studies of Japonisme in British theatres. Gilbert and Sullivan's *The Mikado* (1885) was one of the earliest Japanese-themed performances to receive great acclaim when it first opened at the Savoy Theatre in London. Ryota Kanayama regarded *The Mikado* as a 'virtual reality' that was not even a 'parody' of Japan but was completely made up in Britain (*Invitation to the Savoy Theatre* 48). Likewise, *The Mikado*'s storyline itself was Britain's response to Japan and the wider world, as the production was deeply influenced by the political stance of the British Empire (44–45). Noboru Koyama also discussed Japanese-themed performances in 1885 and stated that some Japanese people who came to London to take part in the Japanese Native Village helped with the production of *The Mikado* (291). His research revealed that Japanese-themed performances from 1885 onwards played a key role in developing Japonisme from 'collecting habits' into popular entertainment.

In her study of *The Mikado* and its reception in America, Josephine Lee argued that the objectification of the characters of *The Mikado* made Japonisme familiar to the British and American middle-class household by suggesting that 'characters resemble the docile objects of the parlour and dining room' (19). Here, Lee associated *The Mikado* with Japonisme in decorative art and interior design, and the costumes were not evaluated as 'clothing' in an intimate relationship with western bodies. By contrast, fashion historians Elizabeth Kramer and Akiko Savas saw Japanese-themed performances through a costuming framework in the catalogue for *Kimono: Kyoto to Catwalk*, an exhibition held at the Victoria and Albert Museum in 2020. They described how *The Mikado* and *The Geisha* 'brought a vision of "exotic" Japan to a wider audience' (181). A more detailed analysis of each costume in Japanese-themed performances was conducted by Yukiko Komeima and Kei Sasai in 2012. They concluded that the design, colour and patterns of the kimonos in *The Mikado* and *The Geisha* played an important role in portraying each character and narrating the story (161–170). While Komeima and Sasai focused on the design of the costumes, the analysis of the transformations using kimonos experienced on stage is left unstudied.

What this study is eagerly focusing on is how the people in or around the kimono both physically and psychologically undergo physical and emotional change. Therefore, it explores the relationship between kimonos on stage and the people in and around them, seeking to show the power of kimono as a sartorial experience in the West End theatre productions. The three performances discussed in this section also play an important role in suggesting and reflecting how kimonos were understood among upper- and upper-middle-class British society. The process of transforming British bodies became easier and easier as the kimono became more familiar in Britain.

The first Japanese-themed musical comedy performed in Britain was *The Mikado*. It opened in 1885, which was one of the most fertile years for Anglo-Japanese cultural history. The Japanese Native Village was opened in Knightsbridge, London, in January of that year, and it displayed Japanese tea houses, temples and various forms of entertainment, which will be discussed in Chapter 4. Two months later, on 14 March 1885, *The Mikado* was first performed at the Savoy Theatre in London. Lee wrote that 'The Mikado served as the basis of knowledge of what "Japanese" meant' within the western society (Lee viii). It was not simply a fragmentary scene but encapsulated the whole idea of 'Japan' as imagined in the British mind at the time. The audiences of *The Mikado*, thus, expected both/either peculiar and nostalgic 'Old Japan' and/or the picturesque and fashionable exoticism. The imaginary 'Japan' recreated in *The Mikado* was a 'pure invention' as Oscar Wilde once noted (52). Kanayama defined *The Mikado* as 'Utopia' or an 'amusement park' that could transport the audience to an imaginary world, and he also continued that this 'Utopia' was the ultimate representation of 'otherness' invented by the Orientalism (The Mikado as Utopia 17). The costumes also supported the completion of this imaginary Japan by transforming the actors' bodies into foreign ones. Actors were fully dressed in hybrid costumes, which completely hid their bodies in them to take the actors and the audience away from the dull reality to a fantasy land.

While *The Mikado* is set in the fictional Japanese town of Titipu, all the Japanese characters were originally played by white actors. The story begins with Nanki-Poo, son of The Mikado of Japan, escaping his marriage to an elderly woman, Katisha, by disguising himself as a travelling musician. Nanki-Poo meets and falls in love with a young Japanese girl, Yum-Yum, who is engaged to Ko-Ko, the Lord High Executioner of Titipu. The Mikado is concerned that there have been no recent executions in Titipu; thus, Ko-Ko is forced to behead someone within one month. Ko-Ko himself was actually 'condemned to death for flirting', but he found Nanki-Poo, who is preparing to commit suicide in despair over losing Yum-Yum and makes a bargain with him (Sullivan 5). Nanki-Poo can marry Yum-Yum for a month if he allows himself to be executed at the end of his allotted time. In Act II, The Mikado and Katisha arrive in Titipu. Ko-Ko hands them a fake death certificate and Katisha discovers that it belongs to Nanki-Poo. The Mikado declares that he will execute all who are responsible for the death of his son. To avoid the tragedy, Nanki-Poo persuades Ko-Ko to marry Katisha, who initially rebuffs Ko-Ko but is soon moved by his love song. The Mikado is astonished to find his son is alive, but Ko-Ko's absurd explanation is deemed satisfactory. The musical concludes with everyone in Titipu celebrating the happy ending.

The people associated with the construction of the Japanese Native Village helped with the production of *The Mikado* (Koyama 291). The production also imported Japanese bodily movements. According to the Victorian impresario whose company produced *The Mikado*, Richard D'Oyly Carte's interview published in the *Pall Mall Gazette* in September 1885, Gilbert asked a Japanese dancing master and two Japanese girls to

38 *Translating Bodies*

teach him 'all they knew' during the process of creating the opera ('An Interview with Mr. D'oyly Carte' 12). Carte stated that they 'acquired the Japanese wriggle and the Japanese giggle and other commodities of an equally fragile but desirable nature' (12). A Japanese visitor who saw *The Mikado* when it travelled to New York confirmed that the actors in *The Mikado* 'would hardly [be] distinguishable from the ladies of my [his] own country' (Takeda 27).

Grace E. Lavery focused on the 'problematic geolocation' of *The Mikado*, explaining that '*The Mikado*'s jovial ambiguity about its location makes claims about the real world (that which we might call the *epistemological* ambition of realism) while refusing to represent that world realistically (realism's a*esthetic st*rategy)' (36–37, 39). While *The Mikado* implied the society and the lives of contemporary Britain, the actual 'Japan' was difficult to find.[19] Lavery argued that there is a 'movement *between* a fantasy of knowledge and the fantasy of its dissolution' in *The Mikado*, saying that it was never straightforward, categorised as either 'about Japan' or 'not about Japan' (36). The costumes of *The Mikado* well supported the complex nature of this opera in the way that they might have been apparently 'Japanese' to the contemporary audience, while the materials and designs were thoroughly intermixed; therefore, the costumes belonged to the ambiguous place between Japan and Britain.

The costume was designed by the famous designer, William Charles Pitcher (1858–1925), also known as 'Wilhelm' in London ('Wilhelm'). The actual construction was done by the London-based costumier Madame León.[20] In his interview, Carte revealed how the costumes of *The Mikado* were put together, stating that he 'bought up in London and Paris everything that was worth having' ('An Interview with Mr. D'oyly Carte' 12). He probably meant the second-hand clothes and textiles imported from Japan that had been sold in curio shops in London and Paris since the 1870s. Carte also explained that some of the costumes were too old to be used for his production, so he 'cut off the elaborate embroideries and had them put on brand-new grounds by appliqué work' (12). Fukai and Sasai wrote that the materials from Liberty's were used for the costumes of *The Mikado*; thus, pieces of second-hand Japanese kimonos were probably appliquéd on Liberty's fabrics to complete each costume (Fukai *Japonisme in Fashion* 174; Sasai 234).

Although there are not many sources to study the actual costumes of the first production in 1885, the photographs of the first revival of *The Mikado*, played at the Savoy Theatre in November 1896, give a more comprehensive view of these patchworks. A weekly high society journal, *The Sketch*, featured this revival for two weeks in a row on 8 and 15 January 1896, in which a number of photographs of the actors were published. It is unknown if they also used the costumes from the first production, but the costumes in these photographs seem to be a mishmash of varied materials. For example, the three little maids' costumes look very close to real Japanese kimonos, but they are mismatched, implying their costumes were separately chosen from the random things acquired in Paris and London (Figure 1.16).[21] The costume of the elderly lady, Katisha, also has a distinctively hybrid style (Figure 1.17). Unlike the other female characters' kimonos, Katisha's kimono is greatly altered from the original kimono form, having two layers of garments with the top-kimono opened in front to show the skirt-like under-kimono. This open-front style probably came from the tea gown trend that had been fashionable in Britain since the late 1870s. It was possibly made up of two different materials because the outer kimono has a different embroidery from the inner kimono.

Figure 1.16 'The Three Little Maids from School' in *The Sketch*, 15 January 1896, p. 615. ©Illustrated London News/Mary Evans Picture Library, London.

The costumes of the male characters, too, clearly show the appliquéd parts on their costumes. The kimono worn by Ko-Ko, for example, has rounded motifs placed onto the hem of his brocaded kimono (Figure 1.18). The same brocaded fabric was also used for the costume of Pooh-Bah (Figure 1.19). *The Mikado*, therefore, demonstrates the hybrid nature of Japonisme with the western actors acting and dancing in a 'Japanese way' while dressed up in the costumes that were patchworked in an appropriative manner. When second-hand kimonos and textiles were brought from Japan to Britain from the 1860s onwards, they had been used and collected as decorative objects to adorn the house, completely separated from the human body. In *The Mikado*, on the contrary, those empty kimonos were cut into pieces and put together to be brought back to life by the actors who played at being 'Japanese' by mimicking the behaviours they had learnt from 'real' Japanese people.

Kimonos on stage offered a completely foreign experience in *The Mikado*. Combined with the movements, kimonos could build a more tactile and intimate relationship with human bodies. Nevertheless, this 'experience' was utterly unfamiliar to both the wearers and the audience. Wrapped in hybrid kimonos that were neither fully Japanese nor British, they moved and posed in a 'Japanese' way as they were instructed. In the end, *The Mikado* created neither the idealised 'Old Japan' nor the picturesque and fashionable Japan, but it was something in-between the reality and the fantasy. A British body was thoroughly transformed into a 'foreign' one by acting and dancing in unfamiliar ways in

Figure 1.17 'Miss Rosina Brandram as Katisha' in *The Sketch*, 8 January 1896, p. 565. ©Illustrated London News/Mary Evans Picture Library, London.

an entirely alien costume. The cut and mixed kimonos here had the power to transform the bodies as well as make the town of Titipu more complex and, therefore, ambiguous.

In April 1896, only a few months after the first revival of *The Mikado*, another British-made Japanese-themed musical comedy, *The Geisha: A Story of a Tea House*, opened at Daly's Theatre in London. It was produced by George Edwardes (1855–1915) and the production ran for 760 performances. *The Geisha* is set in Japan and concerns Lieutenant Reginald 'Reggie' Fairfax of the British Royal Navy. Reggie spends his time at the Tea House of Ten Thousand Joys, where he meets many beautiful geishas, including O Mimosa San, the chief geisha of the tea house. Molly Seamore, who is engaged to Reggie, hears that her fiancé is infatuated with O Mimosa San and decides to follow him to Japan to win him back. Disguising herself as a new geisha named Roli Poli, Molly is inadvertently put up for sale along with other geishas after a local overlord closes the tea house in a jealous rage. The overlord, called Marquis Imari, tries but fails to buy O Mimosa San for himself at the sale but instead purchases Molly disguised as Roli Poli. On the wedding day of Marquis Imari and Molly, O Mimosa San covertly switches a veiled Molly with a veiled French girl, called Juliette, who is secretly in love with Marquis Imari. The performance concludes with Juliette and Marquis Imari, O Mimosa San and her lover Katana and, lastly, Molly and Reggie all getting married and having a happy ending.

The female costumes in *The Geisha* were slightly less 'costumey' and more fashion-focused compared to the ones in *The Mikado*. O Mimosa San was played by Marie

Figure 1.18 'Mr. Walter Passmore as Ko-Ko' in *The Sketch*, 15 January 1896, p. 617. ©Illustrated London News/Mary Evans Picture Library, London.

Tempest (1864–1942), one of the most successful singers and actors of her era. One of her costumes was described in an issue of *The Sketch* on 29 April 1896 as:

> a Japanese dress of softest grey, lined with vividly beautiful blue and all embroidered with pink and blue and white flowers, with white butterflies hovering over them and long-legged birds with scarlet and white plumage poised gravely here and there ('Dress at the Play' 42).

O Mimosa San's kimono for the final scene was also described in detail as 'the black ground almost covered with an embroidery of green and red flowers wrought with gold and silver, while a lining of vivid red gives added effect' (42). No descriptions have been found explaining how and where these kimonos were made, except for in the *Illustrated London News*, which reported that all the kimonos were 'made in Japan' (Scott 572). The photographs of Tempest in the grey and black kimonos were reproduced in an issue from 20 May 1896, in which there seems to be no attempt to mimic Japanese geishas. Instead, it shows Tempest in her most attractive and entertaining manner. In one photograph, for example, Tempest as O Mimosa San is photographed riding a bicycle (Figure 1.20). Another of Tempest's kimonos was described as being made out of a pair of shimmering yellow curtains with embroidered apple blossoms in pale-pink and white (Florence 126). Apparently, the costume designers had been looking for kimonos in yellow (Tempest's

42 *Translating Bodies*

Figure 1.19 'Mr. Rutland Barrington as Pooh-Bah' in *The Sketch*, 15 January 1896, p. 613. ©Illustrated London News/Mary Evans Picture Library, London.

favourite colour), only to find that it was unobtainable in Japan. The problem was solved by the 'transformation of the curtains' (126). It seems that Tempest, who was called 'a barbarian in her love of bright colours', was quite particular about what she wore (126). The example of her yellow kimono implies that the stage costumes of highly successful actors like Tempest could involve her opinions and preferences.

Letty Lind (1861–1923), who played Molly Seamore, first came on stage in a yachting dress by Maison Jay, one of the most stylish fashion houses in Regent Street, London ('Dress at the Play' 42). The kimono she wore when Molly disguises herself as a geisha was described in *The Sketch* as 'a white satin robe exquisitely embroidered with pink-petalled flowers, tender-green leaves and stately silver-plumaged birds, her dancing revealing a lining of pale blue and a transparent under-dress of white gauze' (42). Figure 1.21, which portrays the scene in which she dances as Roli Poli, most likely depicts the kimono described above. On the same page, there is another photograph of her in the same kimono but without her 'Japanese' wig, which reminded the reader that Roli Poli was an alter ego (Figure 1.22).

In these photographs of Tempest and Lind, their poses do not intend to look authentically 'Japanese', but to be an attractive parody of Japan. In addition, the way women's journals explained and described the costumes of *The Geisha* was different from the way they described the costumes of *The Mikado*, both in 1885 and in 1896, especially regarding how kimonos were incorporated into the contemporary fashions. Because there were many western characters dressed in fashionable clothing as well as Japanese geishas in beautiful kimonos in *The Geisha*, kimonos were also seen as 'fashionable' rather than being regarded as 'foreign'. In fact, the *Illustrated London News* reported that '[t]he

Translating Bodies 43

Figure 1.20 Marie Tempest riding a bike in the role of O Mimosa San in 'The Geisha' at Daly's Theatre in 1896 in *The Sketch*, 20 May 1896, p. 139. ©Illustrated London News/ Mary Evans Picture Library, London.

fashionable tea-gown of the future will surely be a Japanese Kimono with a lovely obi' (Scott 572).

The tea gown trend had already been swirling in the Victorian fashion by 1896. Tea gown that was used for five o'clock tea adopted some features of Japanese kimono from the late 1870s. A layered open-front gown was one of the typical styles of tea gowns. While they were originally designed as a more comfortable garment, they gradually became more elaborate and fitted. According to Ashelford, tea gowns 'could be worn as an informal dinner dress' by the end of the 1880s (242). Japanese-inspired tea gowns were also seen in some high-society journals as early as 1878, but the 'Japanese' elements were often too modest to actually be spotted (Sasai 235). Before 1896, truly kimono-shaped gowns or second-hand Japanese kimonos with less-constructed silhouettes had only been enjoyed among the artistic groups and rarely worn daily in most upper- and upper-middle-class households. It was later in 1896, the year *The Geisha* opened at Daly's, when a truly kimono-shaped gown was introduced as a tea gown, which will be further discussed in Chapter 2. In 1896, the Liberty Christmas gift catalogue advertised a kimono-shaped gown for the first time with an illustration labelled a 'Japanese Kimono (or Native Dress)' (Figure 2.7).[22] While no direct connection between Liberty's kimono and the costumes in *The Geisha* has been found so far, it may not be a coincidence that a garment shaped like a Japanese kimono began being sold as tea gowns from 1896.

Indeed, the costumes worn by the actors in *The Geisha* were connected to consumer culture at the end of the Victorian period, as suggested by the women's journals that introduced and featured the costumes in great detail. Furthermore, the *fin de siècle*

44   *Translating Bodies*

Figure 1.21 'I can dance to any measure that is gay'. Letty Lind in The Geisha at Dalys Theatre in 1896 in *The Sketch*, 13 May 1896, p. 99. ©Illustrated London News/Mary Evans Picture Library, London.

catalysed the rise of musical comedies that attracted and were accessible to a broad audience (Breward 70). The most noteworthy group among this audience were unmarried upper- and middle-class women 'for whom the stigma of attending the theatre had been removed' (70). The performance itself, therefore, played the role of a fashion magazine, enchanting the female audience with the stylish and wearable garments presented on stage. The attractive costumes in *The Geisha*, thus, were interwoven with the growing trend for kimono-shaped gowns in Britain. The kimonos in *The Geisha* were not displayed as an alien and foreign 'costume', but as more personal garments that could feel more imitable to a British audience.

In the story of *The Geisha*, the kimono was personally experienced by an English character through disguise. Since there were no 'English' characters who dressed in a kimono in *The Mikado*, Molly was probably the first English character who wore a kimono on stage. The sale of the indentured geishas during the last scene of Act I was a key event that brings up the discussion of what this 'disguise' signifies in the story. Molly Seamore dresses herself in a kimono and transforms into a new geisha, Roli Poli, to win Reggie back. At the sale, there is a binary opposition between who buys and who is bought. One character with the power to buy geishas is Lady Constance Wynne, an English aristocrat who travels to Japan in her yacht, buys O Mimosa San to save her from Marquis Imari at the sale. Lady Constance's character was most likely inspired by British female travellers such as Isabella Bird and Anna Brassey (1839–1887), the wife of politician Thomas

Figure 1.22 'Just look at me, what a pretty thing I've done.' Letty Lind in 'The Geisha' at Daly's Theatre in 1896 in *The Sketch*, 13 May 1896, p. 99. ©Illustrated London News/Mary Evans Picture Library, London.

Brassey (1836–1918), who travelled the world with her husband in their yacht and visited Japan in 1877. Lady Constance is characterised as an extraordinary woman with financial and social power.

Molly Seamore, on the contrary, is being sold to Marquis Imari because she is dressed as a geisha. Molly Seamore and the Japanese geishas are characterised as women who are destined to be owned by someone more powerful than them. The common view of Japanese women in Victorian Britain was that they were child-like, sensual and 'in need of Western guidance' (Kramer 20). The word 'geisha' had entered the English vocabulary in the 1870s, but it was this particular musical comedy that 'did the most to cement the image of the geisha in the West' (Downer 223). As Downer explained, one song in *The Geisha* had lyrics that were 'distinctly saucy', leading to 'the image of the geisha as a creature of deliciously dubious morals [being] established in the western mind' (224). In *The Geisha*, the image of a Japanese geisha was suggested by adding the 'saucy' and immoral characteristics evident in the musical to the perception of Japanese women as child-like, sensual and in need of guidance.

In Act II, Roli Poli is able to return to being Molly Seamore with the help of O Mimosa San. As she escapes from Marquis Imari, Molly exclaims 'you [Marquis Imari] thought I'd marry a Japanese Marquis, when I can get an English sailor?' as though she has a

46   *Translating Bodies*

choice in the matter (Richards 265). Molly, who earlier found herself in a position where she was being sold, now speaks assuredly of her fate as she returns to being an English woman.

In 1896, there was a great deal of discourse regarding a woman's social identity in Britain. The feminist ideal of the 'New Woman' emerged in the late 1890s, with the media being dominated by both discussion and criticism of the movement. Independence was the fundamental idea behind these New Women, who demanded political, physical and sartorial changes that acknowledged their equality to men. The New Woman was the kind of woman who supported women's suffrage, had a job, behaved independently, played sports and rode a bicycle (Sasai 144). This was contrary to the Victorian feminine ideal that saw a woman as the 'Angel in the House'. As such, the New Women were ridiculed by some for not meeting this ideal but admired by others for their convictions. Although there is no discernible sign of Molly's affiliation to the movement, her coming to Japan by herself is certainly not the kind of behaviour one would expect of a Victorian 'Angel in the House'. The newly established image of a modern English woman, influenced by the rise of the New Women in late Victorian society, helped characterise Molly's role in *The Geisha*. Molly's 'modern' and, therefore, 'active' character is exemplified even further after she is revealed to not be a Japanese geisha. While Molly Seamore embodies the western image of a Japanese geisha when she is wearing a kimono, her characterisation as a modern young English woman is emphasised when she reveals her true identity.

In *The Geisha*, Molly's fate is, thus, changed through the influence of a single Japanese kimono. In other words, kimonos in *The Geisha* offer a personal experience to one English woman that alters her attitude and identity. Her social identity on stage is switched between a modern English woman and a passive Japanese woman through putting on and removing a kimono.

In 1905, another Japanese-themed musical comedy opened at the Criterion Theatre. It was called *The White Chrysanthemum* and was written by Leedham Bantock (1870–1928) and Arthur Anderson (1873–1942). This fun and lyrical production opened on 31 August 1905 and ran for 179 performances until 10 February 1906. It is the love story of an English woman, Sybil Cunningham, and her sweetheart, Lieutenant Reginald Armitage, of the British Royal Navy. Reginald, called 'Reggie' for short, proposes to Sybil before leaving for Japan. He initially goes to Japan for a promotion so that his strong-willed father, an Admiral, might permit him to marry his beloved Sybil. Sybil follows Reggie and arrives in Japan chaperoned by Betty Kenyon, a young widow and the two are given living quarters, while Reggie awaits his promotion. While in Japan, Sybil puts on a kimono and pretends to be a 'Japanesy' girl known as O San or The White Chrysanthemum, so that she and Reggie can avoid getting into trouble with Reggie's father (Dangerfield 139). They are supported in their ruse by Reggie's friend and fellow officer, Lieutenant Chippendale Belmont, while Reggie's father finds another woman, the wealthy American heiress Cornelia Vanderdecken, for Reggie to marry. There are some ups and downs in the story, but, by the end, it concludes with three happy couples: Reggie and Sybil, Cornelia and Chippendale and, finally, Betty and Reggie's father.

The difference between *The White Chrysanthemum* and other Japanese-themed performances is, quite obviously, the lack of male Japanese characters, with the exception of some rickshaw pullers. The male main characters are all English except for a Chinese servant called Sin Chong. Most of the men, including Reggie, are in naval uniforms in white that are clearly in contrast to those of the female characters, who wear flowing gowns with lots of frills, ribbons and colourful embroideries. Masculinities and femininities through costume design are strongly defined and exaggerated, with Japanese kimonos being emphasised as particularly feminine costumes.

Costumes are highly important in *The White Chrysanthemum*. The western-style dresses and the kimono-like gowns worn by Isabel Jay (1879–1927), who played Sybil/O San and the six chorus girls that played Japanese girls, could all fit into the contemporary vogue in Britain. One kimono worn by Jay was one of the highlight pieces of this production. The cut of her kimono was moderated to meet contemporary western fashion with a low-shoulder silhouette, a fluted skirt and train (Figure 1.23). Jay loosely wraps her kimono, so that her *décolletage* and round pendant are shown. As her kimono has a skirt-like silhouette (similar to Katisha's kimono in *The Mikado*'s first revival), what she wears underneath is revealed as she moves. Likewise, the six Japanese girls in the musical wear kimonos in the same manner and their matching underskirts, with embroideries, are on view as they sit, move and dance (Figure 1.24). Also in *The Play Pictorial*, there is a photograph of Sybil putting her kimono over her fashionable white dress (Figure 1.25).

As seen in Figures 1.23–1.25, in *The White Chrysanthemum*, Japanese kimonos were not considered a garment that completed a look on its own, but as a gown to be flung on. Indeed, kimonos were rarely worn on their own when they were used as indoor gowns in Britain in this period. Akiko Savas confirmed that indoor kimono-shaped gowns began to be sold at department stores from 1900 (Savas 164). An article in the *Illustrated London News* from about ten years prior suggesting that the kimonos in *The Geisha* would be the fashionable tea gown of the future became a reality in the early twentieth century (Scott 572). The term 'kimono', 'kimino' or 'kimona' was widely used to describe Japanese kimonos, kimono-shaped gowns and kimono-inspired western dresses in Britain. Among them, kimono-shaped gowns started to be used as indoor gowns by upper- and middle-class women in the early twentieth century, which will be further discussed in the following chapter.[23] When kimonos were worn at home, they were almost always worn over western dresses.[24] During the 1900s, kimonos, thus, became recognised in Britain as a gown to be worn over a dress. Not only were the kimonos in *The White Chrysanthemum* identical in design to those sold in British stores as indoor gowns, but those kimonos were also worn in the way they would have been worn in British homes in 1905.

In a review from the *Illustrated Sporting and Dramatic News*, a critic wrote bitterly about the plot of *The White Chrysanthemum*. While the anonymous writer remarked that '[t]he play is beautifully mounted and delightfully dressed and its costumes of east and west are in pleasing contrast', they expressed their disappointment at the story ('Our Captious Critic' 81). Sybil's morality, above all, was the most contentious issue in the review. Sybil is chaperoned by a widow, Betty, and stays with Reggie in Japan until his father allows him to marry her. The writer criticised Sybil for being in 'a position which is not conducive to sympathy' because she 'apparently dwells in the same house' with Reggie (81). The writer continued by stating that 'the whole thing is most disagreeable for the heroine, who ought to have been married right off or sent to a hotel' (81). While some brave women were able to transcend social norms during the early twentieth century, Edwardian society inherited most of its strict morality from the previous period. According to the criticism quoted above, Sybil's behaviour, such as dwelling in Reggie's house in Japan and disguising herself as a Japanese woman, was far from that of a respectable woman. In the musical, however, Sybil could get away with such behaviour without suffering the devastating social consequences.

In the early twentieth century, numerous characteristics had been ascribed to Japanese women in the West. The childishness and passiveness demonstrated by the Japanese

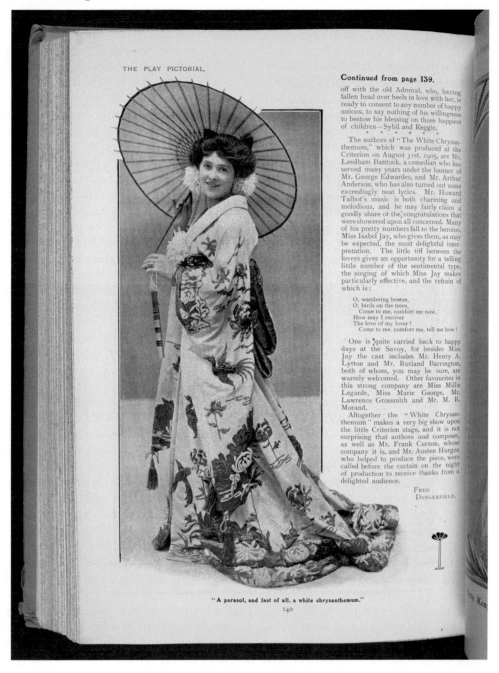

Figure 1.23 'A Parasol, and Last of All, a White Chrysanthemum' in *The Play Pictorial*, 1905, p. 140. © British Library Board, London, P.P.5224.db 39, Vol. VI, 1905, p. 140.

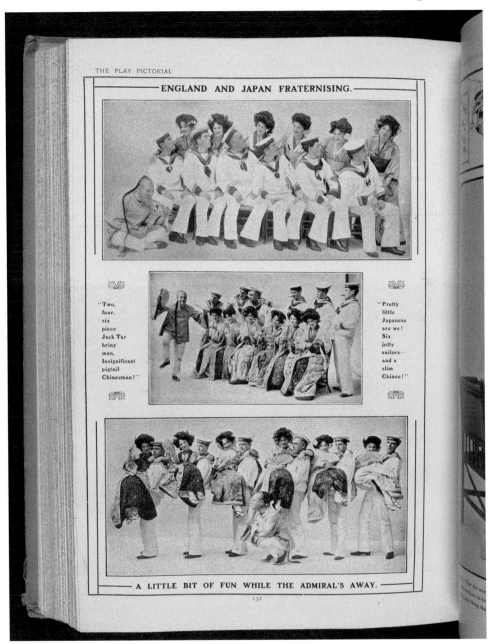

Figure 1.24 "A Little Bit of Fun while the Admiral's away' in *The Play Pictorial*, 1905, p. 152. © British Library Board, London, P.P.5224.db 39, Vol. VI, 1905, p. 152.

women at the tea houses of the Japanese Native Village, the three little maids of *The Mikado* and the indentured geisha girls from *The Geisha* were the most commonly known portrayals of Japanese women.[25] After the success of *The Geisha* at Daly's in 1896, 'geisha' became the term used to describe a typical Japanese woman. The term not

50 *Translating Bodies*

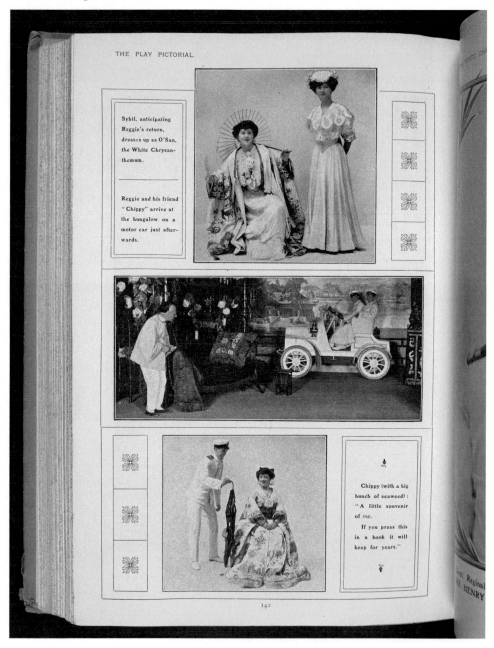

Figure 1.25 'Sybil, anticipating Reggie's return, dresses up as O'San, The White Chrysanthemum' in *The Play Pictorial*, 1905, p. 142. © British Library Board, London, P.P.5224.db 39, Vol. VI, 1905, p. 142.

only inherited the original image of Japanese women as child-like and passive, but they were also seen as a 'creature of deliciously dubious morals', as quoted earlier (Downer 224). In *The White Chrysanthemum*, the fixed image of Japanese women inherited from

The Geisha was projected onto the characters in kimonos. The six Japanese girls in the musical, for example, embody the typical idea of cute, dainty and slightly frivolous geisha girls. Figure 1.24 titled 'A Little Bit of Fun While the Admiral's Away' depicts the six Japanese girls being carried off in the arms of British sailors. These girls were there to adorn the stage, but they also cemented 'the indelible image of the geisha in her kimono as a child-like creature, with little to offer than her body' (224).

In *The White Chrysanthemum*, the kimono plays an important role in transforming Sybil from an English lady to a Japanese woman and vice-versa. Upon arriving in Japan, Sybil transforms into O San by flinging on a kimono, which makes it possible for her to put herself in a situation that would normally be considered immoral if she had remained dressed as an English woman. Sybil uses a Japanese kimono to hide herself from her fiancé's father but takes her kimono off when she is alone with her chaperon and her lover, Reggie. Kimonos in *The White Chrysanthemum* are all 'opened', revealing what is worn beneath and constantly alluding to the motion of taking the gown off. Kimonos were presented as an open integument, which fully covered the British bodies but could easily be slipped off. Indeed, the image of childish, powerless and saucy Japanese geishas that was imposed on Japanese kimonos could hide Sybil from the social norms she should have been facing, but it could also be slipped off more easily and freely. In the story of *The White Chrysanthemum*, the kimono is essentially a cloak of invisibility.

In the final scene, Sybil wears a beautiful dress of white chiffon. Her fashionable clothing reminds the audience that Sybil is a respectable English woman who is worthy of marrying Reggie. This is in great contrast to Puccini's *Madame Butterfly*, performed in London in July of the same year (1905), in which a Japanese woman who marries an American naval officer is betrayed and decides to kill herself in despair. In Sybil's case, the kimono can be cast off as she pleases, which reminded the audience that her body is not trapped in a Japanese kimono but is instead imprisoned in her white chiffon dress. British social norms and morality were forced upon her at all times and kimonos only temporarily hid her from them.

The kimonos in *The Mikado*, *The Geisha* and *The White Chrysanthemum* were experienced by both the performers and the audiences. Being presented in the West End theatres, not only kimonos were widely exposed to a large audience in London but also their images were circulated via newspapers and journals.

The Mikado made a breakthrough in Britain for kimonos to be experienced rather than collected as objects. Kimonos were seen 'live' with the duplicated physical behaviours of Japanese people. The costumes were a combination of Japanese and British materials. By being combined with Japanese attitudes and behaviours that were instructed by some people from Japan, the intermixed presence of the kimonos in *The Mikado* offered an extraordinary experience and invited the audience to a 'virtual reality' world that was a 'pure invention' as Oscar Wilde defined. The bodies that were fully costumed in alien clothes were all completely transformed into 'foreign' ones. The hybrid costumes in *The Mikado* exoticised 'Japan' even more strongly by locating them in the ambiguous in-between place and that image has circulated across the country since 1885.

In *The Geisha*, on the contrary, kimonos were more personally experienced, so they affected the wearer's identity on stage. As kimonos came to be more and more familiar as one of the styles of tea gowns among contemporary fashion-conscious people in 1896 onwards, it was not the 'foreign' land but rather a fashionable and artistic trend that the kimonos in *The Geisha* represented. Thus, not only were the kimonos of O Mimosa San and Molly selected because they were fashionable but they were

52   *Translating Bodies*

also greeted with great enthusiasm by the female audience. The familiarity towards kimonos, indeed, led a kimono to be personally experienced by an English woman, Molly. Her behaviour and how others saw her were changed as Molly was disguised in a kimono. Kimonos in *The Geisha* teach that although kimonos as a fashion style became familiar (thus was worn by an English character on stage), kimonos still served to identify a stereotypical idea of Japanese women in Britain. Therefore, Molly's kimono could transform not only her body but also her identity on stage, the British idea of Japanese geisha was imposed upon Molly and she was unable to escape this idea without help.

Transformation through a kimono was done more easily and freely than ever before in *The White Chrysanthemum*, performed in 1905. Sybil also disguised herself as a Japanese woman by flinging on a kimono as Molly had done in *The Geisha*, but in Sybil's case, her transformation was done on stage several times. Furthermore, Sybil's kimono was open at the front most of the time, so it played a role in temporarily hiding her instead of imposing the British idea of Japan upon her. In *The White Chrysanthemum*, the image of a Japanese woman as it existed in British society was also attached to a kimono. Still, the openness of Sybil's kimono implied that it was always in the process of being taken off. The utility of a kimono in *The White Chrysanthemum* implies that kimonos became much more familiar to the British audiences by 1905, so kimonos (and the ideas of Japan that were imposed upon them) were seen to be owned and controlled by the wearer and could easily be put on or taken off as they pleased. Here, the kimono's power was weakened as it turned into one of the fashion items in Britain. Sybil's kimono only served as a cloak of invisibility on stage. Kimonos as stage costumes altered their function from a foreign experience that transformed a whole stage to a more personal experience that translated the attitudes and identities of the individual. Western-style kimonos have evolved into a predominantly 'open' gown, always implying an 'undressing' process that enabled an easy and instant transformation.

The representations of kimonos in paintings and theatres discussed in this chapter were proportional to contemporary fashion at the time. Both were affected by the adoption of kimonos or kimono-like garments in Britain. However, the theatre performances depicted the acts of dressing and undressing as central to developing the story. Because the bodies in kimonos are alive: they walk, dance and speak; the kimono's aspect as 'a garment to take off' was experienced much more tangibly in theatres. Kimono served as a significant item for western women in *The Geisha* and *The White Chrysanthemum* since the transformation through kimonos played an important role in helping, endangering and hiding the wearers. In *The White Chrysanthemum*, it had to be a kimono that could be easily put on and off on stage to repeatedly hide and transform Sybil. The original characteristics of a Japanese kimono were differently translated in each performance; thus, each kimono had a different effect on the stories and the wearers.

The Victorian paintings built an initial idea of 'what kimono was' within the artistic circle and the high society. By being represented as decorative objects, things to wear and things to be taken off, kimono offered a new sartorial experience to the wearers and the audiences. Often without deliberate intentions, it was a different relationship between the body and the garment that was suggested by the kimonos.

At the West End theatres, kimonos also offered a unique interpretation of living bodies and garments on stages. The tangible experiences of kimonos conducted on the theatre stages completed transformations that could never be done otherwise.

The numerous examples show how kimonos were practised, as well as how kimonos guide human bodies to look, behave and be seen in a certain way, thereby allowing kimonos to actively shape or frame bodies in the works discussed in this chapter. In this case, kimonos experienced in paintings and theatres of the West End were so much more than just a representation. These examples rather show that the manipulative power of kimonos affected the depicted bodies, the scenes and the audiences.

Notes

1 Georges Didi-Huberman makes a powerful argument against Kenneth Clark's theory on 'nude' and 'naked' in *Ouvrir Vénus: Nudité, rêve, cruauté*. Didi-Huberman argues that the 'nude' is never separated from the 'naked', so that the art history needs what Clark denied; *attraction* and *désir*. See Didi-Huberman 24–25.
2 Tissot's friend, Edgar Degas (1834–1917), painted a portrait of Tissot in 1867–1868. In this work, Tissot is surrounded by art works including a Japanese-style painting. It shows Tissot's passion and interest in Japonisme. The portrait is now at The Metropolitan Museum of Art, New York.
3 Despite the face of the model is said to have been modelled on a Japanese doll, Krystyna Matyjaszkiewicz also writes that this work could be the lost 'Portrait de Madame Desoye' listed in Tissot's sales notebook of 1871. See Emery 11.
4 Robert Upstone confirms that one of the bridesmaids was Ellen Smith. The woman on the right was Frederick Sandy's gypsy mistress, Keomi. See Upstone 101.
  The black child in the foreground was one whom Rossetti met 'at the door of an hotel'. See Rossetti ed.
5 Frederick Richards Leyland (1831–1892) purchased it from unidentified collector in 1872 and then Alexander Reid (1854–1928) purchased it at Christie's auction on May 28th 1892. In 1894, Sir William Burrell (1861–1958) purchased it from Reid and finally it joined Freer Gallery of Art, Smithsonian Institute in 1920. See museum record, https://asia.si.edu/object/F1903.91a-b/. Accessed 29 November 2021.
6 See museum record, https://asia.si.edu/object/F1892.23a-b/. Accessed 29 November 2021.
7 See museum record, https://asia.si.edu/object/F1904.75a/. Accessed 29 November 2021.
8 Baldry argued that it was Albert Moore who Baldry personally knew ranked the highest in drawing draperies among the contemporaries. See Baldry 237–238.
9 In case of Fragonard's *Le Verrou*, Minato sees that the folds and drapery of the bedsheet capture pleasure in this painting. He argues that the nature of this work is not hidden under the bedsheet but abides on the surface of it. See Minato 106–110.
10 Yamaguchi describes that Moore's draperies are the space between body and beauty that is hidden in its form. Drapery is in between the representation and the abstract, waiting for beauty to come out on its surface. See Yamaguchi 'Beyond Drapery' 157.
11 See museum record, https://asia.si.edu/object/F1904.75a/. Accessed 16 June 2022.
12 Whistler did not fully agree with the original idea of Aesthetic dress as 'a means of gaining access to past eras of beauty, nobility and naturalism'. He was more interested in Aesthetic dress as 'a current and novel mode of artistic expression'. For more on Whistler's principal of Aestheticism and Aesthetic dress, see Wahl 50–52.
13 *Spring* by John Grimshaw is now in private collection.
14 There is a preparatory study for *The Japanese Gown*, titled, *Kimono*, painted in 1889 that is stored in York Art Gallery in York, England. The model in *Kimono* is Rose Amy Pettigrew, who was once in a romantic relationship with Steer. See *Philip Wilson Steer, 1860–1942* 42–43.
15 Richard Francis Burton (1821–1890) published the translation of *One Thousand and One Nights* in English in 1885. His version is known for having detailed information on Arab sexual practices and customs in its footnotes. For more on the popularisation of *Arabian Nights* in Britain, see Colligan.
16 The original story is an ancient Greek comedy by Aristophanes performed in 411 BC. Beardsley's illustrations are included in the 1896 version of *The Lysistrata of Aristophanes* published by Leonard Smithers in 1896.

54   *Translating Bodies*

17 Beardsley wrote a letter to Rothenstein on 20 November 1893 to say thank you for a book of Japanese erotic prints (Beardsley calls it a *Book of Love*). See Beardsley 56.
18 This illustration was not accepted by the publishers so Bearsley had to provide a different design. Salomé's naked semi-naked body was considered problematic, but what was the most criticised was the seated figure on the right, possibly in the act of masturbating. For more information, see the museum record. https://collections.vam.ac.uk/item/O186116/the-toilette-of-salome-i-print-beardsley-aubrey-vincent/ Accessed 30 November 2022.
19 Lavery pointed out about the Labouchere Amendment that was passed in 1885 as being connected with the plot that 'flirtation was punishable by death' in *The Mikado*. See 41.
20 A journal from the Bailiwick of Guernsey, *The Star*, reports *The Mikado*'s first arrival at Guernsey on 17 September 1885. An article wrote that the costumes were 'made up under the artistic eye of Madame León' from the designs provided by Wilhelm. Madame León's name is also listed as a costumery of several Gilbert and Sullivan's operas. See Wearing 186, 273, 337 and 415.
21 Their *obis*, especially, are distinctively different. While Peep-Bo's obi looks thin and stiff, the obis of Yum-Yum and Pitti-Sing look as though they were made from kimono fabric.
22 Prior to 1896, American fashion journal, *The Delineator*, which also sold copies in Britain, introduced a paper pattern for a kimono-like gown in 1890 and Liberty introduced 'Japanese Printed Cotton Crepe Gowns' without an illustration in their catalogue published in 1892. However, in 1896 Liberty first introduced a kimono-shaped gown named 'Kimono' as a tea gown with an illustration in their catalogue for the very first time. See Suoh.
23 Women in the artistic circle, as seen in Chapters 1 and 2, actively adapted both real Japanese kimonos and the kimono-shaped gowns prior to the 1900 as indoor gowns, they slowly began to be enjoyed even outside of the artistic circle around the turn of the century.
24 An illustration in a fashion column from the *Pall Mall Gazette* on 16 November 1907 shows an open-fronted kimono being worn over a dress. See 'Kimono Tea-Gown in Green and Silver' 10.
25 Shintaryo Tawata explained that the scene of 'women' welcoming 'men' suggested in *The Geisha* and the tea house at the Japanese Native Village were the perfect examples of how-society-should-be to the Victorian audience, which can also link to the expectation of the British travellers as imperialists. See Tawata 241.

Works Cited

Anon. 'An Apostle of the Grotesque'. *The Sketch*, 10 April 1895, pp. 561–562.

Anon. 'An Interview with Mr. D'oyly Carte'. *Pall Mall Gazette*, 7 September 1885, p. 12.

Anon. 'Art. The New English Art Club'. *The Spectator*, 16 April 1887, pp. 526–527.

Anon. *Ashton Weekly Reporter, and Stalybridge and Dukinfield Chronicle*, 28 June 1862, p. 1.

Anon. 'Aubrey Beardsley from a Japanese Standpoint'. *Modern Art*, vol. 3, no. 1, 1895, pp. 22–24.

Anon. 'Caprice in Purple and Gold: The Golden Screen'. *The National Museum of Asian Art at Smithsonian Institute*, https://asia.si.edu/object/F1904.75a/. Accessed 31 January 2021.

Anon. '"Curiosa"'. *Tate Britain*, https://www.tate.org.uk/whats-on/tate-britain/exhibition/aubrey-beardsley/exhibition-guide. Accessed 31 January 2021.

Anon. 'Dress at the Play'. *The Sketch*, 29 April 1896, p. 42.

Anon. 'Kimono Tea-Gown in Green and Silver'. *Pall Mall Gazette*, 16 November 1907, p. 10.

Anon. 'La Japonaise au Bain, 1864'. *Musée des Beaux-Arts de Dijon*, https://musees.dijon.fr/japonaise-bain-1864. Accessed 29 May 2022.

Anon. 'Our Captious Critic – 'The White Chrysanthemum,' at the Criterion Theatre'. *The Illustrated Sporting and Dramatic News*, 16 September 1905, p. 81.

Anon. 'The Beloved ('the Bride')'. *Tate Britain*, https://www.tate.org.uk/art/artworks/rossetti-the-beloved-the-bride-n03053. Accessed 1 November 2019.

Anon. 'The Princess from the Land of Porcelain (*La Princesse du pays de la porcelain*)'. *The National Museum of Asian Art at Smithsonian Institute*, https://asia.si.edu/object/F1903.91a-b/. Accessed 31 January 2021.

Anon. 'Variations in Flesh Colour and Green – The Balcony'. *The National Museum of Asian Art at Smithsonian Institute*, https://asia.si.edu/object/F1892.23a-b/. Accessed 31 January 2021.

Anon. 'Wilhelm'. http://www.vam.ac.uk/content/articles/w/wilhelm/. Accessed 12 February 2021.

Aristophanes. *Aristophanes Lysistrata*, edited by Jeffrey Henderson, Oxford UP, 1987.

———. *The Lysistrata of Aristophanes*. London, Leonard Smithers, 1896.

Baldry, Alfred Lys. 'The Treatment of Drapery in Painting'. *The Art Journal*, 1909, pp. 231–238. https://archive.org/details/sim_art-journal-us_1909/page/n5/mode/2up

Beardsley, Aubrey. *The Letters of Aubrey Beardsley*, edited by Henry Maas et al., Fairleigh Dickinson UP, 1970.

Breward, Christopher. 'Popular Dressing: 1890–1914'. *The London Look: Fashion from Street to Catwalk*, edited by Christopher Breward, Edwina Ehrman and Caroline Evans, Yale UP, 2004, pp. 61–77.

Clark, Kenneth. *The Nude: A Study in Ideal Form*. Pantheon Books, 1956.

Colligan, Colette. '"Esoteric Pornography": Sir Richard Burton's Arabian Nights and the Origins of Pornography'. *Victorian Review*, vol. 28, no. 2, 2002, pp. 31–64.

Dangerfield, Fred. 'The Story of the White Chrysanthemum'. *The Play Pictorial*, vol. 39, no. 4, 1905, pp. 138–140.

Didi-Huberman, Georges. *Ouvrir Vénus: Nudité, rêve, cruauté*. Editions Gallimard, 1999.

Downer, Lesley. 'Geisha: Perpetuating the Kimono Mystique'. *Kimono: Kyoto to Catwalk*, edited by Anna Jackson, V&A Publishing, 2020, pp. 221–225.

Emery, Elizabeth. *Reframing Japonisme: Women and the Asian Art Market in Nineteenth-Century France, 1853–1914*. Bloomsbury, 2020.

Florence. 'Celebrities' Clothes'. *The Sketch*, 12 August 1896, p. 126.

Fowle, Francis. 'The Reading Girl'. *Tate Britain*, 8 December 2000, https://www.tate.org.uk/art/artworks/roussel-thereading-girl-n04361. Accessed 1 November 2019.

Fredeman, William E., editor. *The Correspondence of Dante Gabriel Rossetti*. D.S. Brewer, 2003.

Fukai, Akiko 深井晃子. *Japonisme in Fashion: umi wo watatta kimono* ジャポニスム・イン・ファッション―海を渡ったキモノ [*Japonisme in Fashion: Kimonos in Overseas*]. Heibonsha, 1994.

———. *Kimono to Japonisme: seiyou no me ga mita nihon no biishiki* きものとジャポニズム：西洋の眼が見た日本の美意識 [*Kimono and Japonisme: Japanese Sense of Beauty Seen by West*]. Heibonsha, 2017.

———. 'Radical Restructure: The Impact of Kimono'. *Kimono: Kyoto to Catwalk*, edited by Anna Jackson, V&A Publishing, 2020, pp. 198–207.

Gere, Charlotte. *Artistic Circles: Design and Decoration in the Aesthetic Movement*. V&A Publishing, 2010.

Gidoni-Goldstein, Ofra. 'Kimono and the Construction of Gendered and Cultural Identities'. *Ethnology*, vol. 38, no. 4, 1999, pp. 351–370.

Gilroy-Ware, Cora. *The Classical Body in Romantic Britain*. Paul Mellon Centre for Studies in British Art, 2020.

Godwin, Edward William. *Dress and Its Relation to Health and Climate*. London, William Clowes & Sons, 1884.

Hollander, Anne. *Seeing Through Clothes*. U of California P, 1993.

Issac, Veronica. 'The Enigma of Ellen Terry (1847–1928)'. *Women's History*. https://womenshistorynetwork.org/the-enigma-of-ellen-terry-1847-1928-dr-veronica-isaac/. Accessed 1 November 2019.

Kirk, Anna Marie. 'Japonisme and Femininity: A Study of Japanese Dress in British and French Art and Society, c. 1860–c. 1899'. *Costume*, vol. 42, 2008, pp. 111–129.

Komeima, Yukiko 米今由希子 and Sasai Kei 佐々井啓. '19 seiki kouhan no igirisu engeki ni mirunihon no fukusyoku' 19 世紀後半のイギリス演劇にみる日本の服飾 ['Japanese Costumes in British Musical Comedies in the Late 19ᵗʰ Century']. *Nihon Jyoshi Daigaku Daigakuin Kiyou* 日本女子大学大学院紀要 [*Journal of Japan Women's University*], vol. 18, 2012, pp. 161–170.

56   *Translating Bodies*

Koyama, Noboru 小山騰. *London nihon-jin mura wo tsukutta otoko: nazo no kougyoshi Tanaka Buhikurosan* ロンドン日本人村を作った男 – 謎の興行師タナカー・ブヒクロサン 1839–1894 [*The Man Who Built the Japanese Native Village in London: The Showman of a Mystery, Tanaka Buhikurosan, 1839–94*]. Fujiwara Shoten 藤原書店, 2015.

Kramer, Elizabeth. '"Not so Japan-Easy": The British Reception of Japanese Dress in the Late Nineteenth Century'. *Textile History*, vol. 44, no. 1, 2013, pp. 3–24.

Kramer, Elizabeth and Akiko Savas. 'The Kimono Craze: From Exoticism to Fashionability'. *Kimono: Kyoto to Catwalk*, edited by Anna Jackson, V&A Publishing, 2020.

Lacambre, Geneviève. 'Les Milieux Japonisants à Paris, 1860–1880'. *Japonisme in Art, An International Symposium*, edited by Chisaburo Yamada, Kodansha International, 1980, pp. 43–55 (translated by the author).

Laughton, Bruce. *Philip Wilson Steer 1860–1942*. Clarendon Press, 1971.

Lavery, Grace E. *Quaint, Exquisite: Victorian Aesthetics and the Idea of Japan*. Princeton UP, 2019.

Lee, Josephine. *The Japan of Pure Invention: Gilbert and Sullivan's The Mikado*. U of Minnesota P, 2010.

Livingstone, Karen. 'Origins and Development'. *International Arts and Crafts*, edited by Karen Livingstone and Linda Parry, V&A Publishing, 2005, pp. 40–61.

Marillier, Henry Currie. *Dante Gabriel Rossetti: An Illustrated Memorial of His Art and Life*. London, George Bell & Sons, 1899.

Minato, Chihiro 港千尋. *Kangaeru hifu: shottkaku bunka ron* 考える皮膚―触覚文化論 [*Considering Skin: Tactile Culture*]. Seidosha 青土社, 1993.

Nead, Lynda. *The Female Nude: Art, Obscenity and Sexuality*. Routledge, 2002 [First published in 1992].

Pennell, Elizabeth Robins and Joseph Pennell. *The Life of James McNeil Whistler*, vol. 1. W. Heinemann, 1908.

Philip Wilson Steer, 1860–1942: Paintings and Watercolours. The Fitzwilliam Museum and the Arts Council of Great Britain, 1986.

Richards, Jeffery. *Imperialism and Music: Britain 1876–1953*. Manchester UP, 2001.

Rossetti, William Michael. *Dante Gabriel Rossetti as Designer and Writer*. London, Cassell & Company Limited, 1889.

————— editor. *Rossetti Papers 1862–1870*. Sands, 1903.

Sasai, Kei 佐々井啓. *Victorian Dandy: Oscar Wilde no fukusyoku-kan to 'atarashi onna'* ヴィクトリアン・ダンデイ：オスカー・ワイルドの服飾観と「新しい女」 [*Victorian Dandy: Oscar Wilde's Fashion Theory and the 'New Woman'*]. Keisou Shobou 勁草書房, 2015.

Sasso, Elenora. *The Pre-Raphaelites and Orientalism: Language and Cognition in Remediations of the East*. Edinburgh UP, 2018.

Sato, Tomoko and Toshio Watanabe. *Japan and Britain: An Aesthetic Dialogue, 1850–1930*. Lund Humphries, 1991.

Savas, Akiko サワシユ晃子. '20 seiki syotou no eikoku ni okeru nihonsei yusyutsuyou kimono no ryutsu to nichiei gyousha no sougo kousyou ni tsuite 20 世紀初頭の英国における日本製輸出用キモノの流通と日英業者の相互交渉にいて ['Japanese Kimonos for the British Market at the Beginning of the 20th Century']. *Journal of the Japan Society of Design*, vol. 65, 2014, pp. 15–29.

—————. '20 seiki syotou no eikoku no taisyu shosetsu ni okeru kimono to kimono Sugata no josei hyoushou no henka' 20 世紀初頭の英国の大衆小説におけるキモノとキモノ姿の女性表象の変化―キモノブームという視点から― ['Changes in the Representation of Kimono and Kimono-clad Women in British Popular Fiction in the Early Twentieth Century']. *Studies in Japonisme*, vol. 35, 2015, pp. 77–95.

—————. 'Dilute to Taste: Kimonos for the British Market at the Beginning of the Twentieth Century'. *International Journal of Fashion Studies*, vol. 4, no. 2, 2017, pp. 157–181.

Schechner, Richard. *Performance Studies: An Introduction*. 3rd ed. Routledge, 2013.

Scott, Clement. 'The Play Houses'. *The Illustrated London News*, 2 May 1896, pp. 570–572.

Shope, Bradley. 'Masquerading Sophistication: Fancy Dress Balls of Britain's Raj'. *The Journal of Imperial and Commonwealth History*, vol. 39, no. 3, 2011, pp. 375–392.

Sik, Sarah. '"Those Naughty Little Geishas": The Gendering of Japonisme'. *The Orient Expressed: Japan's Influence on Western Art, 1854–1918*, edited by Gabriel P. Weisberg, Mississippi Museum of Art, 2011, pp. 107–126.

Sturgis, Matthew. 'Aubrey Beardsley and Oscar Wilde'. *The Wildean*, no. 13, 1998, pp. 15–27.

Suetees, Virginia, editor. *The Diaries of George Price Boyce*. Real World, 1980.

Sullivan, Arthur. *Libretto of the Japanese Comic Opera in Two Acts: The Mikado*. Boston, Oliver Ditson Company. Accessed 7 December 2021.

Summers, Leigh. *Bound to Please: A History of the Victorian Corset*. Berg, 2003.

Suoh, Tamami 周防珠美. '1880–1910 nen dai no igirisu ni okeru nihonsei sitsunaigi: Liberty shoukai no tsushin hanbai catalogue wo tegakari to shite' 1880–1910 年代のイギリスにおける日本製室内着－リバティ商会の通信販売カタログを手がかりとして ['Japanese-Made Gowns in British Liberty's Catalogues, 1880s–1910s']. *Dress Study*, vol. 51, 2007.

Takeda, S. 'A Japanese Criticism of the The Mikado.' *Chicago Daily Tribune*, 29 November 1885, p. 27.

Tawata, Shintaryo 多和田真太良. *19 seiki seiyou engeki ni okeru Japonisme: "nihon" no hyoushou no hensen* 『19 世紀西洋演劇におけるジャポニズム－「日本」の表象の変遷－ [Japonisme in the Western Theatres of the Nineteenth Century]. 2016. Gakushuin University, PhD thesis.

Upstone, Robert. 'The Beloved ('The Bride') 1865–6'. *The Age of Rossetti, Burne–Jones, and Watts: Symbolism in Britain 1860–1910*, edited by Andrew Wilton and Robert Upstone, Tate Publishing, 1997, pp. 100–101.

———. 'Théodore Roussel (1847–1926), The Reading Girl, 1886–7'. *Exposed: The Victorian Nude*, edited by Alison Smith, Tate Publishing, 2001, p. 252.

Wahl, Kimberly. *Dressed as in a Painting: Women and British Aestheticism in an Age of Reform*. U of New Hampshire P, 2013.

———. 'Picturing the Material/Manifesting the Visual: Aesthetic Dress in Late-Nineteenth-Century British Culture'. *Dress History: New Directions in Theory and Practice*, edited by Charlotte Nicklas and Annebella Pollen, Bloomsbury, 2015, pp. 97–112.

Watanabe, Toshio. *High Victorian Japonisme*. Peter Lang, 1991.

Wearing, J. P. *The London Stage 1890–1899: A Calendar of Productions, Performer and Personnel*. 2nd ed. Rowman & Littlefield, 2014.

Wentworth, Michael. 'Tissot and Japonisme'. *Japonisme in Art: An International Symposium*, edited by Chisaburo Yamada, Kodansha International, 1980, pp. 127–146.

Wilde, Oscar. 'The Decay of Lying: A Dialogue'. *The Nineteenth Century*, vol. XXV, edited by James Knowles, London, Kegan Paul, Trench & Co., 1889, pp. 35–56.

Wood, Christopher. *Tissot: The Life and Work of Jacques Joseph Tissot, 1836–1902*. Weidenfeld and Nicolson, 1986.

Yamaguchi, Eriko 山口惠里子. 'Drapery no mukou gawa: Albert Moore "yume miru onna tachi" he' ドレーパリーの向こう側－アルバート・ムーア《夢見る女たち》へ ['Beyond Drapery: Albert Moore's *Dreamers*']. *Media to Fashion: Thomas Gainsborough kara Albert Moore he* メディアとファッション－トマス・ゲインズバラからアルバート・ムーアへ [Medium et Novus Vestium Mos: Ex Thomas Gainsborough ad Albert Moore], edited by Reiko Onodera 小野寺玲子, Arina Shobou ありな書房, 2020, pp. 123–158.

———. 'Raphael zenpa kyoudai dan ni okeru Primitivism: 19 seiki eikoku no "Rhaphael izen" mondai' ラファエル前派兄弟団におけるプリミティヴィズム：19 世紀英国の『ラファエッロ以前』問題 ['Primitivism in the Pre-Raphaelite Brotherhood']. *Journal of Modern Languages & Cultures* 論叢 現代語・現代文化, vol. 4, 2010, pp. 97–155.

———. 'Raphael zenpa kyodai dan ni okeru Primitivism: materiality no realism' 「ラファエル前派兄弟団におけるプリミティヴィズム－マテリアリティのリアリズム ['Primitivism of Pre-Raphaelite Brotherhood: Realism of Materiality']. *Zen Raphael shugi: kako ni yoru 19 seiki kaiga no kakushin* 前ラファエロ主義－過去による 19 世紀絵画の

58 *Translating Bodies*

革新 [*Pre-Raphaelism: Innovating Nineteenth Century Art through the Past*], edited by Chikashi Kitazaki 喜多崎親, Sangensha 三元社, 2018, pp. 149–208.

———. 'Victoria cho no medievalism to Japanisme no setten: Rossetti kyoudai no ukiyo-e collection wo jirei to shite' ヴィクトリア朝の medievalism と Japanisme の接点：ロセッティ兄弟の浮世絵コレクションを事例として ['The Rossetti Collection of Ukiyoe Prints: The Unification of Medievalism and Japanisme in Victorian England']. *Journal of Modern Languages & Cultures* 論叢 現代語・現代文化, vol. 6, 2011, pp. 113–159.

Yokoyama, Toshio. *Japan in the Victorian Mind: A Study of Stereotyped Images of a Nation 1850–80*. Macmillan, 1987.

Zatlin, Linda Gertner. 'Aubrey Beardsley's "Japanese" Grotesque'. *Victorian Literature and Culture*, vol. 25, no. 1, 1997, pp. 87–108.

2 Creating Fashion

The reference of Japan in British sartorial culture was first developed in association with artistic movements that emerged in the second half of the nineteenth century. 'Tea gown' is one of the earliest and most popular forms that adopted Japanese characteristics, for it was widely worn by women of upper- and upper-middle-class since the late 1870s. This chapter seeks to show the experience of kimonos emerged within the aesthetic circle, the fashionable high society to the world of mass consumption from the late Victorian period to the early twentieth century. It especially focuses on the adoption of kimonos among the upper to middle classes. It is a well-known fact that many wealthy women of upper- and upper-middle classes enjoyed wearing kimono-inspired garments at home, so they became the central figures of the commercial Japonisme at the turn of the century. The kimono was largely modified to meet their (or society's) expectation, so the gowns called 'kimono' had a highly westernised hourglass silhouette during the Victorian period.

In the twentieth century, on the contrary, a new silhouette began to be introduced by the new designers of the luxury couture houses in Paris. And simultaneously, 'kimono' in Britain gradually altered its silhouette from a highly westernised dress to an open-fronted gown that is similar to an original Japanese kimono. Furthermore, kimono began to be mass produced to also allow cheaper kimonos to be circulated across Britain.

Their commercialisation and popularisation had also altered the definition of 'kimono' in Britain. At first, Japanese-like motifs, *obi*-belts and long-hanging sleeves defined the 'kimono', but later 'kimono' came to be interpreted more widely. In the mid-1910s, any gown could be called a 'kimono' as long as it was a loose open-fronted gown. Materials and prices gained a wider range in the early twentieth century, so kimonos became affordable to much wider populations.

At the turn of the century, the kimono was the symbol of wealth and class. As a result, cheaper kimonos that imitated expensive ones began to be produced and sold not only in the cities but also in other parts of the country. Widely commercialised kimonos became a familiar dress by the mid-1910s instead of solely luxury gowns. The materials used rather than the kimono itself became the barometer of wealth and class. However, it is important to note that assuming that kimonos were adopted by all who could afford them could be misleading. Although cheaper kimonos started to be sold in the early 1900s, it was still considered an item that was unnecessary to the everyday life of most working-class people. The lower middle classes, whose numbers were increasing in the early twentieth century, could have enjoyed the newly available cheaper kimonos.

The kimonos that were circulated across Britain can now be found in museums and private collections throughout both Japan and Britain. This chapter introduces some of those surviving kimonos and demonstrates how they are materially and sensory different

DOI: 10.4324/9781003334255-3

60   *Creating Fashion*

from the westernised kimonos of the previous period. Furthermore, the object-based analysis of each garment also shows how expensive and cheap kimonos would have been worn differently at the beginning of the new century.

Aestheticism to Department Stores: Luxury Kimonos, 1879–1914

Several artistic movements in design developed in the late Victorian period, most of which sought to highlight—and encourage the pursuit of—their idea of beauty and to reject the ugliness of industrialisation. Being deeply influenced by the idea of John Ruskin (1819–1900), an English designer William Morris (1834–1896) teamed up with his fellow painter, Edward Burne-Jones (1833–1898), 'to create an alternative to the dehumanising industrial systems that produced poor-quality, "unnatural" objects' ('Introducing William Morris'). Morris was influenced by a chapter of Ruskin's treatises, *The Stones of Venice*, in which Ruskin argued the importance of manual labour rather than making a man like a tool.[1] Morris and Burne-Jones were also deeply influenced by the Pre-Raphaelite Brotherhood, an artistic group formed in 1848 that rejected the artistic ideals established by the Royal Academy and tried to explore a new style of art by learning from the art and design of the Middle Ages (Yamaguchi, 'Primitivism of Pre-Raphaelite Brotherhood: Realism of Materiality' 149). The idea of 'primitive' art promoted by the Pre-Raphaelites and the natural and organic form of design advocated by Morris and Burne-Jones created a trend in Britain toward re-thinking the true meaning of 'beauty', both in art and in life. The Aesthetic Movement, guided by the motto 'art for art's sake', was promoted by artists such as Burne-Jones, James Abbott McNeil Whistler and Albert Joseph Moore (1841–1893) in painting and by Morris in applied arts. In aestheticism, the art and culture of medieval Europe, ancient Greece and the newly accessible Japan were treasured and considered keys to the creation of new art and design.

Samuel Bing, one of the key figures involved in the creation of Japonisme in art and design in Europe, was an art dealer/collector and publisher who noticed in the movement's earliest stages that a new trend in decorative art was emerging from Japan. Perhaps, his most remarkable contribution to Japonisme was his periodical on Japanese art and culture, *Le Japon Artistique*, which was first published in 1888 in France. This journal was printed in French, English and German and included detailed illustrations of artworks, primarily from Bing's own collections (Weisberg 25). The textiles reproduced in *Le Japon Artistique*, for example, sometimes inspired fashion designers and were used for dress designs. The journal was translated into English as *Artistic Japan* and published in Britain starting in 1888. It also inspired aesthetes in Britain. The French Japonisme and the British Japonisme intertwined although, according to Ono, French Japonisme was structurally different from the Japonisme developed in Britain. While *Artistic Japan* put more focus on educating people for the development of industrial designs, the Aesthetic Movement in Britain lied in the cultivation of 'good taste' by extracting the essence of Japan (Ono 15–16).

The Arts and Crafts Movement was born in the late 1880s, based on '[c]oncerning for the diminishing role of the craftsman, caught in a downward spiral since the Industrial Revolution' (Livingstone 40). The Arts and Crafts Movement, too, rejected the ugliness of manufactured objects, but this movement was focused more on practical design for everyday life than on the fine arts. William Morris, who by the 1880s had become commercially successful through his interior designs, was the central figure of the Arts and Crafts Movement (Parry and Livingstone 13). Both the Aesthetic Movement and the Arts and Crafts Movement accelerated a new trend in decorative arts and furnishing design in Britain but soon incorporated the on-going discussion on dress, especially female dress.

Late Victorian Britain saw the rise of the dress reform movements, which promoted clothing standards that were more practical and comfortable than the typical fashions of the time. Dress reform was developed along with the artistic movements described above, as the supporters of those artistic movements also actively promoted the new styles of female dress from around the 1880s.[2] Traditional Victorian female dress typically exaggerated the feminine silhouette through the use of many layers of undergarments, including corsets and heavy skirts. Upper- to middle-class women in Victorian Britain were considered to belong at home, where they were expected to play the role of decorative accessories. Female dress was accordingly far from practical or comfortable, to the extent that medical professionals were often alarmed about this 'unhealthy' fashion. Tight-lacing, above all, was notorious not only because it could cause pain but also because 'it might impair [women's] child-bearing potential' (Ashelford 229). Nevertheless, corsetry was considered essential by women in all social classes. Leigh Summers, who conducted a study on Victorian corsetry, suggested that even the poorest women 'did not necessarily have to go without them', as those who could not afford to buy corsets 'could make their own' (11). Victorian corsets were boned using whalebone or steel and were usually worn very tight enough to press the ribs and organs. The dangerous nature of corsetry was one of the most widely discussed controversies in the late Victorian period. Other Victorian sartorial trends, such as big crinolines and bustles worn underneath the skirt, also made it difficult for women to move freely. The most well-known reform dress was bloomers, the divided garments for women, that came from America in the 1850s. Bloomerism was backlashed in Britain, as *Punch* reproduced numbers of cartoons to mock women wearing bloomers. In 1890s, another kind of reform dress was invented by the central figure of the Rational Dress Society, Florence Wallace Pomeroy (1843–1911), a divided skirt for cyclists. They were, again, bifurcated and allowed women to have more freedom of movement.

While the rational dress movements and the aesthetic movement were deeply intertwined, the aesthetic dresses looked different from those rational dresses explained above. The origins of aesthetic dress lay with the Pre-Raphaelites, who took an 'innovative yet historicised approach to merging art and life' in their work (Wahl, *Dressed as in a Painting* 3). Rossetti, for example, often depicts models in dresses with loose sleeves and waist that went against the conventional styles of the mid-Victorian period (4).[3] Yet, aesthetic dress was a matter not only of fine arts but also of health and taste. The principles of the Aesthetic Movement whereby feminine beauty was identified with healthy bodies (13). Aesthetic dress has a mixed style incorporating several different characteristics of dresses of the past. Kimberly Wahl explained it as follows:

> Initially based on earlier Pre-Raphaelite models, Aesthetic dress was eclectic and historicist, merging antique or medieval models with picturesque elements drawn from later periods: smocking, a high or natural waist, puffed sleeves, squared off necklines from the Renaissance and more often than not, the inclusion of a 'Watteau' panel inspired by the sacque-back styles of the eighteenth century (Wahl, 'Picturing the Material/Manifesting the Visual' 99).

In addition, Japanese costumes were also adopted as a means of achieving the aesthetes' ideal of natural and beautiful dress.[4]

62   *Creating Fashion*

It was through 'tea gowns' that these artistic ideals were transmuted into actual fashion. Five o'clock tea became a new habit among upper- and upper-middle-class ladies and gentlemen by the 1860s (Pool 209). It was recognised as a social ritual that they gathered together in the drawing room for afternoon tea at five o'clock. Afternoon tea was often enjoyed with family members and close friends, so it was less formal compared to dinners and balls. People changed their dresses for afternoon teas, so 'tea gowns' were invented exclusively for this new habit. Kei Sasai explained that these tea gowns were less structured but more formal than morning gowns (199). Tea gowns quickly became fashionable among wealthy ladies from the late 1870s to the 1890s (Sasai 200).

These gowns, designed for semi-public settings, were one of the key means through which Aestheticism was promoted in Britain. In 1881, Mary Eliza Haweis (1848–1898), one of the founders of the Rational Dress Society in Britain and an author who actively published works on female fashion and interior decoration from the late 1870s to the entire 1880s, referred to the close connection between dress and interior design in her publication, *The Art of Decoration* (1881). She wrote that '[f]urniture is a kind of dress, dress is a kind of furniture, which both mirror the mind of their owner, and the temper of the age' and concluded that dress and furniture 'ought to be considered together' (Haweis 17). During the late nineteenth century, the matters of dress and interior design were interrelated for fashionable women. Not only Victorian ladies 'wore' home interior, but the dress was also part of home décor. In this sense, tea gowns worn in the drawing room, which was considered the most feminine space in the house, were one of the important pieces of decorations in the room (Kume 183).[5] Therefore, the aesthetic tea gowns could also play a role in adding some artistic touch to the drawing room as part of the interior decorations, which helped aesthetic style of dresses be adopted rather widely not only among the artistic circles but also among the women of upper and upper-middle classes.

In 1893, a high-society women's journal called *The Lady* featured tea gowns with various aesthetic influences, including 'Elizabethan' and 'Empire' styles, both of which were deeply inspired by historical fashion designs (qtd. in Sasai 207). References to Japanese designs were seen elsewhere in high-society journals as well. There is a fashion illustration of a 'Japanese *Robe de Chambre*' in an article in *The Queen* published on 26 April 1879 (qtd. in Sasai 235). *Robe de Chambre* originally meant 'indoor gown' but was sometimes used as an earlier name for the tea gown in Britain. The 'Japanese *Robe de Chambre*' in *The Queen* features slightly wider sleeves and an *obi*-like sash belt.

The *Myra's Journal of Dress and Fashion*, advertised as 'the cheapest Fashion Journal in the World', although, at sixpence, it was priced the same as *The Queen* and *The Sketch*, also shows a fashion illustration of a 'Japanese Morning-Gown' in an issue published on 1 April 1887.[6] This gown features long hanging sleeves and a sash belt tied in a bow in front (qtd. in Sasai 236). The description says that it can be used as a tea gown (qtd. in Sasai 236). All of these gowns have few Japanese elements, and they rather mostly look like western-style dresses with a slight exotic touch.

Many such Japanese-influenced tea gowns were featured in these high-society journals, but it was not until 1892 that the name 'kimino', possibly meaning kimono, was attached to a tea gown (qtd. in Sasai 239). This gown, called the 'Kimino Tea Gown' (Figure 2.1), looks more Japanese in form compared to the earlier Japanese-influenced tea gowns discussed above. While the earlier gowns have a completely western dress shape with structured bodices and rather voluminous skirts, this 'Kimino Tea Gown' has a much simpler and more linear silhouette, such that the garment seems to 'wrap' the body rather than the body 'fitting' into a structured garment.

Figure 2.1 '"Kimino" Tea Gown' in *The Queen*, 2 January 1892, p. 12. Newspaper image © The British Library Board. All rights reserved. With thanks to The British Newspaper Archive (www.britishnewspaperarchive.co.uk).

64 *Creating Fashion*

Another example is held at the Kyoto Costume Institute in Kyoto, Japan. It is a Japanese-inspired tea gown in pink (Figure 2.2). It has an exquisite embroidery done by a Japanese embroidery technique, presumed to have made around 1895.[7] KCI presumed that it was from Liberty & Co and declared to have a mixture of the design of the eighteenth century and the medieval period, while the large sleeves also remind us of a

Figure 2.2 Tea Gown, c. 1895. © The Kyoto Costume Institute, photo by Richard Haughton.

Japanese kimono.[8] Tea gowns could be designed to fit more loosely and flexibly because they were intended as indoor gowns that would be worn only in a semi-private setting. They were not expected to be worn at evening balls or dinners, where fashion and the traditional sartorial rules mattered more than comfort.

Aesthetic reform was not, after all, a radical movement that aimed at an immediate and total transformation of female dress; it was guided by a higher hope to 'guide all changes into wholesome directions' according to the Healthy and Artistic Dress Union which was established in July 1890 ('Introduction' *Aglaia* 3). It is not known whether the luxury tea gowns depicted in women's fashion magazines were designed with full agreement with the principles of the Aesthetic Movement or whether their designers had simply picked up some of the current 'artistic' trends for fashionable and commercial reasons. Either way, these gowns played an important role in re-awakening '[t]he cravings for beauty', which could only be satisfied by placing oneself 'in a healthy atmosphere of beautiful surroundings', according to the Healthy and Artistic Dress Union (3). The appropriation of characteristics inspired by Japanese costumes, such as wide hanging sleeves, *obi*-like sash belts, cross-front necklines, the employment of Japanese fabrics and embroideries and their incorporation into British tea gown design—as well as those of the ancient Greece and the medieval period—promoted the aesthetes' and reformers' desire to improve the body within by wearing healthier and more beautiful clothing as Arthur Liberty addresses that 'object-lessons' from Japan could develop the taste in dress in the West (Liberty 27). The adoption of the name 'kimino' and the shift in fashion design away from the traditional western silhouette initiated a wave of change in the female dress of British high society. Although late Victorian society was not ready for a dramatic reform of western female dress, the emergence of these aesthetic tea gowns suggests that fashion was already moving in a non-traditional direction that this movement appealed to wealthy women with artistic taste and that an appreciation for Japanese design was deeply involved in this process.

Liberty's, a department store in Regent Street, London, took the initiative in promoting aesthetic women's dress. In 1864, Farmer & Rogers, a draper in London, bought some of the Japanese exhibits from the International Exhibition of 1862 and used them to start an Oriental Warehouse that sold Japanese and other Eastern goods (Adburgham 13). Arthur Lasenby Liberty (1843–1917), who worked for Farmer & Rogers at the time, was fascinated by the Japanese display at the exhibition and became the manager of this Oriental Warehouse in 1866 (13). After leaving Farmer & Rogers, Liberty opened his own small shop called 'East India House' at 218 Regent Street, London, on 15 May 1875 (19).

Liberty himself came to be known as the most significant figure in the Japonisme movement during this later period, as his shop promoted Japonisme by selling many kinds of goods imported from Japan. His employee, William Judd, however, explained that East India House sold only 'coloured silks from the East' when it first opened, implying that Liberty's Japonisme had started with textiles (19). Judd added that these silks were '[t]he sort of thing that William Morris, Alma-Tadema and Burne-Jones and Rossetti used to come in and turn over and rave about' (19). These artists named by Judd were involved in the Aesthetic Movement. By the 1880s, Liberty's shop was selling various kinds of Japanese imports, from porcelain to swords (Arwas 194). Liberty extended his store in 1883 and also opened a new shop on the same street.

Thanks to the artistic and intellectual movements of the second half of the nineteenth century, public interest in 'good taste', as opposed to the vulgarity associated with

66 *Creating Fashion*

industrialisation and mechanisation, grew as never before. There was constant demand from the wealthier middle-class 'to purchase something to improve their daily lives at a low cost', and Liberty was well aware of this demand (Ono 27). After expanding his shop, Liberty started producing original products for the shop, all of which were distributed under the name of 'Liberty' rather than the names of their individual designers (Arwas 194). Liberty & Co. became very successful by commercialising public interest in the pioneering artistic movements of the Victorian era.

In 1884, Liberty & Co. opened a costume department 'with its own studio and workrooms, where dresses would be designed and made in Liberty fabrics' (Adburgham 51). This department was directed by the designer E.W. Godwin (1833–1886) who had studied medieval arts under the influence of John Ruskin (1819–1900) and was also a keen collector of Japanese goods (Ono 28–29). He was also greatly inspired by Greek art, an interest that led him to design 'Anglo-Greek' furniture (32). When Godwin became the director of Liberty's costume department, he was already deeply involved with the Dress Reform Movement. Godwin wrote, in a handbook titled *Dress and Its Relation to Health and Climate* for the 1884 International Health Exhibition, that:

> [s]cience and art must walk hand in hand if life is to be worth living. Beauty without health is incomplete. Health can never be perfect for you so long as your eye is troubled with ugliness (2).

Aesthetic sensibility in dress was rooted in the desire to cooperate with medical advice. The beauty of the human body, according to this belief, could only be accomplished through natural and healthy dress.

The key characteristic of the aesthetic reformers' ideal dress was drapery, as seen in the costumes of the ancient Greek and in the Japanese kimonos depicted in *ukiyo-e* prints. The Healthy and Artistic Dress Union was associated with both the Aesthetic Movement and the Arts and Crafts Movement. In the Autumn 1894 issue of *Aglaia: The Journal of the Healthy and Artistic Dress Union*, an article written by Arthur Lasenby Liberty includes several Japanese *ukiyo-e* prints showing women in kimonos. Liberty stated in this article that 'object-lessons from the Land of the Rising Sun have been foundation stones on which western developments in regard to taste in dress have been built up' (Liberty 27). Furthermore, in introducing a drawing by Albert Moore (Figure 2.3), Liberty explained that '[t]he figures are draped in Eastern fabrics, and the composition is intended as an idealised expression of combined western and Oriental motives in treatment' (Liberty 27). The drapery seen in ancient Greek costumes and that seen in Japanese kimonos were often associated with each other and both played a role in inspiring healthier and more beautiful dress. Soft and delicate Eastern fabrics were, in fact, required to create the ideal drapery form necessary to create an aesthetic dress (Adburgham 14).

The analogy between Greek and Japanese dress had already been declared as early as 1875 when a man named C. A. Bridge referred to the similarity of Greek *chiton* and Japanese kimono in his article titled 'The Mediterranean of Japan' (qtd. in Tanita 105).[9] A Japanese art historian, Hiroyuki Tanita, argued that British people saw purity in Japan and that they were obsessed by the idea of 'Old Japan', so it was linked to ancient Greece in the late Victorian Britain (107). While there are similarities found between Japan and ancient Greece, they also have contrasted characteristics recognised within the Victorian society. Employing ancient Greek dress could possibly be one of the means for the Victorians to locate themselves in the European ancient civilisation that was ideal. Therefore,

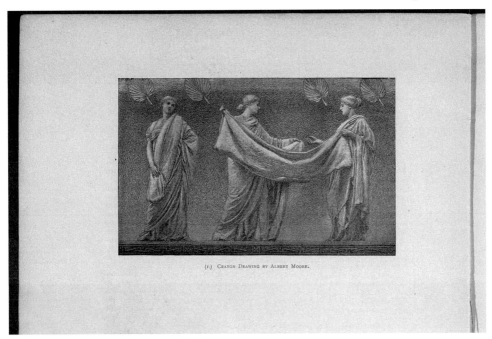

Figure 2.3 Crayon Drawing by Albert Moore in *Aglaia: The Journal of the Healthy and Artistic Dress Union*, 1894, p. 26. By permission of University of Southampton.

it could safely guard them from the fear of *degeneration* that the post-Darwin society was seized with.[10] Employing Japanese dress, on the other hand, could rather expose the anxieties towards Japan, where was undeniably considered an uncivilised non-western country. While it is possible that aesthetes, such as Wilde, Liberty and Godwin, selected Japan from simply aesthetic reasons, the society and the people who adopted those new dress styles could be exposed to those ambivalent images attached to each dress: a safe absolute ideal and a new disturbing nation.

In 1881, Liberty began to issue catalogues in which several varieties of aesthetic dresses were displayed and sold. Japanese-made dressing gowns were sold from 1881 on, explicitly labelled as 'Japanese Silk Dressing Gowns and Jackets', with both men's and women's versions available (Figure 2.4). These quilted dressing gowns featured embroidery depicting clichéd Japanese motifs and were described as having shapes, styles and fittings that were 'carefully adapted for Western use'.[11] They had been made in Japan for western customers since 1873 by the Japanese silk merchant Shobei Shiino (Fukai, *Kimono and Japonisme* 229). Shiino had opened a shop in Yokohama in 1859 when the treaty port was established (Kramer and Savas 179). A dressing gown labelled as having been made by S. Shobey Silk Store is now stored in the Kyoto Costume Institute in Kyoto, Japan (Figure 2.5). This gown, estimated to have been produced in 1875, is made of brown quilted silk with Japanese-style embroidery. Although it has a Victorian-style bustle, it has a looser silhouette, as did most of the indoor gowns sold in Britain in this period. Kramer and Savas explain that these looser fitting gowns 'did not require the complicated sewing techniques of fully tailored gowns and were thus simpler for Japanese artisans to create' (179). While few ladies of the late Victorian period would have worn them without a corset, even in their own homes, these looser indoor gowns at least suggested a

68　*Creating Fashion*

Figure 2.4 'Japanese Silk Dressing Gowns and Jackets' in '*Liberty*' *Yule-Tide Gifts*, 1896, p. 17. By permission of University of Brighton Library Services.

simpler style. In Liberty's catalogue from 1898, Japanese-made women's dressing gowns were offered at prices ranging from 37s 6d to 63s. These are prices that the lower middle class could barely afford, yet the gowns are described in the catalogue as '[i]nexpensive', which implies that Liberty's dresses and catalogues were intended for wealthy customers.

Aesthetic tea gowns were also sold in the company's first catalogue in 1881 (Sasai 212–213). There are two surviving Liberty-made tea gowns stored in the Victoria and Albert Museum. One, made of dark green velvet, has a typical Aesthetic style inspired by the fashions of the late fifteenth century (Figure 2.6). This gown was said to have been made for a member of the Liberty family in 1894. Although this gown appears to fit loosely around the waist, it is described as boned under the bodice.[12] It seems that the aesthetic ideals of 'loose' and 'healthy' gowns were sometimes too radical for most women of the late Victorian period, as Wahl explained, 'Unlike many home-sewn or locally produced examples of Aesthetic dress, which are less structured, boning can be observed in most of the Liberty gowns' (Wahl, 'Picturing the Material/Manifesting the Visual' 107).

In 1896, a gown with a shape similar to that of the Japanese kimono was added to Liberty's catalogues. It was called the 'Japanese Kimono (or Native Dress)', and customers could select from silk, satin or silk crepe for the material (Figure 2.7).[13] The illustration shows a woman in a kimono holding a fan. Her hair, embellished with small fans, is probably a reference to the 'Three Little Maids' from the 1885 comic opera *The Mikado*, which was discussed at length in the previous chapter. This kimono-shaped gown looks

Creating Fashion 69

Figure 2.5 Shiino Shobey Silk Store. At-Home Gown, c. 1875. © The Kyoto Costume Institute, photo by Richard Haughton.

rather authentic and is worn in the Japanese way, with the right side tucked under the left side; this arrangement is called *migimae* in Japan and only the deceased are permitted to wear a kimono closed the opposite way. This kimono was offered in Liberty's catalogue at prices ranging from £2 10s to £10 10s and described as 'adapted for Tea Gowns and Fancy Costumes'.

70 Creating Fashion

Figure 2.6 Liberty & Co. Ltd. Dress, 1894. Victoria and Albert Museum. T.56-1976. ©Victoria and Albert Museum, London.

In 1900, another type of kimono-shaped gown was added to the 'Eastern Embroideries' section of their catalogue. This was called the 'Kimono (or Japanese Robe)' and was offered in 'Liberty' silk-brocade or 'Liberty' printed silk. The catalogue features a photograph of a model on the left who may be wearing this 'Kimono (or Japanese Robe)', but her styling of the kimono is contrary to Japanese custom and her waistline is laced incredibly tight (Figure 2.8).[14] This is priced starting at five guineas if it was made in 'Liberty' silk brocade, or 75/- if it was made in 'Liberty' printed silk. Both are quite expensive such that not all members of the middle class could afford them. As Breward noted, 'Liberty sold a dream of exotic and antique lands to wealthy customers'; these gowns were an aesthetic suggestion aimed at upper- to upper-middle-class ladies (Breward 'Fashion in the Age of Imperialism' 56). Although 'looseness' is not a feature of the kimono pictured in the 1900 catalogue, perhaps, it's simpler design and 'exotic' elements might have helped reawaken 'the cravings for beauty' ('Introduction' 3).

From the late 1880s, even outside artistic circles, these newly introduced Japanese costumes were regarded with anxiety, curiosity and mild 'hope' of a sartorial revolution. In the late 1880s to the 1890s, many articles were published both locally and nationally in Britain introducing and discussing styles of dress in Japan. Among them, there is an article titled 'Dress of Japanese Ladies' consisted of an open letter written by two American women to 'Japanese women who are adopting foreign dress' which was repeatedly reproduced in the different newspapers published in 1888.[15] This article warns Japanese

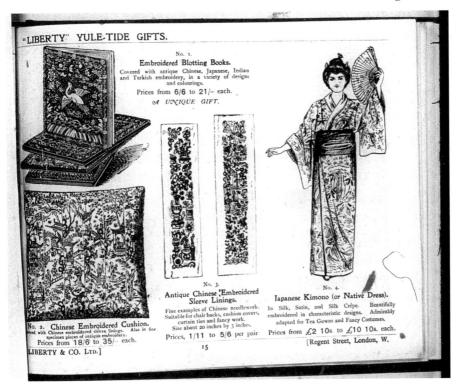

Figure 2.7 'Japanese Kimono (or Native Dress)' in '*Liberty*' *Yule-Tide Gifts*, 1896, p. 15. By permission of University of Brighton Library Services.

women against adopting European dress, pointing out that the heavy skirts, close-fitting bodices and corsets are 'direful in [their] consequences':

> Japanese ladies may be made aware of the dangers in such a course before adopting foreign dress, and that they may be led to stop and consider well before doing what will affect, not only their own health, but that of their sons and daughters ('Dress of Japanese Ladies' 2).

The letter expresses great concern for the health of Japanese ladies, which is put at risk by the adoption of European dress styles, which the two writers clearly believed are 'unhealthy'. This article appeared in many newspapers across Britain from Edinburgh to Canterbury in August and September 1888.[16] It was so widely published that the westernisation of Japanese costume became a matter of public concern in Britain. Furthermore, it is also very significant that this article specifically warned the British readers about the danger of their own dress by using Japan as an example.

Another article on costume in Japan was published in the *Pall Mall Gazette* in 1888. It was titled 'Japanese Dress' and was written by a British travelling commissioner. This article takes a more professional view of the westernisation of costume in Japan, citing a Japanese study conducted by 'Dr. Seiken Takenaka'. Dr. Takenaka, whose details are unknown, seems to have obtained valuable data by conducting a survey in a popular

72 *Creating Fashion*

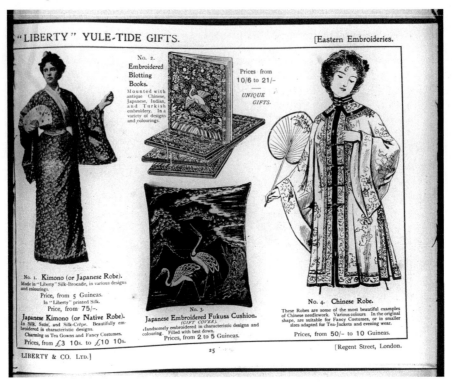

Figure 2.8 'Kimono (or Japanese Robe)' in '*Liberty*' *Yule-Tide Gifts*, 1900, p. 25. By permission of University of Brighton Library Services.

ladies' magazine asking whether Japanese or foreign dress was more suitable for Japanese men and women and requesting that readers contact him with their opinions. His result apparently revealed that 'both Japanese male and female dress is far superior to foreign [dress] in point of durability' ('Japanese Dress' 1–2). The English author reporting on these results notes that 'Japanese dress is best except for boys' clothing and the business dress of men' ('Japanese Dress' 2).

In this long article, which spans two pages, the writer explained what Japanese women typically wore in great detail, including their undergarments and socks. Here, the writer brought up the *himation* belt in ancient Greek dress as an example to explain the Japanese *obi* belt. *Himation* was a type of clothing worn by ancient Greek men and women. It played the role of a cloak or shawl. He wrote that the *obi* 'reveals the taste and cultivation of the wearer almost as much as the throw of the *himation* did in Greece' ('Japanese Dress' 2). He also noted that if a Japanese lady were to remove everything but her *juban*, an undergarment, she would have been 'dressed exactly like a Greek woman' ('Japanese Dress' 2). The connection between the Japanese kimono and the dress of the ancient Greeks was first drawn by the Aesthetes in the 1870s; the article told us that by the late 1880s this association was also acknowledged even outside artistic circles.

According to Dr. Takenaka, the only 'defect' of the Japanese kimono is that it impedes the movement of the legs because the lower limbs are uncovered if the wearer moves rapidly or sits on chairs. The author continues that this can be remedied by 'wearing additional underclothing' or adopting *hakama* [traditional Japanese loose trousers].

However, he notes with regret, adopting *hakama* can lead to the disappearance of the *obi*, which the author believes is 'the beauty of the whole costume' due to its 'long graceful Greek folds' ('Japanese Dress' 2). The author finishes this column by suggesting that Japanese people should learn the details of Greek costume, so that they may achieve the ideally comfortable yet beautiful style of dress ('Japanese Dress' 2).

In 1892, local newspapers in Coventry and Dover ran an article that introduced the customs of Japan and claimed that:

> [w]ith vanity sufficient to produce neatness of appearance and beauty of dress, the Japanese ladies are spared the vagaries of fashion, and custom does not yet necessitate the wearing of hats, bonnets, flowers, stockings, boots, shoes, petticoats, under linen, or jewellery, so that simplicity can still characterise the life of women of even the wealthiest families ('Customs in Japan' 6; 'Little hand cars, or jinrikishas...' 3).

Through this comparison with the admirably simple dress of Japanese women, the writer criticises the fussy dressing styles of the women of his or her own country.

As we have seen, descriptions of and opinions on the costumes of Japan were widely circulated in British newspapers and journals of the late Victorian period. Unlike the actual adoption of aesthetic tea gowns, the readers of those papers are not limited to the women of high society or the wealthier middle classes. The discussions expressed on newspapers also involved the non-aesthetes male readers. The experience of kimonos went beyond the limited artistic circles or the luxury department stores since the late 1880s, raising awareness on the issues on dress and proposing a different way of dressing. Many of these articles praised the simplicity of Japanese costumes and regarded it as a healthier option that could induce a breakthrough in the on-going discussion about female health and women's dress in the West. Furthermore, the analogy between Japanese and Greek dress was often discussed and idealised. This analogy was not a mere whimsical association but actually underlined the contemporary discussions over race, body and the human evolution as discussed earlier. The issue of British women's health and dress was controversial throughout Britain by the end of the nineteenth century, and the costumes of Japan were incorporated into this discussion—and the sartorial revolution that followed—as a healthier alternative.

This section explored the primary development of Japonisme within luxury fashion in Britain. In the examples demonstrated here, the aesthetic aspect of kimonos helped create a new path for British fashion in parallel with the artists' aspiration towards ancient Greek art. Japanese dress was involved in the aesthetes' attempts to liberate female bodies by projecting different femininity. The radical dress reformers promoted bifurcated skirts or other comfortable dress styles, however, did not particularly see Japanese kimonos as 'healthy' (Kramer 14). The aesthetic aspect of kimonos, instead of their actual construction of them, was more important on the adoption of kimono-inspired tea gowns. Even though they were genuinely invented in Britain, kimono-inspired tea gowns had the power to create a space that could 'guide all changes into wholesome directions' as quoted earlier. The actual aesthetic dresses, including kimono-inspired tea gowns, were adopted by the wealthy ladies as well as the women within the artistic circles. It was the luxury department stores such as Liberty's that widely sold those aesthetic dresses. The dresses were priced from £2 at the cheapest, which only allowed some wealthy people to purchase them.

What had been attempted within artistic circles, however, was more widely acknowledged through newspapers and journals, which tell us that the public was aware of the

74 *Creating Fashion*

issues of contemporary western dresses and that Japanese dresses could be one of its solutions. The reaction towards the clothes in Japan was variously expressed within the newspapers and journals in the late nineteenth century. The ideas circulated beyond the artistic circles, helping 'Japanese dresses' to be defined and understood in Britain. The kimono was not an immediate answer to the sartorial problems facing the Victorians, but it certainly gave the elites ideas to tackle these issues. What is significant here is that kimonos were perceived as a sartorial ideology that could provoke arguments both within the artistic circles and in the mass media. By being constantly associated with dresses of the ancient Greece, kimonos were incorporated in the Euro-centric ideal, while they also brought out reactions and responses even by the people who did not physically dress in any of the related costumes.

New Japonisme of the New Century, 1900–1914

As mentioned in the Introduction, Japonisme in fashion trend in Euro-American countries is most acknowledged and popular in form of couture dresses and luxury textiles. It was Charles Frederick Worth, a prominent English fashion designer, who adopted Japanese elements to his dress designs at the end of the nineteenth century. At this time, Japanese motifs were being actively adapted for use in couture dresses and luxury textiles. Unlike British aesthetes who were more interested in forms of Japanese kimono, the exotic Japanese motifs were more adaptable to high fashion during the second half of the nineteenth century. In the new century, however, the Japonisme aesthetic that had been adopted to western high fashion gradually shifted in order to shake off the conventional and traditional dress forms of the West. As seen earlier in this chapter, an increasing number of criticisms over uncomfortable female dresses began to be heard in Britain at the end of the nineteenth century, which was also the case across Europe.

One of the designers who responded to these concerns was Paul Poiret (1879–1944). He opened his own fashion house in 1903 in Paris and designed garments that could be worn without a corset (Fukai 'Radical Restructure' 201). Poiret pioneered a dress design with a straight cutting, an *obi*-like belt arranged at high-waist level or the liner silhouette. His designs from the late 1900s to 1910s show a straight and simpler dress form. One of his mantles designed in 1913 shows his feature design with a crossed-front and wide, loose sleeves.[17] Poiret's designs were popular among British high society. In 1909, one of his dresses, owned by the wife of Herbert Henry Asquith (1852–1928), who served as Prime Minister from 1908–1916, was reported to be worth around £2,000 ('Paul Poiret's Dresses' 5). Poiret's dresses became well-known among the British customers for their radical and modern design from the capital of fashion.

Poiret's radical designs inspired contemporary fashion designers and triggered many other dresses with unconventional silhouettes to be created. Italian-born designer Mariano Fortuny (1871–1949), too, found inspiration in Japanese design and designed several kimono-inspired jackets and gowns from 1910 onwards.[18] A 'kimono coat' stored in the Kyoto Costume Institute, designed between 1910 and 1920, had its pattern taken directly from Japanese *obi* fabric from the late-Edo period (Figure 2.9).[19] This loose open-fronted style of dress utilises original 'Japanese' patterns featuring butterflies, wild ginger and curving lines and utterly loose open-fronted style of dress.

Other couture designers such as Jeanne Paquin (1869–1936) and fashion house Callot Soeurs also designed dresses with liner silhouettes in the 1910s. The early twentieth

Figure 2.9 Mariano Fortuny. Kimono Coat, 1910s. © The Kyoto Costume Institute, photo by Richard Haughton.

76   Creating Fashion

century was a turning point in couture fashion, as the debate over female dresses was further developed and realised through actual dressmaking.

The trend in luxury fashion from the Continent and the popular demand for ready-made clothes in Britain influenced one another. By the beginning of the twentieth century, the gowns with liner silhouette which looks much closer to the original Japanese kimono, instead of the westernised kimono-inspired dresses, had been firmly established as a type of indoor gown in Britain, instead of being considered solely a traditional costume of the Far East. Different varieties of gowns were called 'kimonos' during the early twentieth century, but the most common design was that of a long open-front gown with a sash, padded hem and flamboyant embroideries of flowers and birds.

In Japan, Takashimaya was one of the firms that produced and exported a large number of them to the West. Takashimaya was only a small second-hand clothing shop when it first opened in 1831 in Kyoto, selling pre-owned kimonos to Japanese customers. After Japan opened her ports to foreign countries in 1859, Takashimaya gradually widened its business and started to make their own products instead of just reselling used ones. They welcomed their first foreign customer in 1876 and started to see a future in foreign trade.[20] The company would go on to display their products at the International Exhibitions from 1888 in Barcelona and opened their first trade store in 1900 in Yokohama.[21] According to a 1902 article in the Takashimaya-published *Shinisho*, the company had begun producing and exporting 'kimonos' for western customers since around 1900 (qtd. in Fukai *Kimono and Japonisme* 233). They also opened a branch in London in 1906, which demonstrates that not only were Takashimaya-made kimonos available, but also that the business was successful in England by then.

The Kyoto Costume Institute has one such Takashimaya kimono made for the western market (Figure 2.10). It is made from fine grey silk with embroideries of a big peacock and cherry blossoms scattered around it. The kimono's silhouette is slightly flared out due to the underarm triangle insertions. Museum records show that it was made between 1904 and 1908. This peacock kimono must have been one of the more expensive kimono-shaped gowns that Takashimaya had to offer.

The Takashimaya Historical Archive in Osaka holds a 1911 English-language catalogue which shows a number of both female and male kimonos in various materials. The most expensive kimono in the catalogue was made of heavy silk crepe with silk lining, a matching sash belt and embroidery (Iida & Co., "Takashimaya" 28). It has a similar style to the peacock kimono mentioned earlier. Figure 2.11 shows the pages that reproduce female and male kimonos made for export. One of them is an expensive kimono on a stand. It is priced from 27.50 yen (£2 15s) to 40 yen (£4); the price probably varied depending on the available linings and embroideries.[22] Importantly, this catalogue has a small section introducing a 'cheap line' of kimonos. The cheapest was the half-length kimono made of 'Cheap printed Cotton Crepe' priced at 0.85 yen (about 1s 2d). The full-length one in cheap cotton is 1.30 yen (about 2s 1d). All of the garments sold by Takashimaya were designed and produced in Japan and some of the items used traditional Japanese techniques and materials such as *yoryu* [type of silk crepe], *kabe* [type of silk crepe] and *yuzen* [resist dyeing technique to design on fabric].[23] Considering an average labourer in London at the time earned 7d hourly, 1s was still a lot for most of the people of Britain (Bowley 10). Even so, the evidence that 1s 2d kimonos were sold in 1911 is highly significant in demonstrating the spread of Japanese kimonos at a more popular level rather than being solely a luxury item.

Figure 2.10 Iida Takashimaya. At-Home Gown, c. 1906. © The Kyoto Costume Institute.

78 Creating Fashion

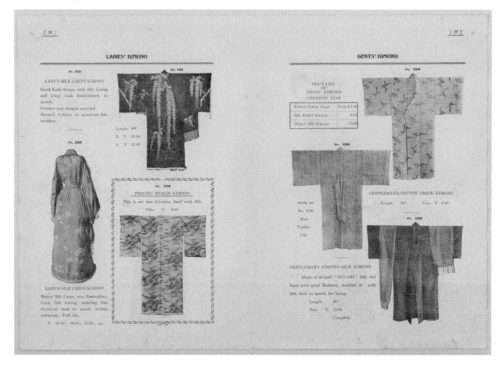

Figure 2.11 Takashimaya. *Novelties in Japanese Articles*, 1911, pp. 28–29. With kind permission of Takashimaya Historical Archive, Osaka.

Takashimaya was keen on keeping a record of their exported products from the 1900s. One of the biggest collections is the albums filled with the photographs of these exports. According to Takashi Hirota, who conducted a study on Takashimaya and their trade business with western countries, the photographs in the albums were taken from the end of the Meiji period (1868–1912) through the Taisho period (1912–1926) and into the early Showa period (1926–1989) (Hirota *Photo Albums of Exported Textiles Produced by Takashimaya* 2–3). Many kimonos that had become popular as indoor gowns in Britain were photographed and kept in these albums. Most of them show cliché Japanese motifs: chrysanthemums, wisterias, cherry blossoms, irises, camelias, birds and butterflies. Notably, a number of roses also appear on these gowns (Figure 2.12).

The variety of motifs arranged on kimonos is also reflected in Takashimaya's illustrated pattern book of exported kimonos, presumably made between 1909 and 1916 (Hirota *About 'Kimono Designs for Foreigners'* 45). Roses are also often used in the book. Roses were not only a popular motif in western society for many centuries, but they also became popular in Taisho-era Japan as a 'modern' western motif (Sakuragi 21). The many rose-motif kimonos made for the western market implies that stereotypically 'Japanese' motifs were not necessary for a garment to be recognised as 'Japanese' in the West.

Takashimaya's exported kimonos nevertheless stayed closer to traditional Japanese kimonos in their form. Even though some of them have triangle insertions for creating a flared hem, the kimonos have a much squarer, straighter silhouette than any European

Creating Fashion 79

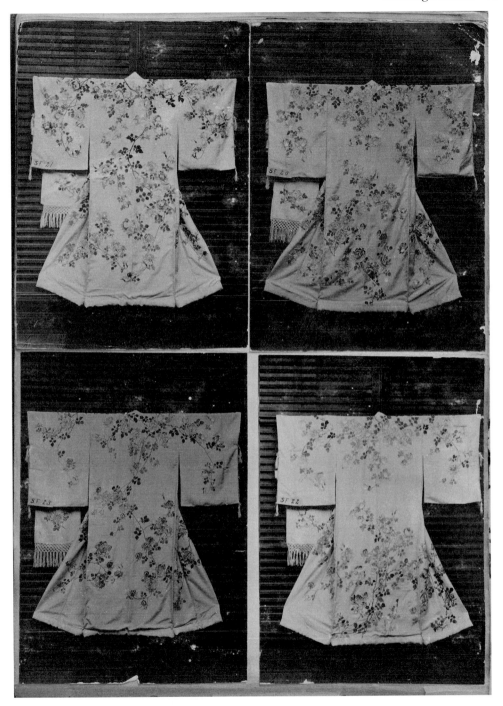

Figure 2.12 Takashimaya. The photographs of kimonos made for the West in *Takashimaya Photo Album of Export Goods*, circa 1910–1929. Takashimaya Historical Archive, ツ 45. With kind permission of Takashimaya Historical Archive, Osaka.

80 *Creating Fashion*

dresses of the period. While the westernised tea gowns sold at the British department stores had been called 'kimonos' from the 1870s, Takashimaya's nearly authentic garments were also called 'kimonos' in the contemporary market. Takashimaya's production of various kimonos with different lengths, materials and prices led the 'kimono' to be interpreted much more widely in Britain, rather than defining it as one particular style of costume.

According to Akiko Savas, who researches kimonos sold in Britain in the early twentieth century, kimono-shaped gowns were also available everywhere in London from small shops to grand department stores (Savas 'Japanese Kimonos for the British Market at the Beginning of the 20th Century' 17). Many were imported from Japan, as seen in Japanese trade records stating that 50,000 to 450,000 'silk night gowns' were exported annually to England from 1902 to 1920 (qtd. in Savas 18). Savas believes that this 'silk night gown' was, in fact, a kimono made for the western market.

While not known whether they were made in Japan or in Britain, some of the department stores in Britain were selling many types of kimono-shaped gowns in the early twentieth century. One of the largest and most luxurious department stores in London, Harrods, sets out an oriental department in 1895 until October 1921, where they sold Japanese goods (18). A 1909 Harrods catalogue advertised 'Chic Kimonos & Wraps' shows four different kimono-shaped gowns, including a half-length cotton kimono priced at 3s 11d and a far more expensive full-length Japanese silk kimono with embroidery priced at 59s 6d (Kramer and Savas 191; Savas 'Japanese Kimonos for the British Market at the Beginning of the 20th Century' 17). Other famous stores such as Whiteley's and Gamage's also began selling kimonos in the 1900s.

A kimono held by the Worthing Museum and Art Gallery in Sussex represents a surviving example of the more expensive kimonos (Figure 2.13). It is dated to 1900, but little else is known about it except that it was donated in 1961. Made from very fine silk and decorated with colourful and flamboyant embroideries of wisterias and chrysanthemums, this kimono is padded all over with heavy padding at the hem. It has a similar style to the peacock kimono of Takashimaya (Figure 2.10). The stiffness of the fabric helps the kimono to stay rather straight. It is a full-length kimono but was shortened, probably by the owner. There is a matching sash-belt with embroideries of chrysanthemums on one end and wisteria on the other. The form of this kimono is remarkably close to a traditional Japanese kimono, with a straight silhouette from top to bottom, but the cut is still different from a traditional Japanese one. It is difficult to tell if it was made in Japan or elsewhere, but it was certainly designed specifically for westerners.

The Chertsey Museum in Surrey also holds a kimono of very fine silk (Figure 2.14). It is in pale pink with embroidered roses lending it a hybrid atmosphere. This kimono is also padded, making it stiff enough to maintain its liner silhouette when wrapped around the body of the wearer. It was altered by stitching the front closed, so that it has to be pulled on over the head. According to the costume keeper at the Chertsey Museum, Grace Evans, it was said to have been worn by Queen Mary (1867–1953) in the 1930s during the final illness of King George V (1865–1936). While cheaper kimonos were already on the market by the early twentieth century, a kimono could keep its air of luxury through the right fabrics and embroideries. Graceful pink roses, instead of 'exotic' Japanese flowers and birds, were probably a more suitable choice for a queen.

Another silken kimono is held in the Tunbridge Wells Museum and Art Gallery in Kent (Figure 2.15). It represents a slightly more modest design than the former examples and was presumably also less expensive. It is not stuffed with paddings as the examples

Figure 2.13 Satin Kimono, 1900. Worthing Museum and Art Gallery. 1961/706. Personal photograph by the author, with kind permission of Worthing Museum and Art Gallery.

above and is only padded at the hem, creating a much softer silhouette when wrapped on a stand as done in the photograph. Camelias and plum blossoms in a similar colour to the silk are embroidered on the ⅓ of the garment.

Although the luxury kimonos made of fine silks are more likely to have been preserved by many museums, some cheaper examples can also be found in local museums and private collections. One such example is in Bexhill, a sea-front resort in East Sussex which developed rapidly between 1883 and 1902 (Porter 22, 30). The local museum houses a large collection of costumes, including a great number of kimonos that were made for the western market. One of them is made of coarse silk crepe in pink, with embroidered camellias, wisterias, chrysanthemums, and butterflies (Figure 2.16). It is not padded at all,

82 *Creating Fashion*

Figure 2.14 Dressing Gown, 20th century. Chertsey Museum. M. 1986.15. Image courtesy of the Olive Matthews Collection, Chertsey Museum. Photo by John Chase Photography.

Figure 2.15 Kimono, 1833–1866. Tunbridge Wells Museum & Art Gallery. Museum Number TUNWM: 1993.149. © Tunbridge Wells Borough Council t/a The Amelia. Personal photograph by the author.

84 *Creating Fashion*

Figure 2.16 Kimono. Bexhill Museum. Personal photograph by the author, with kind permission of Bexhill Museum, Bexhill-on-Sea.

so it is very light weight. There is also a similar kimono in green (Figure 2.17). These kimonos were presumably sold between the late 1900s and the 1920s when indoor gowns were popularised and became available even in the countryside. The local newspaper also advertised kimonos being sold at the local department store, Miller & Franklin, in 1914.[24] The kimono in the advertisement is 2s 11¾d, but they also add that they have other gowns in their showroom priced up to 5 guineas. This suggests that a variety of kimonos were even available at the local department store in a small seaside town by 1914. One of the cheapest kinds of kimonos has survived in the Tunbridge Wells Museum (Figure 2.18). It has no lining, no padding and no hanging sleeves. Dated between 1890 and 1910, this ¾ length cotton kimono has a yellow bird, irises and cherry blossoms hand-embroidered in cotton, and a cotton sash is attached at the back. This was possibly made at home using paper patterns. The *Acton Gazette*, London's halfpenny local newspaper, for example, advertised a kimono paper pattern for 6½d on 30 January 1914 ('Practical Nightdress' 8). The kimono in the *Acton Gazette* is described as a cheap and easy-to-make garment that is 'both useful and dreamy, and as will be seen by one glance at the sketch the making of the one in question will not tax too severely either one's time or one's pocket' (8). These examples suggest that those cheaper kinds of kimonos had already been popularised before the First World War. Although it must have been unusual for the members of the working-class, who made up most of the populations in the early-twentieth-century Britain, to actually adopt kimonos in their everyday lives, cheaper ones were at least affordable to much wider classes. The expensive gowns, on the

Figure 2.17 Kimono. Bexhill Museum. Personal photograph by the author, with kind permission of Bexhill Museum, Bexhill-on-Sea.

other hand, were still being produced for wealthy customers. The 'kimono' itself was no longer a privilege in the 1910s, but rather the quality of the garment reflected the owner's financial and social status.

Kimonos also triggered a physical and sartorial change for British women in its mass production and consumption from around 1900 on. Western dresses and Japanese kimonos are fundamentally different, not only in form but also in meaning. Western dress was structured and made to be worn by human bodies, thus it remained 'clothing' even when not being worn. Kimonos, on the other hand, were traditionally used as household goods as well as garments in Japan for centuries, such as being hung to make a screen or being used as a duvet on a cold night. The kimono's existence as 'clothing' has always been blurred because it often altered its role in Japanese culture.

Kimono's ambivalent characteristics greatly deviated from the western sartorial standards of the early twentieth century, therefore, at the beginning of the twentieth century, the adoption of flat, liner and shapeless characteristics of kimonos within the British sartorial culture suggested a different experience of 'wearing a garment' towards the wide range of consumers. The kimono-shaped gowns in Britain require human bodies to be worn, but they do so by draping over the body instead of shaping it to a certain shape. They were 'worn' but also 'barely worn' in western contexts because a kimono is essentially a formless garment. British encounters with kimonos shook the overall meaning of 'clothing' and the body inside it.

The influence of kimonos on British dresses and bodies became all the more obvious as kimonos permeated across the country. While luxury kimonos such as the ones in

86 *Creating Fashion*

Figure 2.18 Kimono, 1890–1910. Tunbridge Wells Museum & Art Gallery. Museum Number TUNWM: 1993.239. © **Tunbridge Wells Borough Council t/a The Amelia. Personal photograph by the author.**

Worthing and Chertsey are not restrictive, they were heavily padded and too stiff to create the 'drapery' which Arthur Liberty suggested as the key to create beautiful dress in *Aglaia* quoted earlier in this chapter. The cheaper kimonos like the one in the Tunbridge Wells Museum and in the Bexhill Museum, on the other hand, were much lighter and softer that allowed them to loosely drape around the wearer's body. Object-based observation of various surviving kimonos shows how the ideas and discourses around kimonos reflected on the actual garments. While both expensive, stiff kimonos and cheaper, softer kimonos do not necessarily mould the wearers' bodies, the cheaper and softer ones could frame any body: corseted or uncorseted, skinny or large, tall or short, still or moving. While thin kimonos might have been too revealing for women of higher social status meaning they did not adopt them, while other, cheaper kimonos brought new possibilities to contemporary relationships between the female body and dress in the early-twentieth-century Britain.

Virginia Woolf (1882–1941) was one of the modernists who repeatedly addressed the peculiarity of the Victorian period and the improvement people and society made in the new century. Her famous remark, 'on or about December 1910 human character changed', expressed the difference she felt in Britain from the previous period (4). She continued, 'All human relations have shifted [...]. And when human relations change there is at the same time a change in religion, conduct, politics, and literature. Let us agree to place one of these changes about the year 1910' (5). 1910, she meant by the first Post-Impressionist Exhibition organised by Roger Fry at London's Grafton Galleries in November 1910 to January 1911, which presented progressive art from France.[25] In her outstanding novel titled *Orlando: A Biography*, Woolf also wrote that everything is simplified and visible in the twentieth century.[26] According to her, all the 'lingering shadows' and 'odd corners' that had been existed in Victorian period had vanished (267). Here, Woolf specifically mentioned the invention of electricity, but the concept of simpleness and visibleness was also a key notion in the early-twentieth-century kimonos. The excess decorations and the persistent effort to mould female bodies had become out of date towards the 1910s. The silhouette of the kimonos in Britain became much liner and simpler than the conservative Victorian kimonos.

This section discusses the adoption of kimonos in the early twentieth century. In this period, kimono-shaped gowns, which were less westernised and much closer to the form of original Japanese kimonos, started to be widely adopted as indoor gowns by upper- and upper-middle-class women. The utility was also widened and those gowns were worn not only as tea gowns but also as night gowns by this period. British department stores and retailers were importing, producing and selling 'kimonos' specifically designed for the western market. The materials used for those kimonos varied from fine silk to coarse cotton and the price also varied from a few shillings to several pounds. Kimonos for the western market were also produced in Japan; Takashimaya, a department store established in Kyoto, was one of the large firms that produced and exported a number of kimonos overseas.

This chapter shows the beginning of Japonisme within the world of luxury fashion developed specifically in Britain from the 1870s and further discusses the original ideas rooted in this development. Seeing clothes in Japan as one of the more aesthetic inspirations, aesthetes and some progressive women adopted 'Japanese-inspired tea gowns' for the future improvement of contemporary sartorial standards. Furthermore, aesthetes in Victorian Britain often associated Japanese dress with a dress of 'ancient Greek' and tried to seek a solution for more aesthetic and comfortable way of dressing by studying

88 *Creating Fashion*

and adopting them.[27] Interestingly, while both the radical dresses of the Victorian dress reform movements such as the bloomers and the bicycle dresses and the aesthetic suggestions of new dress styles ultimately aimed at the improvement of health and the liberation of female bodies, their final products were completely different. The former was criticised as revealing the mannish nature of women, while the latter sought a different kind of femininity by referencing various kinds of dress including that of Japan.

The aesthetes' attempts in dress came to be widely adopted by the wealthy women with artistic taste at the end of the nineteenth century when the aesthetic style dresses, including the ones that were inspired by Japanese kimonos, became visible in high society journals and were available at the department stores. These 'kimonos' made for the western market were, at first, highly conservative in style that invented Japanese-inspired 'tea gowns' that did not surprise the Victorian consumers too much. The dress shape of these kimonos for the non-aesthetes remained traditional with hourglass silhouette during the nineteenth century until the famous designers adopted loose open-fronted character of a Japanese kimono to create new silhouette of the new century.

Since the beginning of the twentieth century, loose square-shaped kimonos were also widely adopted among the women of upper and middle classes. While the luxury silken kimonos with elaborate embroideries were produced for the wealthy customers, cheaper kimonos and paper patterns were also available to those who could not afford the former. Thus, kimonos became a more popular garment and circulated across Britain in the early twentieth century. As argued earlier, the cheap kimonos were light, thin and soft. It was generally opened in front to show what's beneath; it did not mould a wearer's body into a garment. It was 'barely worn' in the traditional western sartorial standard even though it was wrapped with a sash. The openness and softness of the cheap kimono-shaped gowns—not as a movement but quite unintentionally—emancipated female bodies in parallel to the innovations attempted in the luxury Couture fashion from Paris. Therefore, in the early twentieth century, the 'human relations' changed as well as the relationship between clothes and body. Cheap kimonos delivered this spirit of the period to more populations in Britain to those who could not afford any of those expensive garments.

Notes

1 Ruskin argued that 'a man of the working creature' was far from a machine-like tool. If one tried to make a man work like a tool, it was equivalent to the 'unhumanization'. See Ruskin 11.

2 The Rational Dress Society was organised in 1881 in London. The leading members were Lady Harberton, Mary Eliza Haweis and E. M. King. For more on the Rational Dress Society, see Wahl 12–13.

3 Rossetti drew loose gowns that allowed the free motion of the bodies in *Portrait of Elizabeth Siddal* in 1854 and *Mariana* in 1868–1870. See Wahl 2–7.

4 Unlike the aesthete's views, the Rational Dress Society established in 1881 took a prudent view on adopting Japanese kimono as 'unsuited for active life' because it 'imped the free movement of its wearers' in *The Rational Dress Society's Gazette* published in April and July in 1889. See Kramer 14.

   While Japanese kimonos were seen as an inspiration by aesthetes, not all dress reformers appreciated exotic dresses as inspiration. Victorian dress reform was complex in the way that it did not immediately adopt one kind of garment but blending forms and concepts of different ideas and existing examples.

5 In a typical late Victorian middle-class household, rooms were regarded as either public and masculine or private and feminine. Rooms such as the study, entrance hall and billiard room were masculine, whereas the drawing room and morning room were considered feminine. For more on gen der in the Victorian household, see Kume 183.

6 Myra's journal is advertised as 'cheap' in the *Kilburn Times* published on 25 February 1881. See the *Kilburn Times* 4.
7 The object is named 'Tea Gown' and the museum number is AC6993 91-12-14. It is done in *nikuirinui* technique. See the object description in the KCI Digital Archives. https://www.kci.or.jp/en/archives/digital_archives/1890s/KCI_116. Accessed 30 November 2021.
8 See the object description in the KCI Digital Archives. https://www.kci.or.jp/en/archives/digital_archives/1890s/KCI_116. Accessed 30 November 2021.
9 Tanita referenced 'The Mediterranean of Japan' by C. A. Bridge published in *Fortnightly Review* 18 n. s., 1875, pp. 205–216. See Tanita 105.
10 Max Nordau (1849–1923), a Hungarian author, condemned late nineteenth century artists, writers, poets, and composers, including Oscar Wilde (1854–1900), in his influential work *Degeneration*. It was first written in German in 1892 and was translated into English in 1895. This work was dedicated to Cesare Lombroso (1835–1909), an Italian criminologist, who pursued the concept of criminal atavism. Because *Degeneration* was based on these contemporary scientific concepts, Nordau attempted to advise readers to exhibit the right morality, right knowledge, and right sense of beauty to enable them to continue to evolve and progress, while others degenerated. See Nordau.
11 The advertisement of 'Japanese Silk Dressing Gowns and Jackets' is repeatedly reproduced in Liberty's catalogues. One of them is in *"Liberty" Yule-Tide Gifts* (1896), p. 17.
12 See V&A's museum record. http://collections.vam.ac.uk/item/O15543/dress-liberty-co-ltd/. Accessed 12 December 2021.
13 See Anon *"Liberty" Yule-Tide Gifts* (1896) 15.
14 In the UK, female top or jacket is closed with the left side under the right and the male ones are closed in the opposite way.
15 One of the authors is probably Rose Elizabeth Cleveland (1846–1918) who served as the first lady of United States of America in 1885–1886.
16 The article was published in the London-based newspapers such as the halfpenny *The Evening News* and the penny *St James's Gazette*, and some local penny newspapers such as *Derbyshire Courier*, *Croydon Guardian and Surrey Country Gazette* and *The Shields Daily Gazette* just to name a few.
17 The mantle is held at the Victoria and Albert Museum in London. The accession number is T.165&A-1967.
18 Fortuny found inspiration in ancient Greek dresses too. He invented 'Delphos,' pleated gown made with soft silk satin or taffeta fabrics of China and Japan. Here again, the analogy between ancient Greek and Japan led the invention of modern and liberating style of dress. See Asami, especially section 3, for more information on Delphos and kimono-inspired garments.
19 This Japanese textile was reproduced in Samuel Bing's *Le Japon Artistic* vol. 2 published in 1888. The same textile was also referenced by luxury textile company in Lyon called Bianchini-Férier in 1907. For more information on Fortuny's kimono coat and Japanese textiles in the West, see Kyoto Costume Institute 96–97.
20 The first foreign customer was said to be an employee of Smith Baker & Co., an American trading firm that had a branch in Kobe. They bought a number of Japanese gift-wrapping fabrics called *fukusa*. See Takashimaya Ltd., [*180 Years of Takashimaya*] 11.
21 Takashimaya exhibited embroideries to the International Exhibition in Barcelona in 1888, in Paris in 1889, Chicago in 1893, Paris in 1900, St Louis in 1904 and London in 1910. They were granted awards in all of them. In Paris in 1900, Sarah Bernhardt bought one of their 'velvet *yuzen* hanging' with embroidered birds and ocean waves. See Takashimaya Ltd. [*180 Years of Takashimaya*] 11, 87.
22 According to the catalogue, 1 Yen = 2/-.
23 The description of 'Ladies' Kimono' section of Takashimaya's English catalogue in 1911 says that the kimonos were designed by '[their] own artists' and customers will find 'the material of excellent quality' with the 'workmanship all that could be desired'. It implies that their kimonos were made in Japan using Japanese techniques. See Iida & Co. "Takashimaya" 22.
24 Kimono of Miller & Franklin is advertised in *The Bexhill Chronicle*. See *The Bexhill Chronicle* 6.
25 The exhibition, *Manet and the Post-Impressionists*, displayed the works of Édouard Manet (1832–1883), Georges Seurat (1859–1891), Paul Cézanne (1839–1906), Vincent van Gogh (1853–1890) and Paul Gauguin (1848–1903).

90 *Creating Fashion*

26 Woolf wrote, 'Look at the lights in the houses! [...] One could see everything in the square-shaped boxes; there was no privacy [...] It was harder to cry now. [...] Ivy had perished or been scraped off houses. Vegetables were less fertile; families were much smaller'. See *Orlando* 267.

27 This 'ancient Greek' meant by the idea of the 'ancient Greek' understood and translated in Britain by the end of the nineteenth century. Most of the 'ancient Greek' sculptures that were available in Britain were the 'Roman copies of Greek originals' which was reproduced during Roman times (2nd century B.C–4th century A.D.). In Victorian period, according to Cora Gilroy-Ware, 'the classical and the classicizing art' were 'embraced by industrial culture'. The understanding and the interpretation of 'ancient Greek' in Victorian period, therefore, was not straightforward. It was complex and intermixed. See Gilroy-Ware 115.

Works Cited

Adburgham, Alison. *Liberty's: A Biography of a Shop*. George Allen & Unwin, 1975.

Anon. 'Customs in Japan'. *The Coventry Herald and Free Press*, 29 April 1892, p. 6.

Anon. 'Dress of Japanese Ladies'. *The Evening News*, 27 December 1888, p. 4.

Anon. 'Introducing William Morris'. *Victoria and Albert Museum*, https://www.vam.ac.uk/articles/introducing-william-morris. Accessed 12 December 2021.

Anon. 'Introduction'. *Aglaia: The Journal of the Healthy and Artistic Dress Union*, no. 3, edited by The Healthy & Artistic Dress Union, London, Hope-Hoskins, 1894, p. 3.

Anon. 'Japanese Dress (from Our Traveling Commissioner) Tokyo, August 29. The Great Dress Question'. *The Pall Mall Gazette*, 26 December 1888, pp. 1–2.

Anon. 'Little hand cars, or jinrikishas…'. *The Dover Express*, 6 May 1892, p. 3.

Anon. 'Paul Poiret's Dresses'. *North-Eastern Daily Gazette*, 8 May 1909, p. 5.

Anon. 'Practical Nightdress'. *Acton Gazette*, 30 January 1914, p. 8.

Anon. *The Bexhill Chronicle*, 16 May 1914, p. 6.

Anon. *The Kilburn Times*, 25 February 1881, p. 4.

Arwas, Victor. *The Liberty Style*. Academy Editions, 1979.

Asami, Yoshiko 阿佐美淑子, Hayato Arikawa 有川隼人 and Nao Minamida-Azakami 南田菜穂, editors. *All about Mariano Fortuny*. The Mainichi Newspapers 毎日新聞社, 2019.

Ashelford, Jane. *The Art of Dress: Clothes through History 1500–1914*. National Trust Books, 1996.

Bowley, Arthur Lyon. *Wages and Income in the United Kingdom Since 1860*. Cambridge UP, 1937.

———. *Wages in the United Kingdom in the Nineteenth Century*. Cambridge UP, 1900.

Breward, Christopher. 'Fashion in the Age of Imperialism: 1860–90'. *The London Look: Fashion from Street to Catwalk*, edited by Christopher Breward, Edwina Ehrman and Caroline Evans, Yale UP, 2004, pp. 46–59.

Fukai, Akiko 深井晃子. *Japonisme in Fashion: umi wo watatta kimono* ジャポニスム・イン・ファッション―海を渡ったキモノ [*Japonisme in Fashion: Kimonos in Overseas*]. Heibonsha, 1994.

———. *Kimono to Japonisme: seiyou no me ga mita nihon no biishiki* きものとジャポニズム：西洋の眼が見た日本の美意識 [*Kimono and Japonisme: Japanese Sense of Beauty Seen by West*]. Heibonsha, 2017.

———. 'Radical Restructure: The Impact of Kimono'. *Kimono: Kyoto to Catwalk*, edited by Anna Jackson, V&A Publishing, 2020, pp. 198–207.

Gagnier, Regenia. *Individualism, Decadence and Globalization: On the Relationship of Part to Whole, 1859–1920*. Palgrave Macmillan, 2010.

Gere, Charlotte. *Artistic Circles: Design and Decoration in the Aesthetic Movement*. V&A Publishing, 2010.

Gilroy-Ware, Cora. *The Classical Body in Romantic Britain*. Paul Mellon Centre for Studies in British Art, 2020.

Godwin, Edward William. *Dress and Its Relation to Health and Climate*. London, William Clowes & Sons, 1884.

Haweis, Mary Eliza. *The Art of Decoration*. Chatto & Windus, 1881.

Hirota, Takashi 廣田孝. '"Gaikokuzinmuke kimono zuan" (Takashimaya shiryoukan syozou) nit suite (sono 1)' 『外人向着物図案』 (高島屋史料館所蔵) につい て (そ の 1) ['About "Kimono Designs for Foreigners" (Takashimaya Historical Museum) part 1']. *Journal of Apparel and Space Design* 生活造形, vol. 51, 2006, pp. 45–52.

———. *Takashimaya 'Boueki -bu' bizyutsu sensyoku sakuhin no kiroku syasinsyu* 髙 島 屋 「 貿 易 部 」 美 術 染 織 作 品 の 記 録 写 真 集 [*Photo Albums of Exported Textiles Produced by Takashimaya*]. Kyoto Women's University 京都女子大学, 2009.

Iida & Co., 'Takashimaya'. *Novelties in Japanese Articles*. Iida & Co., 1911.

Kramer, Elizabeth. '"Not so Japan-Easy": The British Reception of Japanese Dress in the Late Nineteenth Century'. *Textile History*, vol. 44, no. 1, 2013, pp. 3–24.

Kramer, Elizabeth and Akiko Savas. 'The Kimono Craze: From Exoticism to Fashionability'. *Kimono: Kyoto to Catwalk*, edited by Anna Jackson, V&A Publishing, 2020.

Kume, Kazusa 粂和沙. *Bi to taishu: Japonisme to igirisu no zyosei-tachi* 美と大衆ージャポニスム とイギリスの女性たち [*Beauty and the Mass: Japonisme and Women in Britain*]. Brucke ブリ ユッケ, 2016.

Liberty, Lasenby. 'On the Process of Taste in Dress: III in Relation to Manufacture'. *Aglaia: The Journal of the Healthy and Artistic Dress Union*, no. 3, edited by The Healthy & Artistic Dress Union, London, Hope-Hoskins, 1894, pp. 27–31.

Livingstone, Karen. 'Origins and Development'. *International Arts and Crafts*, edited by Karen Livingstone and Linda Parry, V&A Publishing, 2005, pp. 40–61.

Nordau, Max. *Degeneration* [translated from the second edition of the German work]. London, William Heinemann, 1895.

Ono, Ayako. *Japonisme in Britain: Whistler, Menpes, Henry, Hornel and Nineteenth-Century Japan*. Taylor & Francis, 2003.

Parry, Linda and Karen Livingstone. 'Introduction: International Arts and Crafts'. *International Arts and Crafts*, edited by Karen Livingstone and Linda Parry, V&A Publishing, 2005, pp. 10–37.

Pool, Daniel. *What Jane Austen Ate and Charles Dickens Knew: From Fox Hunting to Whist – the Facts of Daily Life in 19th-Century England*. Touchstone, 1993.

Porter, Julian. *Bexhill-on-Sea: A History*. The History Press, 2004.

Ruskin, John. *The Nature of Gothic: A Chapter from The Stones of Venice*. George Allen, 1900.

Said, Edward W. *Orientalism*. 1978. Penguin Books, 2003.

Sakuragi, Eriko 櫻木英里子. 'Meiji, Taisho, Showa ki no kimono ni mirareru bara moyou: nihon kokunai ni okeru youka no fukyu tono kankei' 明治·大正·昭和期の着物に見ら れ る薔薇模様ー 日本国内における洋花の普及との関係ー ['Kimono of the Rose Design in the Meiji, Taisho and Showa Periods: The Relationship between the Spread of Western Flower in Japan']. *Bulletin of the Faculty of Home Economics, Kyoritsu Women's University* 共立女子大学家政学部紀要, vol. 62, 2016, pp. 21–34.

Sasai, Kei 佐々井啓. *Victorian Dandy: Oscar Wilde no fukusyoku-kan to 'atarashi onna'* ヴ ィ クトリアン. ダンデイ： オスカー. ワイルドの服飾観と 「新しい女」 [*Victorian Dandy: Oscar Wilde's Fashion Theory and the 'New Woman'*]. Keisou Shobou 勁草書房, 2015.

Savas, Akiko サワシュ晃子. '20 seiki syotou no eikoku ni okeru nihonsei yusyutsuyou kimono no ryutsu to nichiei gyousha no sougo kousyou ni tsuite 20 世紀初頭の英国における日本製輸出 用キモノの流通と日英業者の相互交渉にいて ['Japanese Kimonos for the British Market at the Beginning of the 20th Century']. *Journal of the Japan Society of Design*, vol. 65, 2014, pp. 15–29.

———. '20 seiki syotou no eikoku no taisyu shosetsu ni okeru kimono to kimono Sugata no josei hyoushou no henka' 20 世紀初頭の英国の大衆小説におけるキモノとキモノ姿の女性表 象の変化ーキモノブームという視点からー ['Changes in the Representation of Kimono and Kimono-clad Women in British Popular Fiction in the Early Twentieth Century']. *Studies in Japonisme*, vol.35, 2015, pp. 77–95.

92 Creating Fashion

———. 'Dilute to Taste: Kimonos for the British Market at the Beginning of the Twentieth Century'. *International Journal of Fashion Studies*, vol. 4, no. 2, 2017, pp. 157–181.

Summers, Leigh. *Bound to Please: A History of the Victorian Corset*. Berg, 2003.

Takashimaya Ltd 株式会社髙島屋. *Okage nite 180* おかげにて一八〇 [*180 Years of Takashimaya*]. Takashimaya Ltd. 株式会社髙島屋, 2013.

Tanita, Hiroyuki 谷田博幸. *Yuibi syugi to Japanism* 唯美主義とジャパニズム [*Aestheticism and Japanism*]. Nagoya UP 名古屋大学出版会, 2004.

Wahl, Kimberly. *Dressed as in a Painting: Women and British Aestheticism in an Age of Reform*. U of New Hampshire P, 2013.

———. 'Picturing the Material/Manifesting the Visual: Aesthetic Dress in Late-Nineteenth-Century British Culture'. *Dress History: New Directions in Theory and Practice*, edited by Charlotte Nicklas and Annebella Pollen, Bloomsbury, 2015, pp. 97–112.

Weisberg, Gabriel P. *Art Nouveau Bing: Paris Style 1900*. Abrams, 1986.

Woolf, Virginia. *Mr. Bennett and Mrs. Brown*. London, The Hogarth Press, 1924.

———. *Orlando: A Biography*. London, The Hogarth Press, 1928.

Yamaguchi, Eriko 山口惠里子. 'Raphael zenpa kyoudai dan ni okeru Primitivism: 19 seiki eikoku no "Rhaphael izen" mondai' ラファエル前派兄弟団におけるプリミティヴィズム：19世紀英国の『ラファエッロ以前』問題 ['Primitivism in the Pre-Raphaelite Brotherhood']. *Journal of Modern Languages & Cultures* 論叢 現代語. 現代文化, vol. 4, 2010, pp. 97–155.

———. 'Raphael zenpa kyodai dan ni okeru Primitivism: materiality no realism' 「ラファエル前派兄弟団におけるプリミティヴィズム─マテリアリティのリアリズム」 ['Primitivism of Pre-Raphaelite Brotherhood: Realism of Materiality']. *Zen Raphael shugi: kako ni yoru 19 seiki kaiga no kakushin* 前ラファエロ主義─過去による 19 世紀絵画の革新 [*Pre-Raphaelism: Innovating Nineteenth Century Art through the Past*], edited by Chikashi Kitazaki 喜多崎親, Sangensha 三元社, 2018, pp. 149–208.

———. 'Victoria cho no medievalism to Japanisme no setten: Rossetti kyoudai no ukiyo-e collection wo jirei to shite' ヴィクトリア朝の medievalism と Japanisme の接点：ロセッティ兄弟の浮世絵コレクションを事例として ['The Rossetti Collection of Ukiyoe Prints: The Unification of Medievalism and Japanisme in Victorian England']. *Journal of Modern Languages & Cultures* 論叢 現代語・現代文化, vol. 6, 2011, pp. 113–159.

Yokoyama, Toshio. *Japan in the Victorian Mind: A Study of Stereotyped Images of a Nation 1850–80*. Macmillan, 1987.

3 Making it 'Picturesque'

This chapter focuses on the examples that the kimonos appeared in much more public spaces rather than staying in the drawing room. It looks into the kimonos at the Victorian fancy dress balls, Japanese-themed charity bazaar in Bath in 1882 and the amateur theatricals of the early twentieth century.

Fancy dress balls offered an imaginary space that the participants could express a 'different self' through their extraordinary costumes. There were several varieties of Japanese-themed fancy dress costumes during the Victorian period, varying from a radically altered one to an authentic Japanese kimono. But, all of them were not selected to hide, disguise or conceal wearers' identity but rather to discover one. Japanese elements on fancy dresses were identified with wearers for their self-presentations.

As seen in the previous chapter, women of upper and upper-middle classes were the main consumers of the conservative and fashionable Japonisme that was created for them during the late Victorian period. However, they simultaneously actively offered the experience of kimonos to other people in their own community by organising Japanese-themed charity bazaars and amateur theatricals. Here, it also focuses on the timeline of the emergence of Japonisme in Britain as well as looking into some examples of the actual events regarding kimonos to demonstrate how some British women of upper and upper-middle classes played a much more active role in 'initiating' experiences of kimonos rather than just accepting them.

Fancy Dressed Described, 1887, 1896

As seen in Chapters 1 and 2, sartorial Japonisme, which started with fine arts and high fashion exclusively among the artists or the upper classes, gradually slid down the social ladder and adapted more broadly across Britain in the early twentieth century. As it widely permeated, kimono was also appreciated by much wider types of cultures in Britain. Elenora Sasso demonstrated the steps of Orientalism by quoting Edward Said as to 'capture it, treat it, describe it, improve it' and 'radically alter it' (qtd. in Sasso 1). According to Sasso, radically altering the Orient 'involves the creation of new Oriental structures in order to allow for new interpretations' (1). The examples referred to in this chapter show how kimonos were altered within popular culture in Britain, and those altered kimonos helped recreate a different kind of 'Japan' beyond the conservative appropriation of it. This section focuses on kimonos worn as a fancy dress which demonstrates how kimonos found in the fun costume balls were often 'radically altered', and therefore, they restructured the clichéd understanding of 'Japan', 'Japanese' and 'Japonisme' while they also varyingly performed about the wearers within the ephemeral space of imaginary.

DOI: 10.4324/9781003334255-4

94 *Making it 'Picturesque'*

During the Victorian period, fancy dress balls were one of the most popular entertainments enjoyed among people of all classes. The fancy dress was carefully planned and ephemeral, usually worn for only one night. Clothing was the central figure at the fancy dress balls as attendees dressed up as real or imaginary figures. Bradley Shope explained that Victorian fancy dresses 'reflected a trans-local reasoning that spoke symbolically of the person beneath, and infused sophisticated patterns of thought into the design of costumes' (377). Rebecca N. Mitchell, who studies Victorian fancy dress balls, also argued that they 'offered attendees the chance to represent their own personas or negotiate their social present' instead of offering a complete disguise (292). According to Mitchell, historical costumes that were modified to *fin de siècle* silhouettes were popular as fancy dress at the high society balls in the late nineteenth century. In this manner, 'fashion provided a means of self-reflective historicization, and fancy dress offered an expansive historical and iconographic range through which Victorians could imagine or reimagine their own time' (296).

However, in addition to the exploration of time, the geographical search of a 'different self' was also the key to Victorian fancy dress balls. The partygoers picked up the characteristics of foreign cultures that had already been translated in Britain. Cultural cross-dressing was extremely popular in Victorian Britain, and people loved the fleeting moment of impersonation. What their fancy dresses represented was the hybrid world of fancy which consisted of imaginary time, country and people. Fancy dress, as a meeting place of different cultures, has always brought about discussions and debates on inequality of power between who appropriates and who is appropriated. In her research on cultural cross-dressing, Inge Boer wrote that 'it is necessary to realize that cultural cross-dressing is deeply implicated in unequal relations of power, where the cultural "other" does not call the shots and has little or no recourse to influence the process of being represented' (434). Indeed, in Victorian fancy dress balls, the wearer's own persona as expressed through the dress was much more significant than its origins. Furthermore, the oriental-themed fancy dresses were greatly modified to complete the world of fancy. Fancy dresses were the fun ephemera; therefore, they appropriated Japan in a different way from the trend within the mainstream fashion.

Department stores and voluminous publications inspired Victorians to choose their costumes for fancy dress balls. The series of *Fancy Dresses Described* by Ardern Holt, which went through six editions from 1879 to 1896, was one of the most popular fancy dress how-to books in the period (Mitchell 297). Rich texts and illustrations describe the trends of each period and country, and each dress could be made to order by Debenham & Freebody, one of the most famous department stores in London. While there were many fancy dress designs of British historical heroes, fictional characters and abstract concepts, there are a lot of imperial references, such as 'Chinese', 'East Indian Woman' and 'Ethiopian Serenader' to name just a few. Notable and often stereotypical characteristics of each 'race' or 'culture' are extracted, distorted and reconstructed to form fascinating or eccentric costumes. Authenticity was not the main concern in Holt's books; the design of Victorian fancy dresses lay in the assimilation of the different concepts.

Since it was all about the wearers' self-presentation, it was highly important for the partygoers to look 'fashionable' in the contemporary sense, even though they were wearing historical or oriental costumes. Holt expressed in the introduction how fancy dress

Making it 'Picturesque' 95

balls were the perfect occasion to 'show off' and how the designs introduced in the book allowed the reader to do so:

> It behoves those who really desire to look well to study what is individually becoming to themselves, and then to bring to bear some little care in the carrying out of the dress they select, if they wish their costumes to be really a success. There are few occasions when a woman has a better opportunity of showing her charms to advantage than at a Fancy Ball. (Holt 1887 9)

Re-imagination and modification were the two key ingredients of the fancy dress costumes introduced in the book. About fourteen Japanese-related costumes are described across six editions, but none of them have the style of the authentic Japanese costume. What is interesting about the Japanese-themed costumes is that they represent a fictitious 'Japan' that was rather familiar to the Victorian contemporaries. As already discussed in the previous chapters, Japonisme, in Britain, was first embraced by artists who supported the Aesthetic Movement in the late 1860s but was gradually commercialised. By the end of the 1870s, Japanese-themed dresses and decorative objects were sold at luxury department stores for wealthy customers with artistic tastes. Furthermore, some Japanese- or aesthetic-themed theatrical performances were also performed in the West End, which further invited this particular 'Japan' into the everyday lives of British high society.

In the editions of Holt's books, there are several versions of fancy dresses inspired by 'Japanese' designs. The fifth edition holds the largest numbers of Japanese-related costume ideas. There are 'Japanese' in 'China' category, as well as 'Japanese (Fancy)', 'Japanese Lady', 'Japanese Lantern' and dresses inspired by the characters in the Gilbert and Sullivan's comic opera, *The Mikado* (Holt 1887 57, 124, 155). While the costumes inspired by *The Mikado* have a style close to the original stage costumes, the other 'Japanese' fancy dresses are completely fictitious.

The description of 'Japanese (Fancy)' writes that '[p]ale blue silk trousers set in claret velvet bands; cream china silk tunic embroidered in colours; claret velvet bodice with tulle sleeves worked in gold and silver; three Japanese fans for head-dress' (Holt 1887 124). It is probably even needless to say that this costume sounds nothing like Japanese, only the 'three Japanese fans for head-dress' possibly came from the style of female characters from *The Mikado*.

What is utterly interesting is the silk trousers designed for this costume. The debate of freeing women from their uncomfortable dresses derived from the United States and aroused much controversy in Britain throughout the second half of the nineteenth century and beyond. The Bloomers of the 1850s and the bifurcated skirts that were invented for riding a bicycle in the 1890s for the New Women in Britain were both, to some extent, inspired by the female trousers worn in the Ottoman Empire; thus, they were closely associated with the Dress Reform Movement that aimed to emancipate women from the unhealthy female fashion of the time.

Most Victorian women, however, rarely wore trousers in their everyday lives. Fancy dress balls offered a space for them to dress in an unusual way. The trousers in Oriental form were often designed as fancy dresses since around the 1870s, as the luxury fashion house in Paris, the House of Worth, for example, designed a fancy dress of baggy trousers in silk in 1870 (Figure 3.1). Those Oriental trousers were usually long and baggy caught in at the ankle that were mainly inspired by Turkish fashion. Until those styles

96 *Making it 'Picturesque'*

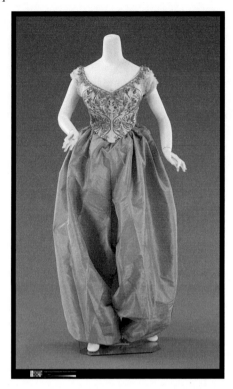

Figure 3.1 Charles Frederick Worth, House of Worth. Fancy dress costume, ca. 1870. 2009.300. 1363a, b. Brooklyn Museum Costume Collection at The Metropolitan Museum of Art, Gift of the Brooklyn Museum, 2009; Designated Purchase Fund, 1983.

were applied to luxury couture fashion by one of the most famous and luxury fashion designers of the early twentieth century, Paul Poiret, around the 1910s, the fancy dress ball was one of the opportunities for non-feminists or the non-dress-reformers to employ baggy trousers, while none of the attendees wore male trousers of their own country but wore the female ones of the far-away land.

The photographs of Princess Alexandra of Edinburgh dressed in kimono-style garment and Turkish-inspired trousers as fancy dress taken in 1889 are held at the Royal Collection Trust (Figure 3.2). It is from Queen Victoria's portrait album of royal children. Aris Kourkoumelis writes about the Princess Alexandra's costume that:

> Interestingly, while in one portrait, the princess is depicted as if performing a traditional fan dance, in the other she is cross-legged, in contrast to the more usual Japanese kneeling position. Equally, her conspicuous bloomers and slippers belie her Japanese persona. The dissonance of both clothing and pose demonstrates the shaky understanding of Japanese culture in mid-nineteenth-century Europe. (126)

Her attire and crossed-legged pose demonstrate her attempt to dress up as an oriental person, blending an interpretation of Japan, Turkey and other oriental places. Furthermore, her choice of costume might have expressed the progressive side of her who was

Making it 'Picturesque' 97

Figure 3.2 Eduard Uhlenhuth. *Princess Alexandra of Edinburgh* in *Portraits of Royal Children Vol. 38 1889–1890*, 1889. Albumen print mounted on album page. 13.7 × 8.8 cm. Royal Collection Trust. RCIN 2904829. © His Majesty King Charles III 2023.

not afraid to wear bifurcated dress in public by casually referencing the dress reform or feminism trend of the contemporary society.

Fancy dresses are not only performative but also highly connected to the wearers' social and personal identity. Benjamin Wild, who studies fancy dresses from the Middle Ages to the present day, adopts the 'critical costume' approach by Rachel Hann who researches performance design and costume to consider the physical form of fancy dresses and 'psychological affect of costume concurrently' (Wild 26). Hann employs a term 'showing dressing' to explain the power of costume to perform by adopting Richard Schechner's notion of 'showing doing' (32).[1] Hann argues, 'The slippage between a costume's performed identity and the individual's "known" identity equates to the idea of showing dressing' (32). Likewise, because of the nature of fancy dress as imaginary, fancy dresses could also perform the identities that are hidden, immanent or fabricated in addition to the 'known' one. 'Blending' different 'oriental' and the contemporary Victorian styles, rules and elements as seen here are one of the common ways as seen in the 'Kimono craze' of the second-half of the nineteenth century in the Euro-American countries. However, here, the process of blending was more connected to the act of 'showing dressing' for the construction of a 'different self' rather than the simple reception of a fad.

Japonisme was centred in material circulation, for the Japanese (and Japanese-ish) goods such as Blue-and-white china wares, fans, paper or embroidered screens, wooden

98 Making it 'Picturesque'

figures and paper lanterns became available in various shops and department stores in the late nineteenth century. In the fifth edition of Holt's book, popular decoration items of Japonisme were transformed into a fancy dress. The design titled 'Japanese', which was placed under the 'China' category, for example, sounds as if it were humanised blue-and-white china. The description reads: 'Square cuirass bodice and tunic of blue and white in Japanese designs. A head-dress of the same, and bracelets with blue plaques' (57). The straight cuirass bodice and tunic might have given an impression of an anthropomorphic blue-and-white vase.

Another object-inspired example is the 'Japanese Lantern'. This is described as having a '[s]triped blue and white short skirt, forming pouf at back' (124). This was not over-the-knee short, but a length that revealed the ankles, or perhaps the middle of the calves at the shortest, which is sometimes seen in fancy dress designs. The top is a 'tunic of gold satin', and the overall look is completed with a hat 'formed like a lantern' (124). What was culturally striking was that the designs of these 'Japanese' fancy dresses did not look like a kimono, nor use some characteristics of it. Moreover, they did not even look like contemporary western-style dresses but rather had a hybrid style of blending various characteristics of the 'Orient' and the fictitious features. Within the world of fancy, the boundary between dress and decorative objects and the distinction between the different cultures were obscured.

Furthermore, what those hybrid fancy dresses expressed was not purely 'exotic' or 'foreign', but it was the decorative objects that slowly came to be part of the upper and upper-middle-class women's everyday for such items could be easily purchased from shops and were regularly reproduced in women's journals. Some wealthy women of this period decorated their rooms with these exotic items. The fancy dresses inspired by the blue-and-white china and the Japanese lantern offered an extraordinary experience by transforming the wearers to the object that was supposed to adorn their households. These examples show a unique and ephemeral kind of Japonisme that was different from either the Japanese-inspired or kimono-shaped tea gown trend or the 'real' Japanese costumes displayed at the Japanese-themed events and theatre performance of the 1880s.

A fancy dress that reflects Victorian tea-gown trend appeared in the sixth edition of *Fancy Dresses Described* published in 1896. The costume is called 'Spring Time in Japan' and it was accompanied by a coloured illustration (Figure 3.3). The description of the costume says that:

> The robe is made of Japanese silk and bordered with apple blossoms, introduced also on the shot velvet bands which surround the waist, and border the neck. The Japanese parasol is also edged with flowers, which likewise ornament the pins placed on either side of the head. The colouring should be bright for Japanese costumes, and the dresses trimmed according to the season of the year. The loose outer robe crosses in front, and only fastens with a broad soft silk belt; wide hanging sleeves, the edge wadded. Two under-skirts, plain and bright coloured (Holt 1896 140).

It seems to be quite similar to the one titled 'Japanese' introduced in the third edition of *Fancy Dresses Described* published in 1882.[2] They strongly reference the Japanese-themed tea gowns that were popularly sold since the late 1870s with two-piece skirts as discussed in the previous chapter. Unlike the other Japanese-related fancy dresses in *Fancy Dresses Described*, the 'Springtime in Japan' and the 'Japanese' are the fancy dress costumes that reflect the pre-existing trend in the contemporary everyday fashion of the

Making it 'Picturesque' 99

Fig. 26.—SPRINGTIME IN JAPAN.

Figure 3.3 Miss Lilian Young, *Springtime in Japan* in *Fancy Dresses Described: What to Wear at Fancy Balls* 6th edition, 1896, p. 141. By permission of University of Brighton Library Services.

100 *Making it 'Picturesque'*

wealthy ladies. The radical alteration that is seen in other Japanese-themed fancy dresses is not found in this example, for the Japanese-inspired tea gowns had already been conservatively modified to fit the Victorian sartorial norms. Having said that the Victorian tea gowns were only worn in the drawing room when having a tea with their close friends or family members, thus tea gowns were not expected to be worn in the public spaces.[3] Therefore, the act of wearing a fancy dress that is similar to a contemporary indoor gown out in the public at fancy dress balls was, to some extent, quite brave. The ordinary and the extraordinary met in one costume, allowing an outstanding self-expression at an ephemeral event.

The 'Japanese' fancy dress costumes in *Fancy Dresses Described* offered an imaginary space where the negotiation of different times, places and trends took place. The performative character of the Victorian fancy dress creates an intimate and unique relationship between the costume and its wearer, offering a very personal experience. Therefore, the deliberate 'misunderstandings' expressed in the Japanese-themed fancy dress could not so much be read as the simple 'subjugation' of Japan by the Victorians as a negotiation of status, persona and position enabled by the hybrid and complex designs. There was an undeniable power relationship between the East and West behind this trend in the way that the real Japan had no say in it at all; however, Japanese elements still had an outstanding agency that facilitated negotiation and self-presentation that could not be negotiated or presented in any other way.

The Devonshire's House Ball, 1897

The Duchess of Devonshire's ball was held on 2 July 1897 to mark Queen Victoria's Diamond Jubilee. A lot of people from the London high society attended the ball, including the Prince and Princess of Wales.[4] Patriotic dressing was expected to the guests at the Devonshire House, for the ball is for celebrating Britain's monarchy. Benjamin Wild explains that the guests at the Devonshire House Ball were divided into different costume groups. He writes that:

> Guests were recommended to arrange themselves into historical and mythical courts. The emphasis on historic characters was edifying as participants learned about their nations and ancestors. It also provided opportunities to demonstrate family associations with historical figures, or to claim them if the guests were cunning (Wild 36).

While the photographs of attendees show many of them in historical costumes (the Prince of Wales as Grand Prior of the order of St John of Jerusalem and the Princess of Wales as Queen Marguerite de Valois), there was also a very exotic streak (the Duchess of Devonshire as Zenobia, Queen of Palmyra and Lady Mary Paget and Constance Gwladys Robinson as Cleopatra). However, those exotic fancy dresses were greatly modified to fit the contemporary fashion of an hourglass silhouette created with a tight-laced corset and gorgeously embellished with diamonds and a low neckline.

Yet among the fashionable revellers dressed as fashionable 'exotic' figures, there was Miss Louise Judith Sassoon (1874–1964), the unmarried daughter of Reuben David Sassoon (1835–1905), dressed as a Japanese lady (Figure 3.4). Louise was the youngest of Ruben's six children and would have been twenty-three years old in 1897. Reuben Sassoon was a businessman who worked for his father's company, David Sassoon & Co., a successful trade firm operating in India, China and Japan.[5] Dressed as a Persian prince,

Figure 3.4 Esmé Collings. *Miss Sassoon as a Japanese Lady*, 1897. Photogravure. 17.9 × 11.3 cm. National Portrait Gallery. NPG Ax41224. © National Portrait Gallery, London.

102 *Making it 'Picturesque'*

Reuben attended the ball with his family. His brother, Arthur Abraham David Sassoon (1840–1912), went dressed as another 'oriental' figure, the Chief of the Janissaries.[6]

Miss Sassoon's kimono especially stands out. It is probably a *furisode* (full sleeve) kimono made in Japan. Her costume is less decorated than other attendees' costumes, which had diamonds and other expensive jewels scattered across them. The features that were fashionably very important for a Victorian evening dress, such as the plunging neckline, a tightly laced waist, and flowing, feminine materials, are absent in her kimono. What she offered instead was a conservatively closed neckline, a straight body and stiff, heavy fabrics. Her costume's liner silhouette created with a wide obi must have made a stark contrast to the corseted *fin de siècle* bodies that surrounded her.

Louise, her father, and her uncle were deliberately dressing up as geographical 'others'; in other words, as exotic. This had a special significance for their actual identities beneath the orientalist costumes. The Sassoon family was a Jewish business family that had originated in Iraq. Ruben's father, David Sassoon (1792–1864), moved to Bombay (modern-day Mumbai) and started an opium business with Great Britain around 1832 before becoming a British citizen in 1853 (Stansky 5). While he did not abandon the dress and mannerisms of Baghdadi Jews, he allowed his children to dress and behave like British people. As extremely rich and famous second- and third-generation immigrants, Arthur, Ruben and Louise did not attempt to dress like the British aristocrats at the Devonshire House Ball. What they did seems as if they projected their identity as outsiders. Their 'exotic' costumes represented the 'oriental' places: Iran, Turkey and Japan.

Although further details are unknown, Louise Judith Sassoon was reported as being presented at the Queen Victoria's drawing room in Buckingham Palace on 16 May 1893 by the wife of Louise' cousin, Edward E. Sassoon (Imperialist 10). In 1914, Louise married a retired British civil servant, Sir Charles Cavendish Boyle (1849–1916), who served as a colonial administrator in several British colonies such as Bermuda, Gibraltar and British Guiana until 1911 (*Burke's Peerage: Baronetage and Knightage* 900). Louise and Sir Cavendish Boyle's wedding took place in Brighton and was widely reported in several newspapers. In an article from *The Globe*, Louise was written to have worn 'a dress of saxe blue flowered charmeuse' for her wedding ('To-Day's Wedding' 9). Furthermore, one photograph of Louise on her marriage reproduced in *The Daily Mirror* published on 9 July 1914 shows her in ordinary western female daywear (a blouse and a skirt), with her hair in a neat bun, a typical women's hairstyle in Britain in the 1910s. She was also reported as having attended several high-society parties and events in London and Brighton in her twenties and thirties. Based on this information, it seems that Louise lived a highly westernised lifestyle. Her everyday wardrobe, therefore, must also have reflected contemporary sartorial culture in Britain. Presenting herself as an exotic figure at the Devonshire House Ball was, thus, an unusual sartorial experience for her. While being 'exotic' was definitely one side of her identity in British society, dressing herself in 'exotic' clothing was still an extraordinary experience.

The way Louise juxtaposed her own identity with other 'exotic' counterparts can be described as, in Elenora Sasso's words, the 'over-orientalisation' (Sasso 6). Fancy dresses allow wearers to play with identities, and in Louise's case, Japanese kimono connoted her Iraqi origin. Mitchell regarded Victorian fancy dress balls as 'respectable' compared to masquerades of the former period, which were corrupted 'by irresponsible people of fashion' (qtd. in Mitchell 297). Impersonation was elevated to a more sophisticated level that also did not overstep Victorian morality. On the other hand, Victorian fancy dress balls were also fraught with the danger of lumping Iraq, Iran, Turkey and Japan together.

Making it 'Picturesque' 103

Louise's kimono reveals her complex position in Victorian high society as a third-generation immigrant; in other words, it demonstrates how Japanese kimono 'over-orientalises' Louise herself and her latent roots at the Devonshire House Ball.

Grand Japanese Bazaar, 1882

A Japanese historian, Noboru Koyama, noted that the 1880s were the height of Japonisme in Britain (200). Not only did objects imported from Japan catch the attention of the Victorians but also 'Japan' was adopted as a popular theme for events and attractions. The biggest Japanese-themed attraction in the 1880s was the Japanese Native Village opened in Knightsbridge, London, in January 1885, which will be discussed in the following chapter. It was the first exhibition that displayed 'real' Japanese people. However, there were also other Japanese-themed bazaars that had been held across Britain, even prior to 1885. The Japanese Bazaar in Bath in 1882 could be named as one of the earliest events that presented the fashionably modified version of 'Japanese' costumes. Although the images seem not to have been widely circulated outside Bath since there were no illustrations nor photographs found so far, the costumes at least created the picturesque 'Japan' and cemented it to the local organisers and visitors. Making everything 'picturesque' is the key concept that the bazaar focused on, portraying the ideal version of Japan.

Prior to the Japanese Native Village, displays that reproduced Japanese villages and streets had already become a fairly popular theme for bazaars across the United Kingdom (Koyama 210). Bazaars were held for fund-raising, often aiming to raise money for charities or for rebuilding or repairing local churches. The Grand Japanese Bazaar held in Bath from 31 November to 7 December 1882, for example, raised about £1,200 for the improvement of the local church, St. Saviour's Church ('Grand Japanese Bazaar at Bath' 6). The advertisement from *The North Wilts Herald* on 24 November 1882 reported that the Bazaar would be opened by the Duchess of Beaufort ('Assembly Rooms, Bath' 1). A group of churchwardens and reverend gentlemen formed the executive committee and local women (including a 'Lady Hayter') hosted stalls (1). The bazaar was held in the assembly hall, which was 'transformed into a Japanese street, with picturesque-looking native houses on each side, the upper storeys being embellished with curious devices, birds, flowers, &c. and the lower being devoted to merchandise' ('Grand Japanese Bazaar at Bath' 6).

The organisers even published an exhibition catalogue, *The Book of Japanese Bazaar*, in 1882. A poem titled 'An Invitation to the Bazaar' reproduced in this book expressed as follows:

> "'Old Fairs' have been, and Concerts too,
> "We'll bring our lures from far;
> "We don't know much about Japan –
> "A Japanese Bazaar!"
> So here it is! as fresh as paint!
> And quite a novel scene;
> Village and Ladies well Japanned
> With nothing poor or mean (8).

The fantasised idea of Japan was more strongly stressed in this poem, writing as if Japan was some kind of design or fashion styles rather than a nation with people and

104   *Making it 'Picturesque'*

culture. This poem set the whole mood in this event, seeing Japan as a fantasy. Thus, the anonymous writer expressed that the visitors would 'admit the illusion to be as perfect as it can possibly be made' and 'may easily imagine that he has stayed into the principal street of a Japanese village on a sort of fair day' (14). Japan in this event was rather an 'illusion' than the real Japan. Thus, the book does not have any fine descriptions or writings on the contemporary state, culture or people in Japan, but it instead has a short story and a local news that have nothing to do with the bazaar or Japan.[7] Even if they ever briefly wrote about Japan and the Japanese in some of the essays collected in this book, most of the expressions are rather absurd.[8] Thus, how to create 'Japan' in the Assembly Room was entirely in the local ladies' and gentlemen's hands (37–42). One lady, called Sophronia in the book, for example, found her Japanese ideal in the works of Oscar Wilde and William Morris; therefore, she decollated the stalls with the plates and vases to express 'her conceptions of what is truly Japanese' (37).

There were thirteen stalls, each presented by the aristocratic or upper-middle-class ladies and named after flowers: the Rose, the Sunflower, the Pansy, the Forget-Me-Not, the Japonica, the Chrysanthemum, the Anemone, the Japanese Lily, the Camellia, the Marguerite, the Poppy, the Flora and Pomona and the Cauliflower (44). Some stalls sold goods (seemed not necessarily Japanese) from furniture to paintings and others offered refreshments and flowers (47–55). These stalls are possibly the most 'Japanned' bits in the bazaar; the other attractions seem nothing like Japanese. There are two stages created in the Assembly Room and there played Tableaux Vivant, concerts, magic shows and a cat show during the event. Tableaux Vivant was explained to have illustrated the scenes taken from Sir Walter Scott's the Waverley Novels and the majority of the music at the concerts were delivered by the Italian band (57, 60).

It is highly significant to note here that the elements of 'Japan' were so little, and nothing was 'authentic' Japanese in this event. Japan was rather purposely translated to complete the 'illusion' in the venue. *The Book of Japanese Bazaar* says nothing about the costumes worn by the participants, but the local newspapers reported them in detail. One article published in *The Bath Chronicle* on the final day of the bazaar, 7 December 1882, wrote that there were some 'Japanese' people within the display, played by young English ladies and boys dressed in Japanese costumes ('Grand Japanese Bazaar at the Assembly Rooms' 3). From the description in the paper, their costumes, too, seem to have lacked authenticity:

> Elaborate pains had evidently been taken with the dress, but it may satisfy some lovers of the beautiful if we at once state that the usual (to our eyes) hideous features of Japanese decoration were omitted. The married ladies in attendance, for instance, had not thought it necessary to pluck out their eyebrows, blacken their teeth, nor to daub white paint upon their faces and necks, but attempts were made to emulate the extraordinary head-dresses affected by the natives of Japan (3).

These modifications were done with the ultimate aim of making the whole display more 'picturesque' than 'generally supposed' (3).

Due to the lack of any visual sources, the texts in *The Book of Japanese Bazaar* and the newspaper articles are the only clues about how the final product looked. *The Bath Chronicle* particularly implied that the hosts of this bazaar were uncertain of the realities of Japanese villages, clothing and people. Strikingly, the article also reported that some ladies combined Parisian fashion with Japanese 'stuffs' (3). This implies that no one really knew the 'correct' way to dress like a Japanese person. Rather, they knew exactly what was the 'right' way to dress fashionably exotic. The Japanese attire at the Grand Japanese Bazaar was significant in that it was the live version of an ideal exotic town. The article in *The Bath Chronicle* repeatedly used the word 'picturesque' to describe the bazaar and the people pretending to be Japanese. They also wrote that the audience 'might, especially if all his knowledge of Japan were derived from books, imagine himself suddenly transported from the fair city of Bath to the land of The Mikado' (3).

The whole space was a make-believe Japan fabricated from their picturesque fantasies and made up of things of which they approved. Not only the entire event was an 'illusion' that was only partly 'Japanned' according to the local ladies' and gentlemen's ideals but also the costumes were deliberately made to look fashionable in the European sense. Thus, the Japanese element was relatively small. It was only the 'head-dresses' and the 'stuffs' that were explained to be Japanese in their costumes. This serves as an example of how the 'Japanese' costume remained divorced from the realities of Japanese life. At the Grand Japanese Bazaar in Bath, the costumes of Japan were considered something to be adapted and appropriated to western fashion for the completion of 'picturesque' illusion.

Making things 'picturesque' was key at the Grand Japanese Bazaar in Bath held in 1882. The village was embellished with all things exotic and the British people play-acted as 'Japanese' dressed in 'picturesque' costumes. Such costumes demonstrated how Japanese clothing was adapted among the upper and upper-middle classes in 1882; the most significant factor was not the authenticity of the dress but its fashionable exoticism. The fantasy recreated at the Grand Japanese Bazaar in Bath, thus, revealed the *beau monde* absorbing the fantasised elements of Japan into their own fashionable habits. These 'Japanned' costumes presented at the bazaar transformed the ladies in Bath to be the fashionable 'lure', but it also helped reinforce the fantasised idea of Japan to visitors' eyes.

Amateur Theatricals, 1900–1914

Amateur theatricals are also the common occasions for the British ladies to 'dress up' in kimonos. The high-society journal, *The Ladies' Field*, often features 'Japanese' entertainments played by the local ladies and gentlemen as part of their philanthropy works during the 1900s. An issue published on 19 January 1901 reproduces a photograph of a group of people in kimono-like gowns with women decorating their hair with flowers and a man wearing a *samurai*-like wig (Figure 3.5). They are the amateur performers consisted of the ladies and gentlemen in Worcester, the journal listing the important names of performers and patrons. In this article, the author makes a sinical remark on amateur theatricals which were one of the common entertainments among the upper and upper-middle-class people in any British towns as:

> AMATEUR performances, arranged ostensibly for the benefit of some particular charity, not unfrequently result in considerably more pleasure to the performers than to the onlookers, while the expenditure is on all sides so lavish that the original object is to a great extent lost sight of in the effort to make a good "show" ('Amateur Theatricals' 19 January 1901, 252).

'Making a good show' seems to have greatly been depended upon the costumes worn by the performers. In the case of the Japanese entertainment in Worcester, they played scenes from the famous West End theatricals such as *the Mikado, the Geisha, San Toy* and

106 *Making it 'Picturesque'*

Figure 3.5 Bennett & Sons, Worcester, Japanese Entertainment at Worcester. 'Amateur Theatricals' in *The Ladies' Field*, 19 January 1901, p. 252. By permission of University of Brighton Library Services.

Circus Girl with permission of Richard D'Oyly Carte and George Edwardes, dressing the performers in Japanese kimonos with their hair decorated with flowers and fans. *The Worcestershire Chronicle*, a local newspaper, also published an article about the event, describing it as: 'an air of picturesqueness was given to the affair by the ladies who assisted on the stage and off' ('Japanese Entertainment at Worcester' 8). The author writes that there were about sixty performers dressed in the 'becoming Japanese costume' that was 'picturesque in the extreme' with bright hues (8).

Gowns inspired by Japanese kimonos were fairly available even in the region by 1900, most of which were adopted as an indoor gown as previously mentioned. Since around the end of the nineteenth century, there were more opportunities for the wealthier people to dress in Japanese-related garments not even for particularly special occasions. While the material-cultural experience of kimonos was available and quite affordable to those who performed and the audiences alike at the amateur theatrical in Worcester in 1901, what makes the kimonos here so 'picturesque' seems as if the costumes' colour that 'afforded a pleasing contrast to the sombre everyday costumes' (8). Pale tone was, indeed, fashionable with female dresses during the 1900 in Europe. There were a vast kind of dress styles, but the colours were often equally neutral in contrast to the bright or dark hues that were fashionable during the mid-nineteenth century. In fact, a journal article about a different Japanese-themed amateur theatrical published on 14 December 1901 writes a great deal about the colour of each performer's costume. An amateur

Figure 3.6 T. Bennett and Sons, Worcester and Malvern, Part of Chorus in Japanese Musical Scenes at Malvern Wells. 'Amateur Theatricals' in *The Ladies' Field*, 14 December 1901, p. 51. By permission of University of Brighton Library Services.

theatrical held in Malvern Wells, a nearby town from Worcester, held in December 1901, played some Japanese scenes taken from the popular musicals of London's West End (Figure 3.6). The author details the colour of the performers' 'kimona' as:

> Mrs. Tennyson d'Evncourt, gowned in an exquisite dark blue satin kimono, lined with crimson and richly embroidered in gold and silver, sang sone Japanese songs, assisted by Miss Mary Moseley, whose equally beautiful Japanese dress was of brilliant crimson satin relieved by white silk and embroidery of gold ('Amateur Theatricals' 14 December 1901, 51)

Dark blue and crimson are the two colours of the surviving kimonos that were also introduced in the previous chapter (Figures 2.14 and 2.16). According to the article, the 'kimonas' are part of the collection of the local art collector, Michael Tomkinson (1841–1921), being lent by him. Michael Tomkinson was a Japonist who held a large collection of goods from Japan. Tomkinson even published two volumes of large catalogues just for his Japanese collections in 1898 titled *A Japanese Collection*. Tomkinson is specific about his Japanese collection to be authentic rather than the 'cheap articles made for the European market' that he argues in Preface that to judge the art of Japan by only seeing the objects made for the European market is 'like regarding Parian statuettes and the atrocities of the modern Italian statuary mason as representative of the European ideal

108 *Making it 'Picturesque'*

of sculpture' (Tomkinson *Volume I* vii). His kimonos are listed in the section of 'Embroideries' and 'Brocades' in Volume I. According to the entry in the catalogue, he holds six robes and a kimono:

- Robe, dark blue satin, embroidered with blossoming plum trees in gold and colours, a crest on the sleeve.
- Robe, scarlet silk crape, embroidered with sacred tortoises, cherry blossom and storks.
- Robe, grey crape, embroidered and stencilled; a view on the seashore, with pines and boats in rain; with crest.
- Robe, white figured silk; wisteria and other flowers and fans embroidered in purple, green and gold.
- Kimono, grey silk; an iris garden in colours, stencilled and embroidered.
- Priest's robe; conventional chrysanthemums and peonies, on a diaper of scrolls, on a red ground.
- Robe; conventional all over pattern in blue, green, red and gold (185).

The 'dark blue satin kimono' of Mrs Tennyson d'Evncourt and the 'Japanese dress was of brilliant crimson satin' of Miss Mary Moseley could be the ones listed above. What is highly significant here is that the costumes used for the amateur theatricals in Malvern Wells were likely the authentic kimonos that came from Japan.

In the examples discussed here, the connotation of 'picturesque' is slightly different from that of the 1882 Grand Japanese Bazaar in Bath. The 'picturesqueness' embodied at the Japanese Bazaar indicated a world of fantasy with romantic feeling towards the idea of 'Japan'. They aimed to invent a picturesque 'Japan' even before Oscar Wilde made his famous remark on Japonisme as 'the whole Japan is a pure invention' in his essay in the January 1889 issue of *The Nineteenth Century* (Wilde 52). As discussed above, the authenticity of their Japanese costumes was not at all significant in this event, and also the participants seemed not to care how 'exotic' or how 'unique' their costumes were, referencing the fashionable style from Paris to the Japanese Bazaar.

At the amateur theatricals of the early twentieth century, on the other hand, people were already familiar with the derivative works such as *The Mikado* and *The Geisha* and the kimono-inspired gowns that were available at the department stores for the upper and upper-middle classes by the beginning of the twentieth century. The participants of the amateur theatricals in 1901, at least, seem to be accustomed to embrace the fabricated 'exoticness' of 'Japan' that was established within Britain by the twentieth century. Furthermore, at the theatrical in Malvern Wells, the performers were dressed in the real kimonos from Japan. The 'picturesqueness' of the amateur theatricals in 1901, perhaps, did not mean the westernised fantasy that holds little sign of Japan but rather mean the staged exoticness that was extracted from the already-fabricated 'Japan'. From the ladies in kimonos, some even sitting on the floor with their legs folded as seen in Figures 3.5 and 3.6, their intent to actively engage in exotic and unique 'Japan' filtered through the numbers of works *about* Japan.

The experience of kimonos within the ephemeral spaces allowed an extraordinary dressing to the women of upper and upper-middle classes. Victorian fancy dresses referenced characters of different times and countries across the world. 'Japan' was a regular theme for Victorian fancy dress balls from the late nineteenth to the early twentieth century. Fancy dress inspired by a Japanese kimono was so popular as later being written in *The Ladies' Field* that choosing kimono for a fancy dress ball was 'somewhat tiresome when there [were] twenty at the same ball' in 1913 ('Fancy Dresses' 306). This section showed how Japanese-themed fancy dresses of the Victorian period were connected to the negotiation and self-presentation. Japanese-themed fancy dresses were often radically altered or blended with other various cultures, which allowed each wearer to explore each of their own identity rather than transforming them into someone else.

Kimonos at the Grand Japanese Bazaar in 1882 and the amateur theatricals of the 1900s, on the other hand, played a role to make the entire venue and the participants 'picturesque', while the term 'picturesque' conveyed a different meaning at the amateur theatricals of the early twentieth century. The less-modified kimonos at the amateur theatricals indicated a translated version of Japan that referenced Japonisme of the previous period.

Understanding high-society approach to kimonos as part of their Japonisme or Orientalism is complicated by their use of Japanese costume as a signifier of self, fashion and wealth, showing different representations of Japanese costumes. The participants of the Japanese Bazaar and the amateur theatricals sought a suitable balance between exoticness and respectability, rareness and familiarity for delivering 'picturesque' Japan to the high-society onlookers. Furthermore, the examples discussed in this chapter show that the women of upper and upper-middle classes were not only the consumers and the receivers of Japonisme but they also sometimes played an active role in creating Japonisme experiences.

Notes

1 'Showing doing' is 'a deliberate scoring of an individual's awareness of their actions'. Thus, it means 'performing: pointing to, underlining and displaying doing' (qtd. In Hann 12). For more on Schechner's approach, see Schechner 28.
2 In the third edition of Fancy Dresses Described published in 1882, a costume named 'Japanese' is described as, 'The colouring should be bright, and the dresses are adorned according to the season of year. Loose outer robe crossed in front, and only confined by broad soft silk belt, wide hanging sleeves, the edge wadded. Two under-skirts, plain and bright coloured; hair rolled back and fastened with flowers and golden pins.' See Holt 1882 75.
3 Japanese-inspired gowns were also employed as dressing gowns during the Victorian period, which were hidden in much more private spaces at home.
4 Queen Victoria could not attend the ball because of her illness but the event was filled with about 700 guests. See Wild 36.
5 David Sassoon & Co. was established in 1832. It succeeded in dominating the opium trade between India-China during the 1860s. David Sassoon & Co. later moved its office in London in 1872. See Stansky 5; Jones 41, 51.
6 His Italian-born wife, Eugenie Louise Judith Sassoon, dressed as La Dogeressa, the title of old Italian aristocrat. Dogeressa means the spouse of the Dodge of Venice. She also represented her 'roots' through her fancy dress.
7 There is a short story titled 'Tales of the Mess' which is about the Convent, a local news about the flood occurred in Bath in 1809 and a writing piece on the habit of kissing titled 'A Chapter on Kissing'. See The Hon. Secretary 16–32.
8 A writer whose initial is 'H. L.', for example, wrote in his essay that 'my womenfolk have given themselves up to the worship of some miserable little Orientals, who, judging from the native pictures which litter every table, are in the habit of walking about with their heads put on backwards. I don't know whether they do so really, but if I only caught them in the flesh prowling about my house I would speedily make the pose of their heads correspond with the pictures!'. See The Hon. Secretary 33.

Works Cited

Anon. 'Amateur Theatricals'. *The Ladies' Field*, 19 January 1901, p. 252.
Anon. 'Amateur Theatricals'. *The Ladies' Field*, 14 December 1901, p. 51.
Anon. 'Assembly Rooms, Bath'. *The North Wilts Herald*, 24 November 1882, p. 1.
Anon. 'Fancy Dresses'. *The Ladies' Field*, 4 January 1913, p. 306.

110   *Making it 'Picturesque'*

Anon. 'Grand Japanese Bazaar at Bath'. *The Western Daily Press*, 1 December 1882, p. 6.

Anon. 'Grand Japanese Bazaar at the Assembly Rooms'. *The Bath Chronicle*, 7 December 1882, p. 3.

Anon. 'Japanese Entertainment at Worcester'. *The Worcestershire Chronicle*, 5 January 1901, p. 8.

Anon. 'To-Day's Weddings'. *The Globe*, 9 July 1914, p. 9.

Boer, Inge. 'Just a Fashion? Cultural Cross-dressing and the Dynamics of Cross-cultural Representations'. *Fashion Theory*, vol. 6, no. 4, 2002, pp. 421–440.

Burke's Peerage: Baronetage and Knightage 107th edition, vol. 1, edited by Charles Mosley, Burkes Peerage & Gentry, 2003.

Hann, Rachel. 'Debating Critical Costume: Negotiating Ideologies of Appearance, Performance and Disciplinarity'. *Studies in Theatre and Performance*, vol. 39, no. 1, 2019, pp. 21–37.

Holt, Ardern. *Fancy Dresses Described; What to Wear at Fancy Dress Balls*. 3rd ed. London, Debenham & Freebody, 1882.

———. *Fancy Dresses Described; What to Wear at Fancy Dress Balls*. 5th ed. London, Debenham & Freebody, 1887.

The Hon. Secretary, editor. *The Book of Japanese Bazaar*. Bath, William Lewis & Son, 1882.

Imperialist. 'Gossip'. *The Colonies and India and American Visitor*, 20 May 1893, p. 10.

Jones, Geoffrey. *Merchants to Multinationals: British Trading Companies in the Nineteenth and Twentieth Centuries*. Oxford UP, 2000.

Kourkoumelis, Aris. '68 Eduard Uhlenhuth (c. 1853–1919), Princess Alexandra of Edinburgh (1878–1942), October 1889'. *Japan: Courts and Culture*, edited by Rachel Peat, 2020, pp. 126–127.

Koyama, Noboru 小山騰. *London nihon-jin mura wo tsukutta otoko: nazo no kougyoshi Tanaka Buhikurosan* ロンドン日本人村を作った男–謎の興行師タナカー・ブヒクロサン 1839–1894 [*The Man Who Built the Japanese Native Village in London: The Showman of a Mystery, Tanaka Buhikurosan, 1839–94*]. Fujiwara Shoten 藤原書店, 2015.

Mitchell, Rebecca N. 'The Victorian Fancy Dress Ball, 1870–1900'. *Fashion Theory*, vol. 21, no. 3, 2017, pp. 291–315.

Sasso, Elenora. *The Pre-Raphaelites and Orientalism: Language and Cognition in Remediations of the East*. Edinburgh UP, 2018.

Schechner, Richard. *Performance Studies: An Introduction*. 3rd ed. Routledge, 2013.

Shope, Bradley. 'Masquerading Sophistication: Fancy Dress Balls of Britain's Raj'. *The Journal of Imperial and Commonwealth History*, vol. 39, no. 3, 2011, pp. 375–392.

Stansky, Peter. *Sassoon: The World of Philip and Sybil*. Yale UP, 2003.

Tomkinson, Michael. *A Japanese Collection, Volume I*. George Allen, 1898.

———. *A Japanese Collection, Volume II*. George Allen, 1898.

Wild, Benjamin Linley. *Carnival to Catwalk: Global Reflections on Fancy Dress Costume*. Bloomsbury, 2020.

4 Educating People

This chapter investigates Japanese-themed events and entertainments that exhibited or displayed 'real living bodies': The Japanese Native Village (1885), The Japanese Exhibition at Whitechapel Art Gallery (1902), The Japan-British Exhibition (1910) and the Japanese acrobatics at the Edwardian variety theatres. Displays and exhibitions of Japan allowed numerous numbers of British citizens to delve into the staged 'Japan' and its culture. The visitors from much wider social classes could see, hear and possibly touch Japanese kimonos being worn by the actual Japanese people or by the dolls; however, unlike the wealthy British ladies who actually dressed up as a 'Japanese lady' at fancy dress balls or the Japanese Bazaar, the experience offered at the displays and exhibitions created distance between the one who 'observed' and 'were observed', often playing a manipulative role in building biased impressions of the latter. But here, it aims to capture not only the one-sided representation of Japan but also how the observers and the participants experienced what was presented to them. Thus, it seeks to show the agency of kimonos at the Japanese-themed displays and exhibitions opened in London and beyond.

The Japanese Native Village, 1885

The Japanese Native Village opened in Knightsbridge in January, followed by the comic opera *The Mikado* at The Savoy. It was one of the biggest opportunities for Londoners to see Japanese kimonos first-hand on 'real' Japanese bodies. The Japanese Native Village was probably also the first opportunity for British citizens to meet Japanese 'commons', most of whom were skilled workers or performers and their families from all over Japan (*About Dispatching Japanese to The Japanese Native Village Opened in London, England*). It was immensely popular and attracted 250,000 visitors within the first few months, even though the one shilling ticket was not easily affordable for most of the British population ('Knightsbridge Green Area' 86).[1] There were eighty-five Japanese people in total and some of them had even come to Britain with their children (Koyama 220).

The Japanese Native Village was organised against the Japanese government's will by a Dutch performer and art dealer, Tannaker Buhicrosan (1839–1894), who was closely associated with the Japonisme movement in late Victorian Britain.[2] The Meiji government did not feel positively about the opening of the village for two reasons: firstly, the idea of displaying Japanese people seemed rather absurd and disrespectful to them and secondly, the ambitious Meiji government questioned the 'quality' of the Japanese people who were displayed in London (226). Koyama pointed out that the Meiji government did not appreciate the 'human zoo' aspect of the Japanese Native Village (225). The government worried that the people hired for the village were not suitable for representing their

DOI: 10.4324/9781003334255-5

112 *Educating People*

own country (226). Without the support of the Japanese government, the process was completely organised and run by Buhicrosan's Japanese Native Village Exhibition and Trading Company (222). The village was reproduced in the glass-roofed Humphrey's Hall, while the Japanese people hired for the village actually lived in the Japanese-style houses built there.

Displaying people from other lands was not new in Britain in 1885. From the 1870s, there were several native villages and similar displays which exhibited actual people or wax figures. John M. MacKenzie wrote that the displays of native villages that were popular in late Victorian Britain 'always performed one function, to show off the quaint, the savage, the exotic, to offer living proof of the onward march of imperial civilisation' (MacKenzie, *Propaganda and Empire* 114). While Japan gradually gained an ostensible 'joint membership of the imperial club' after the Sino-Japanese War (1894–1895) and the Russo-Japanese War (1904–1905), in the 1880s, Victorian image of Japan had still been set against the backdrop of a primitive land (98).

In late Victorian society, the expanding beliefs of social Darwinism supported ideas about racial superiority and inferiority. Social Darwinism was often used to justify racism and eugenics and it accelerated the imperial mood in Britain in the late nineteenth century. The Japanese Native Village was also formed under the predominant imperial mood, which disseminated, albeit unconsciously, imperial attitudes and views on race that were deeply associated with public consumption. An article from *The Daily News* on 26 January 1885 writes about the opinions of the Japanese villagers' at the Japanese Native Village and reveals that the Japanese people found it quite entertaining to observe how the British children soon learn to regard them as 'poor benighted barbarians enveloped in gross mental and spiritual darkness'.[3] The Japanese Ministry of Foreign Affairs collected this very article, which can be found in their collections of materials on foreign diplomacy stored in the Diplomatic Archives of the Ministry of Foreign Affairs of Japan in Tokyo. This suggests that both the Japanese villagers who lived in the Japanese Native Village and the Meiji government in Japan were fairly aware of the racial hierarchy as it was understood in contemporary Britain. The Japanese Native Village, therefore, shared a fundamental purpose with other native villages in Victorian Britain: it was there to acknowledge and exaggerate racial, cultural and social differences between 'us' and 'them'.

However, MacKenzie also argued that Orientalism cannot be discussed without considering 'the reality of reciprocities' ('Orientalism in Arts and Crafts Revisited' 19). In his view, imperialism in British culture always contained a certain doubt and anxiety towards modernism (119). MacKenzie believed the victims of the imperial worldview, therefore, 'maintained their independent agency' and that they exposed 'the essential weakness of imperial power' (118). The 'victim' of this example, in particular, provoked complex feelings about Britain's present and Japan's future. In essence, this was an antimodern reaction that came from the nostalgia for 'the good old days' before Britain's industrialisation.

An article from *The Globe* published during the duration of the exhibit entitled 'The Japanese Villager' expresses a yearning for 'the old-fashioned Japanese villager' that came from nostalgic feelings the British had for their own rural past (1). Although the article does not specifically mention the Japanese Native Village in Knightsbridge, it must have played a role in advertising or promoting it to some degree. The article explained that 'the old-fashioned Japanese villager resembled in many points the old-fashioned English rustic' (1). It continued by saying that Japanese villages were the 'most delighted' because they were 'still far away from what are termed the humanising and refining

Educating People 113

influences of Western civilisation' (1). While the writer warned that real villages in contemporary Japan might be more 'prosaic and unideal' than anticipated, they promised that visitors to Japan would, nevertheless, be charmed by 'their very originality and peculiarity' (2). Anna Jackson, who specialises in Japanese art, also referred to the British understanding of 'Old Japan' that '[t]he East was constructed as something static and unchanging compared with the dynamic, progressive West' (247). She also explained how Japanese decorative arts were criticised by Rutherford Alcock as being on 'the first stage of progress in the arts' in 1878 (qtd. in Jackson 248), while the Japanese craftsmen were 'praised for not attempting innovation' at the Philadelphia Centennial Exposition of 1876 (247), which clearly demonstrated that the reception of Japan and the Japanese art during the late nineteenth century was ambivalent with the sense of superiority and the anxious and nostalgic feeling.

'Old Japan', before the country was westernised, had long been romanticised in Britain, as Elizabeth Kramer confirmed: 'Westerners drew a distinction between "new" and "old" Japan, the former engaged in rapid modernisation, the latter an idealised image of pre-Meiji Japan' (12). The Japanese Native Village possibly played a role in feeding the British people's imagination and helped convince British audiences that 'Old Japan' was real by showing rustic common people in simple clothes acting out an 'ordinary day in Japan'. The encounter with a fantasy that they were convinced existed in a faraway land provoked an inherent anxiety juxtaposed with a sense of superiority over an inferior race. Orientalism in the late nineteenth century contained these contradictory sentimental feelings that romanticised what was lost, while trying to 'protect' the uncivilised other from being westernised. Furthermore, in terms of British 'anxiety', it was also visualised in *The Mikado*. It was deeply inspired and associated with the Japanese Native Village and the story was said to have included a satire on Victorian society. *The Mikado*, opened at the Savoy Theatre in March 1885, represented the fictional Japanese town with actors in kimonos, exaggerating exoticness rather than pursuing authenticity. Both the Japanese Native Village and *The Mikado* reveal the tension between the anxiety towards the contemporary state of Britain and the sense of superiority as a progressive citizen and this tension was subtly hidden by the veil of entertainment.

Even prior to 1885, the image of Japan was fairly well shared in the Victorian minds through the visual sources that had been brought to Britain. One of the most famous visual sources was probably the commercial photographs sold in the sea-side town in Japan, Yokohama. The photography studio had been opened in Yokohama in 1863 by an Italian photographer, Felice Beato (1832–1909), and Charles Wirgman (1832–1891), an English illustrator who had come to Japan as a correspondent for the *Illustrated London News*. Its opening triggered the production and consumption of commercial photographs in Yokohama.[4] These photographs, called 'Yokohama Photography', were purchased by western visitors to Japan as souvenirs. Nancy A. Corwin critically explained that Yokohama photographs 'were skewed by Western notions and helped form and reinforce Western stereotypes of Japan' (34). The photographs, which involved a lot of posing and acting in order to 'reproduce' an everyday scene in Japan, fed the curiosity of Victorian minds. By the late 1860s, Yokohama Photography had established a particular style, including 'the hand-colouring of prints, the use of painted studio backgrounds, the division of portfolios into "costumes" and "views", and the formation of an inventory of popular themes and sights' (Gartlan 29). According to Luke Gartlan, Yokohama Photography 'typifies the kind of studio-based imagery' that reproduced and duplicated the fabricated 'everyday' scenes and people of Japan in the studio instead of capturing

114 *Educating People*

the real, natural lives of people in Japan (30). Most of the costumes worn by the models in Yokohama Photography are far from flamboyant or beautiful and many such photographs reproduce workplace scenes in which women and men are clothed in rather plain and worn-out kimonos. While the kimono had entered British high fashion and fine arts by 1885 and was acknowledged as something 'picturesque' and exotic in late Victorian Britain, the 'real' kimonos of the people in Japan as reproduced in Yokohama Photography were defined as something completely different from the colourful and flamboyant kimonos favoured by wealthy British ladies.[5] There was a fine line in Victorian Britain between the 'picturesque' kimono for western women and the 'plain' kimono for the natives in Japan.

A report submitted to the Ministry of Foreign Affairs from an officer of Kanagawa prefecture in July 1885, containing an interview with a Japanese Native Village 'resident' named Ishizo Nagasawa, reveals many details of how the Japanese villagers lived in London.[6] Among other features, there was a photography shop that sold photographs of the views, objects and Japanese people in the village according to the customers' choice. The act of capturing and collecting the 'real' Japan of late 1860s Yokohama Photography was, thus, also duplicated in the Japanese Native Village in London. In other words, the village itself was a massive backdrop and the people in it were living props recreating the 'live' version of Yokohama Photography.

The production process of Japanese goods became the objects to be observed alongside the finished products themselves. In illustrations of the Japanese Native Village from the *Illustrated Sporting and Dramatic News* and the *Illustrated London News*, artisans and craftsmen sit on the floor in a traditional manner, either cross-legged or with their legs folded beneath them (Figure 4.1) ('The Japanese Village, Knightsbridge' 648; 'The Japanese Village' 203). By contrast, an illustration of the village tea house shows a girl serving tea to a top-hatted gentleman against the backdrop of a western-style café rather than on the matted floor in traditional Japanese style (Figure 4.2) ('The Japanese Village' 203). The tea house was probably the only place in the village where the Japanese and the westerners actually 'met'. While Japanese artisans, craftsmen and performers were all viewed as displays, the tea house was where westerners came inside, sat down and enjoyed not only tea but also the whole process. The tea house was probably where cross-cultural interaction began in the Japanese Native Village. As it was involved in a form of participation, the tea house had to be a hybrid space. When the British audience was actually 'in' the scene, the space had to be more accessible for the western audiences while the romantic, uncivilised land of 'Old Japan' must always exist somewhere distant from them.

Kimonos worn by the Japanese residents were different from the colourful and luxury kimonos British aesthetes collected or the fashionable kimono-inspired dresses worn as tea gowns in late Victorian Britain. According to Nagasawa, these clothes were supplied on their arrival in England, probably by Buhicrosan. They were given sets of Japanese and western-style clothing, including a cotton-wool kimono. As none of the residents was wealthy back in Japan, what they were given was not either extravagant or fashionable but instead a simple kimono that made them look 'authentic'. The Japanese residents of the Japanese Native Village illustrated in Figures 4.1 and 4.2 wear various kinds of kimonos, the artisans and craftsmen are in plain kimono and the female figures (women at the tea house and female dancers) are in subtly patterned kimonos. The article in *The Daily News* mentioned above evaluated the female kimonos worn by the Japanese in the village as not only 'graceful' but also 'not ridiculous' ('The Japanese Villagers' 3). Both

Figure 4.1 'The Japanese Village, Knightsbridge' in The Illustrated Sporting and Dramatic News, 14 March 1885, p. 648. ©Illustrated London News/Mary Evans Picture Library, London.

the illustrations and the descriptions in British journals quoted above imply the modesty of the designs of Japanese kimonos worn at the Japanese Native Village compared to the luxury and decorative 'kimono' understood in Victorian Britain. The costumes of the villagers were significant in projecting what was expected to a 'real' Japanese village reproduced in the Humphrey's Hall: exotic, quaint, uncivilised and nostalgic land of Far East. Kimonos in the Japanese Native Village were not seen as an immediate inspiration for the fashion of the audience, but rather gave an impression of how native people wore kimonos.

Nagasawa also revealed that the Japanese residents of the village were asked to put on western-style clothes when they went out of the village. He continued that they were only allowed to go out from 6am to 10am and from 9pm to midnight, and there were guards at the gate of the village to inspect them when they went out. They could not go out in Japanese attire in order to prevent an 'exposure of the precious show', in Nagawsawa's words. Their kimonos were not considered to belong to the world outside of the Humphrey's Hall. In a situation such as this, the Japanese kimono became a significant marker of authenticity and uniqueness expected in the Japanese Native Village. As the residents were told not to leave the village dressed in kimonos, the kimonos were not there to be exposed to the public but to be kept exclusively for the exhibit. As these kimonos were simple and modest, it seems there was no intention for them to carry a fashionable appeal. Their main role was being simultaneously exotic and ordinary. They

116 *Educating People*

Figure 4.2 'The Tea-House' in The Illustrated London News, 21 February 1885, p. 203. © Illustrated London News/Mary Evans Picture Library, London.

helped convince the British audience that a romantic, nostalgic version of Japan actually existed somewhere in the world.

The analysis of kimonos worn at the Japanese Native Village in late Victorian Britain revealed that the representation of Old Japan had been deliberately recreated in the 1880s. While the fantasised idea of foreign lands always correlated with Victorian racism and imperialism, it also unveiled the mode of cultural appropriation and the Victorian anxiety towards modernism.

The Japanese Native Village displayed Japanese clothing as having nothing in common with contemporary fashion in Britain. Japanese villagers were dressed in simple and plain kimonos to complete the image of a 'native' and 'uncivilised' land in the Far East. The villagers were literally confined within Humphrey's Hall, just as the idealised 'everyday' scenes of Japanese life were 'confined' in a studio for souvenir Yokohama photographs. Japanese people were displayed as models who recreated the fantasy expected by the audience in Britain. However, the fantasy offered at the Japanese Native Village was quite different from that of the Grand Japanese Bazaar in Bath in 1882, which was discussed in the previous chapter. The costumes in the Japanese Native Village were neither picturesque nor fashionable, but plain and simple. Their kimonos were one of the markers of romanticised 'Old Japan' that evoked Victorian anxiety towards losing 'the good old times' of the British past. The imperfect reality of Japan recreated in London cemented their idea of 'Old Japan' as a nostalgic fantasy. Furthermore, these simple and plain clothing of Japanese villagers were not only 'authentic' in a British conservative sense but also familiar to the real Japanese villagers.. While the Japanese Native Village showed the transposition of 'exotic' Japan, which offered a fabricated authenticity to the Victorian audience, the village and the villagers were repeating their everyday lives in Japan in Humphrey's Hall. This space uncovered an ambivalent nature of Japonisme that juxtaposed fantasy and everyday, exotic and authentic, power and anxiety.

Oscar Wilde wrote that 'the whole Japan is a pure invention' in his essay in the January 1889 issue of *The Nineteenth Century* (Wilde 52). He continued, 'The Japanese people are the deliberate self-conscious creation of certain individual artists' (52). In this essay, he referred to the popular and artistic craze for all things Japanese and denied the people's growing expectation of 'Japan' and the people living there. In Wilde's words, 'The actual people who live in Japan are not unlike the general run of English people', thus '[t]here is no such country, there are no such people' (52). Wilde made an ironic remark on Japonisme and assured that the 'Japan' that the British people found so curious and peculiar from the late 1860s was actually a man-made fantasy that deliberately exploited the 'native' or 'uncivilised' impression of Japan.

The 'authenticated' Japanese kimonos at the Japanese Native Village were presented as exotic costumes for observation which set the groundwork for 'real' Japanese in late Victorian Britain. In the 1880s, there was a fine line between the Japanese costumes that could be worn by the British people and that were worn exclusively by the Japanese, both of which were inevitable in feeding the visitors' expectations and completing the commercial event. At the Japanese Native Village, kimonos were not only the significant markers to visualise the organisers' attempt but also the active promoters of the romanticised fantasy of 'Old Japan'.

The Japanese Exhibition at the Whitechapel Art Gallery, 1902

Working classes, especially the poorer citizens in London's East End, are often excluded from the Japonisme experience, especially the sartorial experience of Japan within the academic studies of Japonisme or dress history that are dealing with the period in discussion in this book: 1865–1914. Indeed, it is difficult to find any contacts since there is no evidence that the kimonos were sold at the pawn shops or given to them at charities. There were some shops that were selling kimono-inspired gowns across the United Kingdom, none of them were cheap enough for them to purchase and we also cannot ignore the fact that kimonos were not-at-all useful to the everyday lives of the people with limited means in Victorian and Edwardian Britain. Then, the East Enders did not see, hear, think or learn about Japan at all? Although Japonisme was so widely adopted across Britain, did it not bring any cross-cultural experience to them at the turn-of-the-century?

The truth is, there seems to have a few opportunities for the East Enders to experience—to see, to smell, to hear and, perhaps, to touch—Japanese things. One of these is the Japanese Exhibition that was held at the Whitechapel Art Gallery in Whitechapel, London, from 23 July to 3 September 1902. The gallery held an exhibition on Chinese life and art in the previous year, which was very successful, so the Japanese Exhibition was also expected to be popular. The annual report writes that the Japanese Exhibition was visited by 109,000 people, which is a great number of visitors considering that it was opened only for about six weeks (Whitechapel Art Gallery 6).

The Whitechapel Art Gallery was first opened in February 1901, holding their first exhibition on Pre-Raphaelites and Older English Masters on 12 March 1901, which was open to public on its first day and received a large number of visitors ('Miscellaneous

118 *Educating People*

Items' 8). Although there is no direct connection, the opening of the gallery is deeply associated with the works of Toynbee Hall, a social settlement also located in Whitechapel, London, since 1884. Toynbee Hall was founded by a vicar of the Church of England, Samuel Barnett (1844–1913), and his wife, a philanthropist, Henrietta (1851–1936), to create a hub to raise awareness about the poverty in the East End. The hall and their facilities were rather for the richer people and students than for the local East Enders, but their art exhibitions often welcomed children from the local schools (Toynbee Hall, Whitechapel, 1895 26). The 1901 annual report by Toynbee Hall reports about the opening of the Whitechapel Art Gallery, writing that the foundation of the gallery was the outcome 'of the unceasing efforts of the Warden and Mrs. Barnett to obtain for the neighbourhood a permanent home of Art, that a reference to its final completion must be made here' (Toynbee Hall, Whitechapel, 1901 15). The writer of this report calls the gallery 'the new "House Beautiful"', implying the influence from the aestheticism, and continues by saying that the gallery was appreciated by their 'neighbours' (15).

It is important to make sure who these 'neighbours' were, whether it includes the local poor population as well as the richer students, philanthropists and the patrons. The entrance of the exhibition was free, allowing donations at the door (T.C.O. 300). The high-society journal, *The Queen*, reveals the hint of 'who was there' by making a rather mean comment about some of the visitors of the exhibition as:

> Almost as interesting as the Japanese articles themselves is the East-end foreign Jew's way of looking at a collection. He does not greet it with the careless or comprehensive or sentimental stare of the ordinary Christian, but bends right over it as if he were a watchmaker looking through a magnifying glass to see what part of your watch-works are broken. He is picturing to himself the processes of manufacture. What the article is used for probably does not interest him any more than it interests the lady in the suburbs who uses an hibachi [sic] for a flower-pot holder with or without a tissue paper frill (T.C.O. 301).

It clearly shows that there were some local Jews who visited the Japanese Exhibition. In Whitechapel in the early twentieth century, there was a large number of Jewish populations. The number of Jewish populations grew from the end of the nineteenth century, and it was between 120,000 and 150,000 that settled permanently in Britain between 1881 and 1914, most of whom liked in the East End (Bar-Yosef and Valman 12). Samuel and Henrietta Barnett, as a part of their philanthropy work, also opened a free library in Whitechapel in July 1891 (October 1892 in official) with great aid by John Passmore Edwards (1823–1911), a British journalist and philanthropist (Toynbee Hall, Whitechapel, 1892 25). The library, that was long known as 'the university of the ghetto', was located right next to the Whitechapel Art Gallery that was opened about a decade later and it was completely free to use and opened to the general public. The library was useful to the local community, including the local Jewish populations until it was closed in 2005 (Kennedy). The opening of the Whitechapel Library and the Whitechapel Art Gallery not only meant the Victorian philanthropists enthusiastically provided educational and cultural facilities to the local East Enders', but it also proves that the local people have an intellectual curiosity that enjoyed the benefits of the free library and art gallery. In the article from *The Queen* that was quoted earlier, the author described East End as if it was a foreign country, stating that the street where the Japanese Exhibition was held in Whitechapel is 'more un-English than Rome' (T.C.O. 300).

They also continue that 'the streets are full of foreign Jewesses of the working class, all without hats, and with glossy dark hair, well-groomed in recent fashions' (300). Clearly, they enjoy observing the Jewish people in Whitechapel for they were most likely not what the author and the readers of *The Queen* get to see everyday. The Whitechapel Art Gallery possibly was one of the progressed and inclusive spaces that connected people from different classes with art.

The question that follows to 'who saw the exhibition' is 'what they saw'. Whitechapel Art Gallery holds an exhibition catalogue that was sold for a penny. In the catalogue, there were more than two-hundred articles listed, from maps, paintings, lacquers to rickshaws and the figures dressed in Japanese costumes. *The London and China Telegraph* reports on 29 July 1902 that, 'The idea has not been to obtain a collection of all that was highest and best in Japanese art, but rather to show how the Japanese live and what they make in the more ordinary every-day life' for the 'workers in the East-end to realise what can be done by devotion to an artistic ideal, and how that ideal may be utilised' ('Japan in Whitechapel' 646). The author writes that there were 'clothes' and 'distinctive dresses' along with bronzes and hardware, proving that some kinds of kimonos were on display (646).

According to the records held at the Whitechapel Art Gallery, the Japanese exhibition had some famous figures contributing, including William Michael Rossetti (1829–1919) who lent books from his collection and Alfred Stead (1877–1933), the author of *Japan to-day* published in 1902, who displayed posters and photographs from his collection. Among the lenders, there is Ambrose B. Walford who was listed as a committee member of the Japanese Exhibition in the gallery's annual report of 1902 (Whitechapel Art Gallery, 1902 6).[7] According to the document filled out by Walford himself, he lent numbers of objects for the exhibition that were worth £395 in total and among them there are 'Kimonos'. It is not known if those 'Kimonos' were from Japan, but they likely were since most of the objects displayed at the exhibition were originally from Japan.

The way that the Japanese costumes were displayed at the Japanese Exhibition is worth noting. In the catalogue, kimonos are not listed as they are but displayed on figures (possibly wax-figures). The only clothing that was described in the catalogue is a 'Dress worn by a Daimio or Magistrate when going to superintend the extinguishing of of [sic] a fire' (*Whitechapel Art Gallery Summer Exhibition, 1902. Catalogue* 41). Other entries are titled as 'Figure of woman as "Night"', 'Figure of woman as "Winter"', 'Figures in Dresses of the "No" Dance', implying that the dress was not considered a Japanese *object d'art*, but its social cultural side seem to rather attract the visitors more (34, 46). Kimonos are not-at-all rare to the eyes of the upper and upper-middle classes in 1902 for kimonos from Japan and kimono-like gowns were everywhere from theatres to department stores. They were not specially featured but casually displayed on a figure, aiming to show the 'ordinary every-day life' in Japan. However, some of the kimonos, such as the dress of *No* dance, and the kimonos lent by Ambrose Walford with insurance of £50 each could possibly be nothing like an 'ordinary every-day' kimono of contemporary Japan. Those kimonos are rather a special and the expensive kind. The exhibition could be the first time for a lot of the East-enders to see real Japanese kimonos; nevertheless, the encounter was not like the same as the one that was experienced by the upper and middle classes during the second half of the nineteenth century: the experience that was made to be fashionable, picturesque or idyllic. What the visitors of the Whitechapel Art Gallery experienced was to perceive the expensive kimonos being deliberately blended in the 'ordinary every-day' in Japan.

120 *Educating People*

Furthermore, they also exhibited a doll house with more than twenty Japanese dolls in full costume. The whole set is now held at the Victoria and Albert Museum in London. There is a model of a palace made of cypress and twenty-three enamelled doll figures, all dressed in various Japanese costumes. There are both male and female figures: a Mikado, a princess, samurais and musicians. Figure 4.3 shows the doll figures on *hina-matsuri stage*, being dressed in the court dress possibly from Heian period (about between 794 and 1185). The peach-coloured kimono worn by the doll on the right shows an exquisite embroidery, probably using silk thread. Those dolls are usually displayed for the *Hina-Matsuri* festival (often referred to as a 'doll festival') in Japan, being held on 3 March to celebrate female children and pray for their continued health. The exhibition catalogue of the Japanese Exhibition explains the doll festival in Japan that 'the girls of Japan have a festival in which they display all their dolls' (Whitechapel Art Gallery *Japanese Exhibition 1902* 21). While the whole set of dolls and the model of a palace must have been quite expensive, the exhibit was again situated in accordance with the main theme of this exhibition: showing an ordinary everyday life in Japan by associating it with the custom in Japan.

Interestingly, there was also an exhibit of the Japanese 'race' with a little ethnic and social information of the 'class system' in Japan as written in the description of the 'Model of Japanese Coolie':

> The Japanese are mainly Mongolian, of the same race as the Chinese, but there has been some admixture of Malay blood from the south. In the very north live the "hairy

Figure 4.3 Unknown. Hina-Matsuri Stage, 1800-1900. The Victoria and Albert Museum. 354–1903. ©Victoria and Albert Museum, London.

Educating People 121

Ainus," an aboriginal race, quite distinct from the Japanese. The marks of the Mongolian race are a yellowish skin, scanty straight hair, prominent cheek-bones and oblique eyes. The oval-faced aristocracy, notwithstanding their refined features, share the main Mongolian characteristics with the pudding-faced lower classes. Both men and women are small, but the women and children are graceful and charming. The Japanese may not appear handsome to us, but to them we appear much too big, red haired and green eyed (14).

It could have been a figure of a Japanese man, dressed or partly dressed, that was exhibited to educate the visitors. Whether it was intended to support the Social Darwinian view or was displayed to show the body of the 'worker' in Japan, the 'Model of Japanese Coolie' presents the racial 'difference' between 'us' and 'them'.

The Japanese Exhibition at the Whitechapel Art Gallery housed people from different classes in Britain. The variety of people gathered at the exhibition was much wider than any Japonisme-related events discussed in this book. For the workers in East End, including the poor Jewish community, the exhibition could have been the first time to encounter the things Japanese. For the organisers, lenders and some upper- and middle-class audiences, on the contrary, a Japanese-related subject must have seemed like a cliché by the time of 1902. In that sense, the Japanese Exhibition at Whitechapel Art Gallery, a juxtaposition of miscellaneous objects, disseminates diverse information about Japan.

The ordinary everyday life in Japan was delivered as an update to the existing impression for some, or as a completely new knowledge for others. As written in *The Queen*, the Jewish visitor must have met the displayed kimonos along with other objects from Japan. If the description made in the article of *The Queen* is right, the Jewish visitor probably learnt more from the objects than the 'ordinary Christian' with the careless or comprehensive or sentimental stare (T.C.O. 301). While they walked in the same exhibition and saw the same display, the experience of it was never the same in a different community. Unfortunately, it is impossible to know how each visitor felt about the exhibition; however, there is no way to neglect the local Jewish people's meeting with kimonos in a discussion of Japonisme, for it could never be lumped together with the other experiences.

The Japan-British Exhibition, 1910

The Japan-British Exhibition is one of the largest exhibitions of Japan that was opened in London during the early twentieth century. The exhibition was organised by the Japanese government and the Kiralfy brothers, the successful spectacle producers from Hungary. The Japan-British Exhibition opened from 14 May to 29 October 1910 at White City, Shepherds Bush in London. The opening of this exhibition was delayed by the death of the King Edward VII on 6 May 1910 despite the years of preparations. During the six months, the exhibition attracted more than 8,000,000 visitors (Hotta-Lister 3). Japan's intention was clear and eager: being recognised as a great empire of East. For the Japanese, the aim of this grand exhibition was to 'educate' the British people by showing their vaunted artworks and technologies. Britain, too, had an objective to 'educate' the Japanese to strengthen the trade relationship with East Asia while Britain's contribution at the exhibition was much smaller than that of Japan (Hotta-Lister and Nish 2). Ayako Hotta-Lister argues that promoting Japan as an Island Empire in the East means 'the acknowledged equal partnership, as allies' and 'the similarities, in the natural geographical

122 *Educating People*

position and in the colonial roles of, Japan and Britain' (2). In White City, there were two 'colonial villages': the Ainu Home and the Formosa Hamlet, which demonstrated a newly expressed character of Japan as a colonial empire.

The exhibition site was previously used for the Franco-British Exhibition (1908) and the Imperial International Exhibition (1909). On account of the opening of Japan-British exhibition, they built some Japanese buildings, gardens and gates to add a more exotic touch. The Japan-British Exhibition was, unlike the Japanese Native Village, supported by the Japanese government, so the best kind of staff, artists and other specialists was invited to complete the exhibition.[8] Among the numerous exhibits, what is most striking are the dioramas showing the progression of Japanese history. They displayed wax figures made by one of the most prestigious doll makers of the period, Kamehachi Yasumoto III (1868–1946), and the backdrops depicting each historical period of Japan was drawn by a Japanese painter, Nisei Goseda Houryu (1864–1943) (Hayashi 173). As explained earlier, the Japanese Native Village of 1885 displayed eighty-five Japanese men, women and children for them to be observed almost as a 'human zoo'. The Japanese bodies are displayed to be gazed upon, emphasising the racial as well as the cultural difference between 'us' and 'them'. The dioramas of dolls that were exhibited at the Japan-British Exhibition, on the contrary, turned the observers' eyes away from the Japanese 'bodies'. As an art historian, Michiko Hayashi, pointed out that these dioramas are located somewhere beyond the boundary between art and show, the display is not merely a 'human zoo' but is elevated to a more sophisticated exhibition (173). Placing wax figures instead of actual human bodies could transfer the interest of the audience from the bodies towards the settings. The display at the dioramas put more focus on the manners, customs and history of Japan than the peculiar and uncivilised Japanese bodies.

At the Japan-British Exhibition, the Japanese kimonos, too, were recognised in a different manner from the representation of them at the Japanese Native Village in 1885. In *The Graphic* of 23 July 1910, there are the illustrations of six Japanese ladies at the exhibition dressed in various styles of kimonos (Figure 4.4). The illustrations were drawn by one of the most famous illustrators in Britain, Arthur John Balliol Salmon (1868–1953). Some of them have titles such as 'school girl' and 'dress of ceremony' and each woman dresses differently. Some are wearing a kimono and an overcoat, while others wearing *hakama* [traditional Japanese loose trousers]. In the illustration, beautifully dressed-up Japanese women with the latest Gibson Girl hairstyles are confidently smiling at the readers. Firstly, it is significant to note that the variety of the Japanese women's age, clothes and style introduced in the illustration indicates that the female Japanese dress could have more variety of style than what the western people expected from the word 'kimono'. Secondly, all the women depicted in *The Graphic* are the respectable Japanese lady with names specified in the article. There are also the meanings of their names explained in English at the bottom of the article and the handwritten autographs by each lady are also placed next to the illustrations. The six Japanese ladies are no longer anonymous in this illustration, but they unapologetically pose in their fashionable and smart-looking dresses as a confident and identified individual who travelled across the ocean. This representation of Japanese women at the Japan-British Exhibition implies that the dresses did not have to be plain or simple to stage 'authenticity' and the bodies of the Japanese were no longer some displayed objects in 1910, which was a desirable outcome for the Japanese government who eagerly wanted to change the representations of Japanese people from the discriminatory one towards the 'civilised' one.

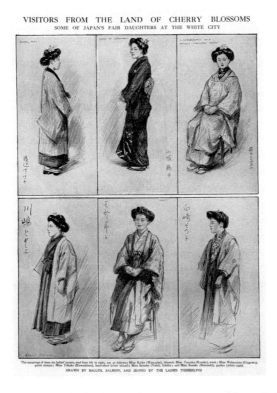

Figure 4.4 'Visitors from the Land of Cherry Blossoms: Some of Japan's Fair Daughters at the White City' in The Graphic, 23 July 1910, p. 137. © Illustrated London News/Mary Evans Picture Library, London.

Against the Japanese government's intention, however, there was a Japanese village called 'Uji village' that was displayed Japanese people at the exhibition of 1910. Kiralfy made sure that the Japanese government included native villages, for he knew they could be the most popular attraction for the British fairgoers (Ziomek 92). It seemed not the initial idea of Japanese government to create Ainu and Formosa villages, but Kiralfy insisted that as well. A historian, Kirsten L. Ziomek, argues that 'the fact that the British planner forced them to include a Japanese village alongside the native villages of their colonial subjects demonstrates the complexities involved in mounting an exhibit of the Japanese empire an international context' (92). These three villages, the Uji Village, the Ainu Home and the Formosa Hamlet, were all placed in the amusement district in the exhibition; however, the Uji village distinctly displayed the Japanese artisans and craftsmen demonstrating their skilled works than showing their everyday habits—from waking up to going to bed—as being done at the Japanese Native Village of 1885. Instead, in Ainu Home and Formosa Hamlet, the discriminatory aspect was much stronger, allowing visitors to observe their bodies and habitats, which ended up highlighting Japan's colonial hierarchy.[9] To some extent, the two 'colonial villages' made the Europeans' gaze away from the 'Japanese bodies' towards their 'power' as one of the colonisers.[10]

The Ainu Home was recreated for the Japan-British Exhibition of 1910, exhibiting three *cises*, traditional houses of Ainu, and ten Ainu people who lived in this man-made village for six months (Miyatake 118). The Ainu Home was organised by a 'syndicate'

124   *Educating People*

that was made up of some English organisers under a strict supervision of the Japanese government (120, 124).[11] Miyatake points out that the Japanese government had a contradictory aim to represent the ten Ainu men, women and children as respectable and civilised 'Japanese citizens' of the New Japan, while the display exaggerated the uniqueness of their race and manners without understanding the culture of Ainu (124). He continues that while the Ainu-themed display at the Louisiana Purchase Exposition in St. Louis in 1904 was understood as 'academically significant', that of the Japan-British Exhibition in 1910 merely served as an 'amusement' (128). The disgraceful representation of the Ainu people and culture in White City in 1910 was mainly as a result of the change of their social status in Japan in 1910 (127).[12] According to an anthropologist, Brian Street, the European visitors 'were taking considerable interest in the Ainu as exotic curiosities, with their long beards, bear ceremonies and "primitive" living conditions, their culture and economy had been destroyed by Japanese domination' by the nineteenth century (123). For the European audience, they were the rare curios to recognise the difference in their 'dress and "ritual" behaviour, as in racial classification' (123). For the Japanese, on the contrary, the Ainu in the exhibition was 'mediated by the view that the Japanese themselves held of their subjugated neighbours' (123).

In spite of the discriminatory representation, the Ainus in London, while facing some troubles, enjoyed sightseeing around London and interacting with the British citizens while they were staying in London for the Exhibition (Ziomek 105–108). The British were much warmer to them than the Japanese, welcoming, communicating and even giving money and gifts to them. One of the local newspapers in Kobe, Japan, *Kobe Shinbun*, published on 15 December 1910 reported that the Ainus were not only given some Western clothes, but they also traded their traditional *attush* robe for western frock coats (108). Without doubt, the Ainu Home at the Japan-British Exhibition had a human-zoo aspect in the way that it displayed and exposed their bodies and controlled their actions, but simultaneously they received some respect as the 'indigenous' people who resembled the white 'races' from the locals in London (Miyatake 129).

The Formosa Hamlet was also built along with the Ainu Home in the amusement district of the exhibition, where twenty-four Taiwanese Aboriginals (the Paiwan ethnic group) were displayed in the same way as the Ainus in the Ainu Home (Miyatake 118). However, as Ziomek argues, the Formosa Hamlet gained less attention because the Paiwan were 'depicted as violent savages', while 'the Ainu were romanticised and beautified' (116). According to the contemporary reports, the Taiwanese Aboriginals were said to have carried weapons such as guns, spears and knives, presenting 'spear throwing contests' and 'a sham fight' to the fairgoers (128, 129). In the postcards and newspaper reports, the Paiwan participants are repeatedly described as 'savages'.

Their staged 'savageness' possibly served as attraction at the Japan-British Exhibition; however, it was also reported that the Paiwan people were keen to learn English, memorising some English phrases and keeping it until they went back to their country (121, 122). They also tried to authenticate the souvenir postcards by signing their names in multiple languages: Japanese, Chinese and English (120). The intellectual side of the Paiwan people at the exhibition was juxtaposed with their 'savageness' and that contradictory characters of them were neither hidden but clearly visible to the audience of the exhibition.

The employment of the Ainu Home and the Formosa Hamlet meant to distinguish the 'primitive' natives and the 'modern' Japanese. When the cultural difference was misused for the political purpose, it could create hierarchy rather than celebrate each other. What

Educating People 125

the Meiji government did was to replicate the discriminatory representation of which they once were the victim to humiliate the entire Ainu and Paiwan culture and people. This could be named as one of the most immature and absurd responses that one could have done to racism. Furthermore, two women, one each from the Ainu Home and the Formosa Hamlet, are reported to have given birth to a baby during the exhibition. Miyatake points out that the mothers of the babies were pregnant for six or seven months when they travelled to Britain and the organisers expected them to give birth during the exhibition. Thus, Miyatake continues that the organisers made an inhumane decision to control and make a show of their sexualities (142–143).

There was a discriminatory undertone over the Ainu and the Paiwan people, placing them under a colonial setting. However, simultaneously, the Ainus and the Paiwan people had an inter-cultural experience in London. They communicated with the British, learnt new languages and cultures and exchanged things during their stay in London. While the people at these colonial villages were exposed to some discriminatory gaze both by the British audience and the Japanese at the Japan-British Exhibition, the Ainus and the Paiwan people had some freedom to explore the city to some extent. In this sense, they were so much more than just a 'body' to be displayed but they rather had and offered a 'cross-cultural experience' with mutual interactions.

Variety Theatres, 1867–1914

During the Victorian period, Japonisme was mostly enjoyed by the upper- and upper-middle classes as art, fashion and entertainment. This included entertainment troupes that came from Japan to perform in Britain. The earliest known example was a group of jugglers that performed at St. Martin's Hall (today's Queen's Theatre) in London in 1867 ('The Japanese Acrobats and Jugglers' 8). Also, Tannaker Buhicrosan, who organised the Japanese Native Village in 1885, actually had already fairly succeeded as a manager of Japanese troupes visiting and performing in western countries before 1885 (Koyama 112). Another troupe called 'Imperial Japanese Troupe' led by an American acrobat performer, Professor Risley, also sailed to Britain from the late 1860s onward to perform acrobatics, juggling and magic tricks (139). These troupes appeared at larger venues, such as the Egyptian Hall in Piccadilly, London, where ticket prices ranged from 1s to 5s, or local Theatre Royals in provincial cities, where tickets cost 1s to 3s (for example, the Assembly Rooms in Cheltenham, Gloucestershire).[13]

The effort of social reformers and the county councils from the 1880s to restrict the alcoholism and indecent manners both on and off stage led the birth of new kind of music hall from the 1890s on: the variety theatres run by paramount theatre chains in London, such as the famous Empires, Palaces and Hippodromes (Double 39, 41). These theatres flourished, accepting not only men and women but also children as their audience. The family was the new audience, drinking was no longer the main activity and the seats were fixed (Summerfield 21). Ticket prices were widened by seats, attracting a mix of audiences from different social classes. Until the birth of variety theatres, ballet and opera had been reserved for the upper class, musicals and acrobatics for the middle class and the free-and-easy melodramas and comic acts for the working class. Variety theatres blurred the boundaries between the performances of different social classes and allowed people to attend performances they had never seen before. In other words, traditional performances that had been developed within each social class were now unified. The Japanese acrobat troupes had usually been performed at the theatres and halls for the

126   *Educating People*

middle classes during the second half of the nineteenth century until when new and socially mixed variety theatres began to be opened.

Not only in London, but variety theatres were also opened in the regions from the 1900s. Dagmar Kift argued that the types of audience of variety theatres were often different from ones in London and in provincial cities (171–172, 174). Many newer theatres in London, such as the Empire and the Palace in Leicester Square, were often filled with upper-class men and the urban bohemians, and the morality of these new halls, again, began to be questioned due to the dubious use of promenades and indecent content and costumes on stage (Walkowitz 427).

In rural regions, on the contrary, newly built variety theatres continued to be deeply rooted in local working-class culture (Kift 172). The provincial variety theatres were also broadly based but were still largely patronised by the members of the working class (172, 174). New chains such as the Empire and the Hippodrome were also built in many provincial cities in the 1900s. This resulted in a broadening of the kinds of performances and allowed members of the rural working class to see performances like Japanese acrobats. Admission prices of variety theatres are generally from 2d to 1s in the countryside and 3d to 10s 6d in London.[14]

According to Arthur L. Bowley's report, the average wages of workers had slightly increased between the mid-nineteenth century and the 1890s, and urban workers were likely to earn more than rural workers.[15] Worker's wages continued increasing towards the twentieth century and the typical earnings of the skilled workers in Britain in 1906 were £97 per year, while that of the semi-skilled workers were £68 per year.[16] In 1906, even unskilled workers' average wages had grown to £63 a year, making it possible for more working-class people to afford the cheaper tickets of the new variety theatres.[17] While some theatres, especially in urban areas, cased out working-class audiences, others offered an opportunity for audiences from broader social backgrounds to enjoy the same acts together.

In those new variety theatres of the 1900s and 1910s, there were two kinds of 'Japan' that were presented on stages both in big cities and in rural towns. While the acrobats and jugglers from Japan successfully welcomed in the variety theatres, there simultaneously existed some Japanese-inspired performers that were played by Euro-American performers. A concert party named 'the Merry Japs' was one of them that was enormously popular during the late 1900s and the early 1910s, performing Japanese-themed miniature musical comedies at the newly built variety theatres across Britain. The Merry Japs were led by a famous music hall actor from Manchester, Marie Santoi (1880–1924) (in private life, Santoi's name was Mary Fuller who died in 1924 aged 44).[18] Santoi was successful in two of her acts: 'A Japanese Tea Garden by Night' and 'A Night in Japan'.[19] She and her party appeared in most of the big variety theatre chains all across Britain, all of which were much appreciated. A local newspaper in West Yorkshire, *The Leeds and Yorkshire Mercury*, reproduces a small illustration of Marie Santoi and the Merry Japs on 4 March 1907 ('Miss Marie San-toi' 8). (Figure 4.5) It shows a centre figure, possibly Marie Santoi, dressed in a short-length gown with shorts, three female-like figures in full-length kimonos and a male-like figure in a militaristic uniform. Although it is merely an illustration, it is significant to note that it is difficult to find any characters dressed in a gown and shorts in any Japanese-themed acts prior to Marie Santoi's. Not only did the acts performed during Victorian period, *The Mikado* and *The Geisha*, but *The White Chrysanthemum*, that opened in 1905, also had no characters dressed as vigorously as Santoi. The Japanese-themed musicals listed above were all played at the West

Figure 4.5 'Miss Marie San-toi' in The Leeds Mercury, 4 March 1907, p. 8. Newspaper image © The British Library Board. All rights reserved. With thanks to The British Newspaper Archive (www.britishnewspaperarchive.co.uk).

End theatres, the costumes presented on stage possibly could not completely derogate from the respectability of the casts and the audience. On the contrary, Marie Santoi, who was successful at the London music halls in her early carrier, created a vigorous Japanese character with a little exposure of skin for variety theatres. Marie Santoi and the Merry Japs toured across Britain until 1915 when their name vanishes from the newspaper advertisements. Santoi's new adaptation of a 'Japanese' person allowed a different representation of one to be available towards broader audiences beyond regions and class.

Japanese acrobat troupes who mainly had performed at the halls and theatres for the middle classes expanded the stages for their performances to the newly built variety theatres in the twentieth century. While the two most famous occasions to observe real Japanese people from Japan (the Japanese Native Village in 1885 and the Japan-British Exhibition in 1910) had mainly been accessible to upper- and middle-class Londoners, variety theatre chains that were built in many regional towns allowed much broader people to actually see the real 'Japanese' in live.

According to the passenger lists of the ships sailed from Yokohama to London, for example, there seems a vast number of Japanese troupes entering Britain in the early twentieth century.[20] Various troupes from Japan visited Britain and toured to perform at the variety theatres throughout the very end of the nineteenth and the early twentieth century. One of the earlier ones found in newspapers was, for example, the act of a troupe called 'Nishiama Matuzi Japanese troupe' who performed at the variety theatre

128 *Educating People*

in Islington, London, called the Holloway Empire in 1902 (The Holloway Empire' 4). Another troupe, 'the Lukushima Japanese troupe' seems to have been successful performing acrobatic acts in a variety of theatres. The Lukushimas toured across the country from Glasgow to Brighton between 1903 and 1911. Their 1½ page advertisements were repeatedly reproduced in *The Music Hall and Theatre Review*, one of which shows an interesting phrase: 'Race Question! Can the Asiatics never be Modernised? YES! THE LUKUSHIMA TROUPE of Japanese Artistes' published in June 1903 ('Race Question!' 368). It is obvious that this slightly racist expression comes from the contemporary view of race that was deeply inspired by the Social Darwinian theory and the eugenics that were still firmly supported in Britain in the early twentieth century. However, explaining a Japanese troupe using a term that had rarely been applied to any Asian countries in the prior period: 'modern', could purely be from the conclusion of the Anglo-Japanese Alliance in 1902. An advertisement reproduced in December 1905 shows children with the national flag of the United Kingdom and the flag of the Imperial Japanese Army, showing that the world of entertainment was also deeply associated with the military alliance. Here implies that 'Japan' projected on variety theatre stages was different (or perhaps 'modern') from that of the late Victorian period.

Looking into the costume of the Japanese troupes, a difference between the costumes worn at the variety theatres in the beginning of the twentieth century and worn at the halls and theatres for middle classes in the 1860s and 1870s can also be pointed out. The troupes in the 1860s and 1870s were mostly men and they dressed in the traditional costumes of acrobat performers in Japan: a kimono and *hakama* trousers as seen in the illustration reproduced in *The Illustrated London News* on 2 May 1868 (Figure 4.6). Yu Kawazoe wrote that the costumes of the Japanese performers of the late 1860s were more 'flamboyant' than the ordinary costumes worn in contemporary Japan (Kawazoe 53). However, both the Japanese performers and their costumes were seen as something utterly peculiar to the British audiences as they were described in *The Illustrated London News* as 'grotesque', 'audacious', 'queerest' and 'hazardous' ('The Japanese Performers at the Lyceum' 437).

In the early twentieth century, on the contrary, the costumes of the Japanese performers were seen differently. First of all, there were a few female performers within the troupes of the early twentieth century. The photographs of the troupes reproduced in the journals show some of the Japanese troupes dressed in embellished kimono-shaped gowns that were closer to those available in Britain. The trend in contemporary British fashion even came to influence the costumes of the Japanese troupes who performed in Britain in the 1900s and 1910s. These costumes seem to have been one of the centrepieces of their performance since their costuming was often advertised as 'gorgeous'.

A troupe called the Fuji Family appeared in the front cover of *The Performer* published on 11 May 1911, for example, dressed up in embroidered kimono-like gowns with no *obi*. The photograph shows six Japanese performers in decorative westernised kimonos. The centre figure seems like a female performer in an elaborate kimono. The male performers' kimonos are a little shorter and reveal their legs, while the female performer is dressed in a full-length kimono, which would have been sold around 50–60 shillings at the department stores in Britain.[21] Two years later, the Fuji Family replaced possibly two of the performers for their advertisement in *The Performer* on Christmas day in 1913, in which the six Japanese men are photographed in heavily embroidered ¾ length kimono-like gowns.[22] Those kimonos, too, were the kind that was popularly sold

Figure 4.6 'The Imperial Japanese Troupe at Lyceum Theatre' in The Illustrated London News, 2 May 1868, p. 433. © Illustrated London News/Mary Evans Picture Library, London.

in Britain. Large camellias and peonies were embroidered into the fabric, and the hem of the kimono was curved as seen in some of the 'exotic' robes available in the West in the early twentieth century.

What is strikingly different from the mainstream adoption of Japanese kimonos in Britain is that the male performers wore decorative kimonos similar in design to the kimonos for the female performers. Their 'gorgeous' costumes could be appealing to female audiences, but they also helped associate decorative and fashionable kimonos with male figures. Both male and female performers of other troupes such as the Banzai Family and the Ko Ten Ichi Troupe, too, were photographed dressed in extravagant, heavily embroidered, open-fronted kimonos that would feed the British expectation of what an attractive Japanese kimono should look like. In other words, the costumes of the Japanese troupes in the early twentieth century represented the picturesque version of 'Japanese' costumes established in the British mind instead of traditional or authentic Japanese dress. And those fashionable kimonos were worn not only by female performers but also by male performers.

A short video captured two Japanese acrobats performing an unusual juggling trick in 1904. What is most intriguing in this a-minute-and-a-half video is that the young man and the boy appear on stage in short kimonos (which look like Japanese *happi* [half-length kimono usually used for festivals]) with heavy embroideries but take those kimonos off as they start their acrobat performance. Under their kimonos, they are wearing

130 *Educating People*

fitted dark-coloured tights, a fitted top and lighter-coloured shorts, which are all very typical of contemporary acrobatic performers in Britain.

Another video that was originally taken in France in 1913 and distributed in Britain also shows Japanese acrobats performing for the western audiences. In this video, five men of varying age come out on stage dressed in an elaborate kimono-like gown with cherry blossoms (Figure 4.7). But as they start their acrobat tricks, they take off the outer kimono to reveal knee-length trousers and a shorter-length kimono also with elaborate floral patterns that are worn underneath (Figure 4.8). Both the outer and the inner kimono gowns have a typical design that was made for the western market and commonly adopted by women in Britain since around 1900. The two younger performers wear a fitted top and a short waistcoat underneath the outer kimonos, but they also take their waistcoats off in the later part of the video. Although, in this video, the act of undressing the outer kimono is not captured as the previous example, it is obvious that they took it off one after another as the performance continues. Unlike the earlier Japanese troupes who were dressed in a traditional kimono and a *hakama* trousers in the 1860s–1870s, showing the 'gorgeous' westernised kimono as they entered and taking it off on stage seem like a part of the performances of the troupes of the early twentieth century.

Japanese male acrobats' employment of the embellished kimono gowns, on the one hand, reveals the disturbance of the conventional idea of clothing that was strictly divided by gender in the western society. Those fashionable kimonos, on the other hand, were taken off for performing dynamic acrobatic acts. Japanese acrobats exposed their

Figure 4.7 Still from *Japanese Acrobats (1913)*. The BFI National Archive. 18813. Courtesy of the BFI National Archive.

bodies under their kimonos in front of the British audience since the twentieth century. In Japan, too, this interesting shift of the costumes of the Japanese male acrobats had also been seen since the Meiji period. Acrobatic troupes during the Edo period were usually fully dressed, showing no skin in front of the audience. It was around the mid-Meiji period (since around the 1880s) when male acrobats began to pose almost naked, showing their muscular bodies to the audience both in Japan and overseas. The image of them was also circulated in Britain as postcards during the 1900s and the 1910s (Figure 4.9)

The male acrobatic performers from Japan who appeared on stage in various theatres across Britain in the early twentieth century, therefore, displayed two contradictory bodies that are wrapped by 'feminine' kimonos and that are showing off 'masculine' physique. In Meiji Japan where many rules and cultures changed, Japanese men cut their hair short and faced a completely new masculinity, and they even exposed their new bodies on stage of the far-away land. As seen in the previous chapters, kimono's role as a 'thing to undress' was again stressed here. However, the act of undressing a kimono on variety theatre stages was not connected to eroticism or sensuality but was rather associated with strength.

Japanese bodies had been variously defined and represented in the western society. They were feminine, dainty and sensual as well as uncivilised, barbarous and audacious. However, what is significant in the Japanese acrobats of the early twentieth century is that it was *they* who took their kimonos off and showed their bodies to the British audience.

Figure 4.8 Still from *Japanese Acrobats (1913)*. The BFI National Archive. 18813. Courtesy of the BFI National Archive.

132 *Educating People*

Figure 4.9 Raphael Tuck & Sons. 'Japanese Acrobats' of Japanese at Home series, 1910. Photographic postcard. Tuck DB Postcards. 6465. https://tuckdbpostcards.org/items/81000/pictures/108895. Accessed 18 March 2023.

Even if their movement was all choreographed, their act of undressing their kimonos imply their emotions to move away from being unilaterally objectified and judged.

Furthermore, as a feminist reformer, Laura Ormiston Chant (1848–1923) once described the female 'Japanese juggler' as having 'strong, unfettered bodies', Japanese acrobats' bodies under their kimonos were strong and confident, unlike the clichéd representations of Japanese people in the West (Chant 55; qtd. in Walkowitz 433). Open-fronted kimonos of the Japanese troupes are used not for hiding but for highlighting what's inside. But in this case, the bodies inside were 'unfettered' as Chant declared. Japanese acrobat performers' prodigious physical ability and athletic bodies are rarely discussed, but they could have been one of the significant images of the 'Japanese' that was accessible in Britain in the early twentieth century.

In the early twentieth century, Japan itself slowly began to be recognised as an Eastern empire that had a growing military power after her victory in the Sino-Japanese War (1894–1895) and the Russo-Japanese War (1904–1905). Japan's earlier image as peculiar, uncivilised, nostalgic, exotic, dainty, sensual and beautiful was juxtaposed with a new image of a military power. In 1902, Japan and Britain signed the Anglo-Japanese Alliance, which cemented this new image even more strongly. According to Summerfield, patriotism continued to be 'highly marketable' in variety theatres of the twentieth century as well (42).[23] Embellishing Japanese bodies with gorgeous anglicised costumes and exposing their extraordinary physical strength could give—even from the patriotic point of view—a strong impression of 'New Japan' that was shifting away from the former stereotypes by revealing Japanese bodies that had previously been hidden. But the fact that the kimonos worn by the acrobats were the kimonos made for the western women created a contradictory juxtaposition.

The experience of kimonos as to 'educate people' was found in the Japanese-themed displays and exhibitions held in Britain from 1885 to 1910. The success of the Japanese Native Village in Knightsbridge accelerated the Japonisme craze in London, which helped the success of the comic opera, *The Mikado*, in London in the same year. However, while *The Mikado* was all about presenting a fictitious 'foreign' town that was in-between the reality and the fantasy, The Japanese Native Village of 1885 exaggerated its role as a native village, so that it intentionally presented the idyllic 'Old Japan'. The 'real' Japanese at the Japanese Native Village was not supposed to dress in the most expensive kimonos made by famous artisans but was to dress in simple kimonos to stage 'authenticity' of a Japanese life.

The Japanese people in London were strictly controlled by the organisers, being instructed on what to wear, what they should do and when. Their bodies in the modest kimonos at the Japanese Native Village were displayed, drawing an insurmountable line between the people who 'observed' and who 'were observed'. However, simultaneously, the manipulative representations of Japan and the Japanese that were exploited at the Japanese Native Village also revealed the anxiety that the contemporary British society held.

A Japanese exhibition was held in the Whitechapel Art Gallery in 1902, which possibly marked the first encounter for the local East Enders to meet the objects including the dresses from Japan. The exhibition completed with the bits and pieces of 'Japan' lent by various donors was placed for an educational purpose to introduce the 'ordinary everyday life of Japan' to the residents of Whitechapel. It attracted many local Jewish communities as well as the art enthusiasts and philanthropists from different social classes. The ordinary everyday life in Japan was delivered as an update of the existing impression for some, or as a completely new knowledge for others. What is important here is to include but also to distinguish the experience of kimonos by the local Jewish community and the upper- and middle-class visitors.

The 1910 Japan-British Exhibition marks the biggest Japanese-themed event that was held in London during the twentieth century. Unlike the two exhibitions that are also discussed in this chapter, the Japan-British Exhibition was directly organised by the Japanese government, making Japanese culture, history and people a part of the political advertisement. The ambitious attempts of the Japanese government aimed to elevate 'Japan' by displacing the British people's gaze from the bodies of Japan towards its manners, customs and history. As seen in the article of *The Graphic* on 23 July 1910, kimonos were recognised as dresses of the respectable Japanese women, being reproduced unapologetically in newspapers. The new victim of the discriminatory representation at the Japan-British Exhibition was the Ainu and Paiwan people who were displayed in the colonial villages in the amusement district of the exhibition site. However, their bodies, rituals and dresses of the Ainu and the Paiwan people were more than just a code to visualise an ethnic hierarchy. The participants of the Ainu Home and the Formosa Hamlet did not accept their places as exhibited objects, but they actively learnt English, explored the town, communicated and exchanged dresses with the local people. The Japan-British Exhibition was unexpectedly interactive not only for the British audience but also for the Japanese participants and the people placed under a colonial setting.

The new variety theatres of the early twentieth century projected a new image of 'Japan' to the diverse audience of Edwardian Britain, and those images were all framed

134 *Educating People*

by the kimono that each performer was wearing. In variety theatres, there were a vast number of acrobatic troupes that came from Japan and their costumes also show new and unique representations. Japanese male performers, for example, dressed in 'feminine' kimonos that were made for the western market. Furthermore, some even took those kimonos off to show their athletic bodies in front of the western audience. The 'feminine' kimonos of the Japanese acrobats did not only have an advertising effect to the British audience, but they also allow the audience to witness an early sign of the 'New Japan' that was actively presented on stage.

The kimonos displayed at each exhibition and theatre were highly manipulative, which were in a strong connection to the representation of the bodies inside. They functioned as frames rather than 'fashion' to draw a line between the 'Asian bodies' and those of the West, reminding people of the power relationship between the East and the West. Furthermore, the kimonos could also reveal the colonial tension within the modern Japan. But kimonos, concurrently, served as subjects that connoted much more complex emotions, relationships and communications between the wearers, organisers and the world that surrounded them.

Notes

1 The admission was one shilling except for Wednesdays, on which the price went up to half-a-crown. See 'Japan in London' 4.
2 Tannaker Buhicrosan who was born in Amsterdam as Frederik Blekman. He visited Nagasaki for the first time in 1859 to work for Sir John Rutherford Alcock as his interpreter. He started to call himself 'Tannaker Buhicrosan' in 1867 when he travelled America and Europe with Japanese acrobat troupes. He was one of the most important figures of developing Japonisme in the West. See Koyama for more information on Buhicrosan.
3 It was written as 'It is not a little entertaining […] to observe how the very children soon learn to regard them as poor benighted barbarians enveloped in gross mental and spiritual darkness'. The article continued that the Japanese villagers 'are not altogether lost in awe and admiration of Western civilization in its own home' and 'they do not think so highly of some of our ways as we ourselves do'. The writer included 'Japanese point of view' on the western civilisation in this article and implied how Japanese people lived in very different way from them, and (in their view) how being civilised was not the only thing Japanese were eagerly after. See 'The Japanese Villagers' 3.
4 The studio was opened in 1863 and it was purchased by Baron Raimund von Stillfried in 1877, who produced photographs even more westernised. See Corwin 34.
5 In the late Edo to early Meiji Japan, less flamboyant colour and patterns were considered fashionable among Japanese women, so that this vogue in Japan also helped distinguish between 'picturesque' kimono for the West and 'simple' kimono for natives. For late Edo and early Meiji fashion, see Mizukami.
   A Yokohama Photography by Felice Beato titled 'A Japanese Girl Dressed a la mode' shows a girl wearing kimono and *obi* with simpler patterns and plain colour. This also implies the different ideas of 'fashionability' of kimono in Japan and in Britain. See Gartlan 30.
6 According to this record, Nagasawa was a carpenter aged 36 at the time he was sent to London.
7 Ambrose Walford is also listed as a member of the Royal Society of Arts in 1906. See 'List of Members with dates of election', p. 50.
8 The opening of the Japan-British Exhibition was conducted by a clear intension of Meiji government to keep the Anglo-Japanese Alliance and the friendship with Britain. For more information on the Japan-British Exhibition, see Hayashi.
9 The displays of the people of Taiwan and Ainu at the Japan-British Exhibition in 1910 was criticised both in Japan and in Britain. While these displays were still successful, they were strictly denounced in Japan as being discriminatory. See Hayashi 194–195.

Educating People 135

10 Ziomek argues that Japan and Japanese were still in a complicated position as a 'non-Western nation' against the Japanese government's will by noting the British people 'conflated the Taiwanese Aborigines and the Japanese' and discussed Ainu people 'as a potential "lost white race"'. See Ziomek 93–94.

11 An English artist, Alfread Parsons (1847–1920) was first appointed as a chair of the 'syndicate' but was replaced by another painter described as 'Julian Hicks'. See Miyatake 120.

12 The assimilation of Ainu people in Hokkaido had already been introduced by the new Meiji government during the late nineteenth century. But it was in 1910 when the Japanese annexation of Korea was completed that the discrimination towards the Ainu people also got worse. See Miyatake 127.

13 According to the advertisement of Royal Tycoon Troupe's first appearance in London at Egyptian Hall in Piccadilly in 1869, admission was from 1s to 5s. The Great Japanese Troupe performed at the assembly rooms in Cheltenham, Gloucestershire from 14th to 17th June 1871, admission was from 3s to 1s. See 'Assembly Rooms, Cheltenham' 4.

14 The admission for the act of Nishiama Matzui Japanese Troupe at the Holloway Empire in Islington, London in August 1902 priced at 10s 6d for the private boxes (for four people), 1s 6d for fauteuils, 1s for grand circles, 6d for pit, 4d for the amphitheatre and 3d for balcony. The admission for the act of Royal Japanese Troupe at Leigh Theatre Royal in Greater Manchester in June 1904 priced at 2d, 3d, 6d and 1s. The admission for the act of Fuji Family at the Palace & Hippodrome in Burnley, Lancashire in October 1910 priced at 3d, 6d, 9d and 1s. See 'The Holloway Empire' 4, 'Leigh Theatre Royal' 1, 'Palace & Hippodrome' 1.

15 'The workers' here are of following industries: agriculture, building, compositors, cotton, iron, mining, sailors and wool. See Bowley 60, 133.

16 'The skilled workers' here means coalface workers, fitters, carpenters, railway engine drivers and compositors. 'The semi-skilled workers' here means semi-skilled pottery workers, railway firemen, bus and train drivers (London), shop assistants, postmen (London) and agricultural labourers. See Burnett 300–301.

17 Burnett writes that builders' labourers were receiving an average of £63 a year, railway porters £50, brewery labourers £50. See Burnett 301.

18 There are vast numbers of advertisements on Marie Santoi and her Merry Japs found between 1905 and 1915, a lot of which are found in *The Music Hall and Theatre Review* that was published for a penny. For an article on her death, see 'Death of Miss Marie Santoi' 15.

19 For the advertisements of Santoi's acts, see 'St. Helens' *The Music Hall and Theatre Review* 83 and 'Amusements' *Gloucestershire Chronicle* 8.

20 According to the passenger lists of the ships sailed from Yokohama to London between 1910 and 1913, there were both male and female acrobat performers arrived in London. For example, a ship called Atsuta Maru arrived in London on 28 April 1910; there were 44 Japanese passengers who were female and 18 of them were recorded as 'performer'. Another ship called Tango Maru arrived in London on 26 October 1911; it carried 'acrobatic party' of 10 Japanese people, and 2 of them were female performers. In both ships, all of the Japanese performers sailed in the third class.

21 The photograph is found in *The Performer* on 11 May 1911, p. 1.

22 The photograph is found in *The Performer*, 25 December 1913, p. 132.

23 Summerfield wrote that in the twentieth century, blatant jingoistic expressions were slightly muted and shifted towards more familiar representations of 'virility servicemen'; however, the expressions of patriotism and Empire continued to be the important theme of popular entertainments. See Summerfield 42.

Works Cited

Anon. 'Amusements'. *Gloucestershire Chronicle*, 13 March 1915, p. 8.

Anon. 'Assembly Rooms, Cheltenham'. *The Cheltenham Examiner*, 14 June 1871, p. 4.

Anon. 'Death of Miss Marie Santoi'. *The Yorkshire Post*, 28 June 1924, p. 15.

Anon. 'Japan in London'. *The Brighton Gazette & Sussex Daily Telegraph*, 30 December 1885, p. 4.

Anon. 'Japan in Whitechapel'. *The London and China Telegraph*, 29 July 1902, p. 646.

136 Educating People

Anon. 'Knightsbridge Green Area: Scotch Corner and the High Road'. *Survey of London: Volume 45, Knightsbridge*, edited by John Greenacombe, London County Council, 2000, pp. 79–88.

Anon. 'Leigh Theatre Royal'. *Leigh Chronicle and Weekly District Advertiser*, 17 June 1904, p. 1.

Anon. 'List of Members with Dates of Election'. *The Journal of the Society of Arts*, vol. 54, no. 2817, 1906, pp. 33–55.

Anon. 'Miss Marie San-toi'. *The Leeds and Yorkshire Mercury*, 4 March 1907, p. 8.

Anon. 'Palace & Hippodrome'. *Burnley Express*, 29 October 1910, p. 1.

Anon. 'Race Question!'. *The Music Hall and Theatre Review*, 5 June 1903, p. 368.

Anon. 'St Helens'. *The Music Hall and Theatre Review*, 4 August 1905, p. 83.

Anon. 'The Holloway Empire'. *The Islington Gazette*, 19 August 1902, p. 4.

Anon. 'The Japanese Acrobats and Jugglers'. *Bell's Weekly Messenger*, 18 February 1867, p. 8.

Anon. 'The Japanese Performers at the Lyceum'. *The Illustrated London News*, 2 May 1868, p. 437.

Anon. 'The Japanese Village, Knightsbridge'. *The Illustrated Sporting and Dramatic News*, 14 March 1885, p. 648.

Anon. 'The Japanese Village'. *The Illustrated London News*, 21 February 1885, p. 203.

Anon. 'The Japanese Villager'. *The Globe*, 13 January 1885, pp. 1–2.

Anon. 'The Japanese Villagers'. *The Daily News*, 26 January 1885, p. 3.

Anon. 'The Original Fuji Family' in *The Performer*, 11 May 1911, p. 1.

Anon. 'Unrivalled Fuji Japanese Family' in *The Performer*, 25 December 1913, p. 132.

Bar-Yosef, Eitan and Nadia Valman. 'Introduction: Between the East End and East Africa: Rethinking Images of 'the Jew' in Late-Victorian and Edwardian Culture'. *'The Jew' in Late-Victorian and Edwardian Culture: Between the East End and East Africa*, edited by Eitan Bar-Yosef and Nadia Valman, Palgrave Macmillan, 2009, pp. 1–27.

Bowley, Arthur Lyon. *Wages and Income in the United Kingdom Since 1860*. Cambridge UP, 1937.

———. *Wages in the United Kingdom in the Nineteenth Century*. Cambridge UP, 1900.

Burnett, John. *A History of the Cost of Living*. Gregg Revivals, 1969.

Chant, Laura Ormiston. 'Amused London No. 1'. *Vigilance Record*, June 1888, pp. 55–56.

Corwin, Nancy A. 'The Kimono Mind: *Japonisme* in American Culture'. *The Kimono Inspiration: Art and Art-to-Wear in America*, edited by Rebecca A. T. Stevens and Yoshiko Iwamoto Wada, Pomegranate Artbooks, 1996, pp. 23–74.

Double, Oliver. *Britain Had Talent: A History of Variety Theatre*. Palgrave Macmillan, 2012.

Gartlan, Luke. 'Shimizu Tokoku and the Japanese Carte-de-visite: Circumscriptions of Yokohama Photography'. *Portraiture and Early Studio Photography in China and Japan*, edited by Luke Gartlan and Roberta Wue, Routledge, 2017, pp. 17–40.

Hayashi, Michiko 林みちこ. *Meiji seifu no taigai bizyutsu senryaku ni kansuru kenkyu:1910 nen nichiei hakurankai wo megutte* 明治政府の対外美術戦略に関する研究—1910年日英博覧会をめぐって [*The Art policy of Imperial Japan During Meiji Period and Its Strategic Expansion Abroad: A Revaluation of The Japan-British Exhibition, 1910*]. 2016. University of Tsukuba, Ph.D. dissertation.

Hotta-Lister, Ayako. *The Japan-British Exhibition of 1910: Gateway to the Island Empire of the East*. Routledge, 2013 [first published by Japan Library in 1999].

Hotta-Lister, Ayako and Ian Nish, editors. *Commerce and Culture at the 1910 Japan-British Exhibition*. Global Oriental, 2013.

Jackson, Anna. 'Imaging Japan: The Victorian Perception and Acquision of Japanese Culture'. *The Journal of Design History*, vol. 5, no. 4, 1992, pp. 245–256.

Kawazoe, Yu 川添裕. 'Nihon-jin ni natte miru, nihon-jin wo yatte miru: shintai ga keisyou suru Japonisme' 日本人になってみる、日本人をやってみる—身体が形象するジャポニズム ['Bring Japanese, Playing Japanese: Japonisme Represented on Bodies']. *Engeki no Japonisme* 演劇のジャポニズム [Japonisme in Theatres], edited by Akira Kamiyama 神山彰, Shinwasha 森話社, 2017, pp. 35–61.

Kennedy, Maev. 'Historical Haven for East End's Great and Hood Closes Its Doors Forever'. *The Guardian*, 6 August 2005.

Kift, Dagmar. *The Victorian Music Hall: Culture, Class and Conflict*. Translated by Roy Kift, Cambridge UP, 1996.

Koyama, Noboru 小山騰. *London nihon-jin mura wo tsukutta otoko: nazo no kougyoshi Tanaka Buhikurosan* ロンドン日本人村を作った男－謎の興行師タナカー・ブヒクロサン 1839–1894 [*The Man Who Built the Japanese Native Village in London: The Showman of a Mystery, Tanaka Buhikurosan, 1839–94*]. Fujiwara Shoten 藤原書店, 2015.

Kramer, Elizabeth. '"Not so Japan-Easy": the British Reception of Japanese Dress in the Late Nineteenth Century'. *Textile History*, vol. 44, no. 1, 2013, pp. 3–24.

MacKenzie, John M. *Orientalism: History, Theory and the Arts*. Manchester UP, 1995.

———. 'Orientalism in Arts and Crafts Revisited: The Modern and the Anti-Modern: The Lessons from the Orient'. *Orientalism Revisited: Art, Land and Voyage*, edited by Ian Richard Netton, Routledge, 2013, pp. 117–127.

———. *Propaganda and Empire: The Manipulation of British Public Opinion, 1880–1960*. Manchester UP, 1984.

Miyatake, Kimio 宮武公夫. *Umi wo watatta Ainu: senjumin tenji to futatsu no hakuran-kai* 海を渡ったアイヌー先住民展示と二つの博覧会 [*Ainu across the Ocean: Displays of Ethnicities and the Two World Exhibitions*]. Iwanamishoten 岩波書店, 2010.

Mizukami, Kayoko 水上嘉代子. 'Chonin no kimono 2 Edo kouki – Meiji syoki no kimono' 町人のきもの②江戸後期〜明治初期のきもの ['Kimono of Townspeople II: Kimono of Late Edo to Early Meiji Period']. *Seni to koigyou* 繊維と工業 [*Journal of Fiber Science and Technology*], vol. 64, no. 8, 2008, pp. 24–27.

Summerfield, Penny. 'Patriotism and Empire: Music-Hall Entertainment 1870–1914'. *Imperialism and Popular Culture*, edited by John M. MacKenzie, Manchester UP, 1986, pp. 17–48.

T.C.O. 'H.E. The Japanese Minister's Models of Japanese Furniture at the Whitechapel Exhibition'. *The Queen*, 23 August 1902, pp. 300–301.

Toynbee Hall, Whitechapel. *Eleventh Annual Report of the Universities' Settlement in East London*. Penny and Hull, 1892.

———. *Eleventh Annual Report of the Universities' Settlement in East London*. Penny and Hull, 1895.

———. *Seventeenth Annual Report of the Universities' Settlement in East London*. Penny and Hull, 1901.

Walkowitz, Judith R. 'Cosmopolitanism, Feminism, and the Moving Body'. *Victorian Literature and Culture,* vol. 38, no. 2, 2010, pp. 427–449.

Whitechapel Art Gallery. *Japanese Exhibition 1902*. Whitechapel Art Gallery, 1902.

———. *Whitechapel Art Gallery Report 1902*. Whitechapel Art Gallery, 1902.

———. *Whitechapel Art Gallery Summer Exhibition, 1902. Catalogue*. Whitechapel Art Gallery, 1902.

Wilde, Oscar. 'The Decay of Lying: A Dialogue'. *The Nineteenth Century*, vol. XXV, edited by James Knowles, London, Kegan Paul, Trench & Co., 1889, pp. 35–56.

Ziomek, Kirsten L. *Lost Histories: Recovering the Lives of Japan's Colonial Peoples*. The Harvard University Asia Center, 2019.

5 Circulating Beyond

This chapter focuses on how Japanese kimonos reached the visual and material culture of the British 'masses', which includes many more populations that had long been considered being excluded from any Japonisme-related habits. Although the cheaper kimonos began to be sold from the early twentieth century, kimonos, especially the rich and fashionable kinds made of fine silk, continued to be regarded as 'the garment of the rich' in Britain.[1] Japonisme in fashion was adopted and developed mostly by upper- and upper-middle-class women. Thus, kimonos were not regarded as necessity but rather as luxury items, with the active experience of kimonos (including purchasing and wearing one) often not accessible to members of the working classes.

It was primarily through postcards that those men and women physically experienced kimonos (including purchasing, personalising and exchanging one) as their own visual and material culture. Postcards were mass produced and consumed, and vast numbers of them were sent every day during the early twentieth century. The images of kimonos, too, widely circulated across Britain as cheap communication. This chapter focuses on how the postcards reproduced the images of the Japanese people or the western people in kimonos and demonstrates how those images of kimonos decorated the everyday messages put on postcards. Furthermore, this chapter also seeks to show how the British senders and recipients experienced and circulated kimonos through the actual hands-on contact with postcards.

Postcards and the Visual Culture of Edwardian Britain

Postcards were first issued in England in 1870 reaching the height of their popularity in the early twentieth century; they were used by everyone, from the working classes to the upper classes (Cure 7). Prior to that, greeting cards, first created by Sir Henry Cole in 1843, were popular among the growing middle classes during the second half of the nineteenth century. Greeting cards were priced from 6d to 2s for a packet, in the late nineteenth century, which was somewhat unaffordable for workers of that period.[2] Greeting cards were never sent without an envelope and they also needed a penny stamp, so sending them was considered a luxury habit.

In the late-Victorian and Edwardian period, unlike letters, the conspicuousness and lack of privacy of the postcard became controversial. In her study on European and American postcards from the early twentieth century, Monica Cure noted that, 'The new postcard was seen as fast, efficient, often political, and potentially dangerous, even though it was represented as a fad' (5). In 1902, the power of that image increased when Britain adopted the 'divided back', with the message and address placed together on the

DOI: 10.4324/9781003334255-6

back and only the picture placed on the front (20). The result of this was 'a reversal of the primacy of message and image' (20). Thus, Cure saw that the birth of the postcard was greeted with both optimism and anxiety because it was seen as 'having incredible potential to stimulate both social and antisocial behaviour' (8 and 21).

The fast and easy-to-send postcard was gradually considered 'the letter of the poor' because it was cheap.[3] Although people of all classes used postcards during the early twentieth century, many of them were sent to the working-class homes. As already mentioned, the postcards were considered not very private; as Julia Gillen noted, postcards 'dangerously violated the private/public divide' (490, 495) because they were 'invading privacy and making visible communications that should be kept hidden' (490). In her study, Gillen obtained postcards sent during the Edwardian period and found that they had been sent to working-class homes.[4] According to the 1905 annual report by the Postmaster General, the number of postcards delivered in the United Kingdom during the year 1904–1905 was 734,500,000 in total, which was an increase of 19.7% compared to the previous year (*51st Report of the Postmaster General* 1). 81% of those postcards were sent for private purposes.

The postcard boom was also heavily associated with tourism in the early twentieth century. Many holidaymakers bought postcards from holiday destinations or took a souvenir photo of themselves and had them printed on a postcard (1). In addition, many postcards that were sold in Britain depicted 'exotic' subjects, such as famous world destinations, exotic people and foreign heroes. One of the most famous postcard firms in Britain, Raphael Tuck & Sons, established in London in 1866, printed numerous types of postcards that contributed to the 'postcard boom' of the early twentieth century. The company now has an online database, in which they hold a large number of postcards from the late nineteenth to the early twentieth century.

Elizabeth Edwards, who researches *carte de visite* photographs that were popular in the late Victorian period, wrote that the human race had been consumed by 'a wide range of "curiosities", exotica and racial and cultural stereotypes' in the second half of the nineteenth century (168). In late Victorian society, according to Edwards, the boundaries between science and popular culture were often blurred, as scientific beliefs and ideas greatly interested the general public. Victorian ideas of race were supported by contemporary 'science', which often justified racism, eugenics and imperialism in Britain. The *carte de visite*, a 'small photograph measuring 2 x 3 ½ inches, mounted on a card', was a popular collectable item widely enjoyed by people of all classes from 1855 to 1880 (174).[5] While the general public, in Victorian times, was aware of the 'gap between the ideal of mechanical objectivity and the realities of photographic practice', the fabricated reality provided by photography 'made photographs convincing carriers of information and ideas' (Tucker 66; Edwards 174).

According to Jonathan Crary, 'to observe' does not mean 'to look at' but 'to conform one's action to' or 'to comply with' (6). The 'observer' is 'embedded in a system of conventions and limitations' and the 'observation' is forced to conform to certain 'rules, codes, regulations, and practices' (6). *Carte de visites*, in most cases, offered this mode of 'observation'; what's depicted generally did not exist to break or transcend the norms and stereotypes, but it instead often reinforced them. Furthermore, it is significant that the 'observers' of *carte de visites* had no power to change or influence what's depicted. What was offered to the 'observers' was to thoroughly receive the imagery.

The photographs frequently depicted non-European bodies, emphasising their 'primitiveness', as if they were scientific specimens. For example, the *cartes* that depicted British

140   *Circulating Beyond*

heroes or celebrities always specified the name of the subject, but no personal information was specified in the *cartes* of 'ethnological performances'. They were described as 'North American Indian [sic]' or 'New Caledonian', which only stressed 'what they were' instead of introducing 'who they were'. Japanese people, too, often appeared on Victorian *cartes de visite*, usually in the form of Kabuki actors or Japanese women in kimonos. Although the *cartes* of Japanese people and those of native Americans or Oceanians cannot be conflated, it is true that, for all such subjects, their names or any further information about the subjects were unspecified. Their world and everyday lives do not seem to exist beyond the photograph. They are displayed as nameless specimens divested of individuality.

As argued by Edwards, collecting the images of different races endorsed a Social Darwinian view of race that was based around the assumption of human beings classified by 'types'. A British scholar who studies photography and media, Michelle Henning, confirmed this idea and writes that photography was one of the factors that invented and accelerated the 'science of eugenics', which 'was later embraced by Nazism' (167). The notable characteristic of *cartes* of 'native types' was the deliberate suggestion and exaggeration of the subjects' 'primitive' presence, by using certain objects and poses as if they were anthropological specimens (174). According to Edwards, photography of the second half of the nineteenth century 'made popular belief in scientific ideas more tangible, effectively more believable' (191).

In Edwardian postcards, on the contrary, the subjects were depicted more vividly alive than on Victorian *cartes de visite*. While Social Darwinism and eugenics continued to be debated into the early twentieth century, the national self-confidence of the British Empire had declined due to the Second Boer War (1899–1902). An English historian, Simon Heffer, described the Edwardian era as the beginning of 'national self-doubt and political turmoil' (214). The huge cost of the prolonged war caused a lack of public trust in the British government. Furthermore, according to the historian who is specialised in the Anglo-Boer War, Fransjohan Pretorius, the badly managed and unhygienic concentration camps built in South Africa, in which 28,000 Boer women and children and 20,000 black people died, caused controversy in Britain. Public sympathy towards the concentration camp prisoners and concern about the terrible state of the poor in their own country led to the defeat of the Conservative Party at the general election in 1906 (Pretorius). Hence, Edwardians, after experiencing a Pyrrhic victory in the Second Boer War, lost confidence as citizens of an absolute Empire and sought to amend their relationship with their colonies and the world (Heffer 214).

Raphael Tuck & Sons printed massive numbers of postcards depicting people in colonial settings in this period, but none of the bodies shown was arranged or juxtaposed as 'scientific references' as they had been in Victorian *cartes de visite*. Although none specify the subjects' names, many of the 'primitive' people were depicted within their own cultural settings, showing how they lived in their own lands. Edwardian postcards did not focus on their 'primitive bodies' but instead on their 'primitive lives'. The representation of 'primitive lives' in postcards reflected British anxiety, as their absolute superiority as an invincible Empire began to waver. Years later, the formerly 'primitive' people also began to be represented as 'allies' on postcards. Thousands of Indian soldiers fought with the British army at the front during the First World War, and postcards during wartime often depicted them on the battlefield or at the camps. The decline of an imperialistic mood in the early twentieth century triggered a change in the role 'exotic' people played in visual culture. British people began to see them as military powers instead of observing them from a distance as undeveloped beings that had nothing to do with Britain's own prosperity.

As discussed in Chapter 4, the shift of the way of seeing 'others' in Britain in the early twentieth century can also be found at the Japan-British Exhibition held in London in 1910. The Japanese Native Village of 1885 displayed eighty-five Japanese men, women and children for them to be observed almost as a 'human zoo'. However, the displays at the 1910 Japan-British Exhibition were much more diverse and it also shows the shift of the British people's interest towards the lives of Japan. While there were some real Japanese artisans and craftsmen demonstrating their skilled works at the exhibition in 1910, their everyday habits—from waking up to going to bed—were not displayed as being done at the Japanese Native Village. In 1910, Japanese bodies were no longer what the British observed, but the interest of contemporary audiences moved on to the next step, towards the 'lives' from the 'bodies' of Japan.

While there had been a romanticised idea of 'Old Japan' favoured in Britain, the impression of a 'New Japan' possessing military power, simultaneously existed from around 1902. Also, Japan was often represented as an ally after the 1902 Anglo-Japanese Alliance. One clear example of this is a set of postcards titled 'Young Japan and Friends', showing two boys holding the flags of their own country: the Japanese Rising Sun and the British Union Jack (Figure 5.1). It sent a clear message to British consumers that Japan and Britain were now in a military alliance. Japan, which also solidified itself as an empire by strengthening their armed forces under the Meiji government's policies, was now more associated with military power than with former connotations.

In the twentieth century, a social and cultural shift could be seen in the visual representations of foreign people; from focusing on their bodies, reflecting the Social Darwinism of the previous century, towards the interest in their lives and acknowledging them as comrades or allies. Because 'lives' were too diverse to stereotype, the people represented

Figure 5.1 Raphael Tuck & Sons. 'L'entente Cordiale' of Young Japan and Friends series. Photographic postcard. Tuck DB Postcards. 6546. https://tuckdbpostcards.org/items/133601. Accessed 12 August 2021.

142 *Circulating Beyond*

in the twentieth-century postcard were depicted not as specimens trapped in the past but rather as living beings, in the present tense.

Kimonos in Edwardian Postcards, 1900–1914

The archive of Raphael Tuck & Sons holds a good deal of surviving photographic postcards depicting Japanese-themed subjects. Among them, a series titled 'Life in Japan' shows Japanese men and women in a variety of poses and settings. Some of them were taken in the studio, but others were taken on the streets. The 'Life in Japan' series includes a geisha, a woman holding a baby, a Japanese man and woman in western attire and so on. What is striking is the diversity of these pictures; some were posed in the studio, as in Yokohama photographs, but others were taken in much more natural, less elaborate settings. As discussed earlier, compared to *cartes de visite* photographs of 'native types'—which all had a similar 'positioning of the body in front of the camera and the presentation of full face or profile, which constituted a form of "scientific reference"'—the photographic postcards depicting Japanese men and women are more focused on their habits, expressions and manners (Edwards 174).

In addition to this shift in visual representation of Japan and the Japanese people seen in Edwardian postcards, material characteristic of postcards also made this experience unique and further allowed the senders/recipients of postcards to be involved in the process of recreating meanings. Being exchanged between individuals, postcards were given tangible messages through the act of writing. Actual hands-on experience with objects created a close physical relationship between a person and an object which recreated, rewritten and revised meanings. Postcards provide, therefore, a more complex process than the images for 'observation' because of the actual contact between the senders and recipients. A postcard is not complete or finished until it has been written on—it cannot fully play its role without being modified. The postcard itself and the subjects depicted on the postcards, in other words, were changeable and diverse; it is not the presentation of one set of ideas or stereotypes about a subject, but a variety of images to suit the individual.

Julia Gillen, who studies picture postcards of Edwardian period, pointed out the multimodality of postcards—postcards were characterised by the combination of message and image—and she wrote that 'the multimodal combination was intended and did have some effect on the recipients' (505). The message and the image correlated and it was the senders who had a choice in deciding how to couple them. Gillen continued, 'the diversity of purposes for which postcards were employed is connected with the affordances of the cards, including their speed of movement and multimodality, and the place of postcards in a self-consciously changing modern world' (505). On postcards, therefore, kimonos were neither just an imagery to convey a single idea or an exclusive experience that was associated with 'exotic' or 'oriental' habits; postcard Japonisme was offered to the British 'masses', which made the purposes and messages even more diverse. This chapter places a particular focus on selected postcards depicting kimonos that were sent to the working-class homes. Although the messages people wrote on postcards often did not directly refer to the picture shown on the front, the image and the message correlated to one another in the way that one goes about decorating or/and defining another.

The combination of the kimono and the message shares a similar effect in the next two examples. A postcard, depicting a Japanese woman carrying a baby on her back, was sent on 22 December 1904 (Figure 5.2). The recipient is 'A M Bayly' of Burnley, Lancashire. Although 'A M Bayly' was not found in contemporary records, this postcard seemed to

Figure 5.2 Raphael Tuck & Sons. 'Geisha Mother with Baby on her Back Holds Hands with Girl beside Large Tree Trunk' of Life in Japan series, 1904. Photographic postcard. Tuck DB Postcards. 1728. https://tuckdbpostcards.org/items/50441. Accessed 12 August 2021.

have been sent to one of the back-to-back houses built for factory workers as seen on present-day maps. Furthermore, according to the census record of Burnley in 1901, a lot of cotton weavers seemed to have lived in the area where this postcard was sent, so the resident of this back-to-back house could have possibly be one too. Although the message written on the postcard is a little hard to read, the sender writes to say thank you for the postcard previously sent from the recipient.

Another postcard shows that a Japanese woman in a voluminous kimono standing at the gate was sent as a thank you note to Miss Violet Walder in West Sussex, who was seventeen years old in 1906 (Figure 5.3). According to the 1901 census record, Miss Walder's father was a wheelwright and a builder and her brother was a carpenter. The postmark on the back says that it was posted on 8 May 1906. The main text says:

> My sister wishes me to thank you for letter and photograph, she is ill in bed with Rheumatic Fever but going on nicely. With love.[6]

The purpose of this card is to give thanks to Miss Walder and the picture of a woman in a kimono was selected to please the recipient. Woman in fashionable dress is the common subject for the Edwardian postcards. Figure 5.2 was probably taken in cold winter and the Japanese woman holds her thick outer kimono up to avoid the hem touching the

144 *Circulating Beyond*

Figure 5.3 Raphael Tuck & Sons. 'Geisha Standing in front of Open Gate' of Life in Japan series, 1906. Photographic postcard. Tuck DB Postcards. 1727. https://tuckdbpostcards.org/items/50435. Accessed 12 August 2021.

ground and to make an aesthetic drapery. Photography is usually created by the photographer and the subject. But pictures on postcards need one more creator to be completed, who holds an absolute power over the image, i.e. they incarnate the image in the process of communicating. Here, the Japanese woman, her kimono, her hand holding it, the drapery and all resided in the sender and the recipient's communication. The image was widely circulated but never extensively shared, enabling a closed visual experience.

There are countless postcards with these everyday conversations and messages and most do not mention anything about the picture printed on the front. One example, however, does refer to the Japanese people depicted in the photograph; a postcard showing a Japanese man and woman in western attire has an interesting message in very informal English (Figures 5.4 and 5.5). Although this postcard does not exactly show 'kimonos', the imagery of Japanese people wearing something other than a kimono should also be considered being part of sartorial Japonisme. It was sent to Mr. Frederick Sutherden near Rye, Sussex on 1 September 1905. Searching on a present-day map, this postcard was sent to an incredibly isolated house surrounded by grassland and a lake, with no other houses nearby. According to the 1911 census record, there were two Fredericks (father and son) who lived at this address and both were fishermen. This postcard was probably sent to the son, who was twenty years old, in 1905. The son later joined the army during the First World War and was killed in action in 1917.[7] The message was written on both sides of the postcard. The text on front says:

Circulating Beyond 145

Figure 5.4 Raphael Tuck & Sons. 'Geisha & Young Man in Western Dress' of Life in Japan series, 1905. Photographic postcard. Tuck DB Postcards. 1729. https://tuckdbpostcards.org/items/50442. Accessed 12 August 2021.

'Oh' anything like this I do enjoy, I only wish, it was my dear Boy.
and the text on back continues,
Ain't this a bit of alright 'Aye' not half.

The message written here uses English slang: 'A bit of alright' means a sexually attractive person, usually a woman. 'Aye' means 'yes', and 'not half' is an abbreviation of 'not half bad' which is used to express agreement. The message on the front and back is similar to the type of conversation between two men when observing a person who they find attractive as if they are recalling a conversation from the past. It is impossible to know what they actually meant by this message, but 'my dear boy' could refer to the Japanese man (or a young boy) depicted in the picture on the front, who looks very young and slightly feminine. It is also possible that the sender and the receiver had previously had a laugh or funny moment about something which the image on the postcard reminded them of.

The consumers' engagement with postcards and the images depicted on the front was intimate; therefore, each card created a unique and one-and-only meaning to circulate as a personal communication. The three pictures of Japanese people depicted in postcards shown here had comforting or joke effect, which was elicited only by being unified with everyday messages.

Raphael Tuck & Sons also published a series of postcards that show two western girls in kimono-like garments in various poses. This series is not named as a whole, but all the

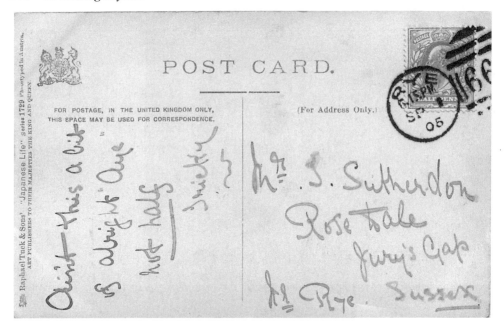

Figure 5.5 Raphael Tuck & Sons. Back of 'Geisha & Young Man in Western Dress' of Life in Japan series, 1905. Photographic postcard. Tuck DB Postcards. 1729. https://tuckdbpostcards.org/items/50442. Accessed 12 August 2021.

postcards show the same two models in the same dress in front of the same backdrop. While the costumes worn by the models look less like authentic Japanese kimonos, the titles of each postcard ('Two Little Japs', 'Two Little Japanese Blossoms' and 'Two Little Geishas') indicate that their costumes were supposed to look 'Japanese'. One, for example, shows the models holding a fan behind their heads, their hair is decorated with flowers and *obi-* belts are wrapped high around their chests. Most importantly, their supposed kimonos have been highly modified – the hems have been sliced open to show a pleated under-skirt which is reminiscent of the Japanese-themed tea gowns fashionable among upper and upper-middle-class women from the 1870s.

Miles and Neath, who discuss the popularity of Japanese-inspired dress in Australian portrait photographs in the early twentieth century, believed that cross-cultural dressing was not only a staging of Orientalist fantasies of 'the exotic other' but reflected their own experiences of modernity and femininity (545–546). Also, Verity Wilson, who has studied 'cross-cultural dressing' in Britain and the United States, argued that 'Clothes from elsewhere had the power to hold back the banality of everyday life' (148). Both arguments can be applied to the postcards of the two girls in kimonos; the girls are experiencing an appropriated and translated idea of 'Japan' and 'the Japanese', in the most tangible way. Wilson also argued that western interpretations of Japanese dress referred 'not so much to styles of clothing but to ways of thinking and perceiving' (144). The costumes worn by the girls in the postcards are far from the reality of actual Japanese life, but they signify an idea and an image of 'Japan' and 'the Japanese' – an image nurtured mostly during the Victorian period, among the upper and upper-middle classes.[8]

Circulating Beyond 147

Figure 5.6 Raphael Tuck & Sons. 'Two little Geishas', 1904. Photographic postcard. Tuck DB Postcards. 571. https://tuckdbpostcards.org/items/49876. Accessed 12 August 2021.

A variety of messages, from birthday wishes to everyday notes, were conveyed on the postcards from this series. One of the postcards showing the two girls in kimonos posing with a fan was sent to Miss May Hookway at St. Germans in Cornwall on 26 December 1904 (Figure 5.6). It is a birthday card with a message written on the front. The recipient is possibly Annie May Hookway who, according to the 1901 census record, lived in St. Germans and was aged twenty-one or twenty-two in 1904. In 1901, Annie May Hookway was working as grocer, draper and postmistress's assistant. What can be seen from this postcard is that it was a birthday card sent to a young working woman, and the picture was probably selected for aesthetic and decorative reasons.

As discussed earlier, dressing up as 'Japanese' allowed the wearers to have an extraordinary experience that has much deeper connection to the western fashion than to the Japanese reality. At children's luxury fancy dress balls, dressing up as the characters from *The Mikado* and *The Geisha* was highly popular among the young girls at the end of Victorian period.[9] Cross-cultural dressing had been vastly embraced by the people from the upper and middle classes from the late Victorian to the early twentieth century. However, these well-discussed experiences of kimonos were greatly different from the everyday lives of the working-class women such as the recipient of this postcard, Miss May Hookway, and the sender, Lena. However, the sender and the recipient actually appropriated the image impregnated with the experience of kimonos through writing, circulating and communicating instead of just 'receiving' the image as an 'observer'. The 'a Happy Birthday' written on the photograph is clearly violating what had been safely

148 *Circulating Beyond*

protected within the image, i.e. the image that had been nurtured within the fashionable cultures of the past.

Another four postcards from this series showing young girls in kimonos seem to be exchanged between the same people. The English written on them is slightly inadequate, which suggests that the sender may have been a young person. The postmarks are both faded, so it is hard to see which was sent first, but all were exchanged sometime in 1907. They are from a 'Winnie' to a 'Miss G. Irwin' of Greenwich, South East London, and the receiver is possibly Gwendolina Ada Irwin, who was twelve years old in 1907. According to the 1911 census record, she was the daughter of John Wallis Irwin who was a coal dealer. It seems that Miss Irwin was collecting postcards and that she and Winnie occasionally exchanged them. One that probably sent on 18 February 1907 reads:

Dear G/ Thank you for p.c./ I liked it very much./ hope you will like this one/ love from Winnie[10]

Another postcard was sent on 27 February 1907 reads:

Dear G/hope you will like this one, thank you for the one you sent me with love from Winnie[11]

Another postcard sent sometime in 1907 reads:

Dear G/ I hope you will like this one. I forgot to get the one you wanted, but will find it next time/ Winnie[12]

The message suggests that Miss Irwin wanted a specific kind of postcard and probably asked Winnie to get one for her. The last example reads:

Dear G/ Thank you very much for postcard I like it very much. I hope you will like this one/ from Winnie[13]

What is important here is that Winnie and Miss Irwin were experiencing their own version of Japonisme through selecting and exchanging these postcards, which they experienced several times. Miss Irwin clearly had developed her own taste in Japonisme postcards.

Since Japonisme first arrived in Britain, kimonos have been depicted in a variety of ways. Many previous researchers have studied how kimonos (and kimono-related garments) have been seen in paintings and on display and have adorned a variety of bodies and bodily movements. Such representations were absorbed and adapted by British fashion. However, it is important to note that only a small number of people experienced kimonos; indeed, most of the population in contemporary Britain experienced none of these activities for themselves. What was depicted in the series of the two girls in kimonos was the representation of Japonisme developed in the period prior to the postcard's arrival in Britain. Postcards, therefore, provided a much more popular and public experience of kimonos, and to a much wider audience.

Most importantly, postcards also offered a personal experience that the sender/ recipient could take an active role in. The sender of a postcard could select the card and add something to it, to make it their own. A card with the sender's own message was a unique, personal and original experience no matter how often the same postcard was duplicated. Furthermore, as seen in the examples of Miss Irwin, individual taste and the ability to choose are part of the experience of the postcard. The kimono-inspired tea gowns were no longer an imagery to 'observe' from a distance, but they are instead in a profound relationship with the consumers. The images on postcards were deliberately chosen and given a new meaning by each sender and caused some various effects on each recipient, allowing some of the members of the working classes to finally experience kimonos and Japonisme instead of just 'observing' what's presented. Therefore, while the British upper and upper-middle classes purchased Japanese goods and clothes from shops and department stores to adorn themselves or their houses, postcards enabled Japonisme to be appropriated by the working-class people and to circulate across Britain, as a cheap and easy means of communication.

Postcards are a form of communication which unite image, message and the sender/recipient all with one piece of card even though these elements are not always consistent. Whether the sender refers to the picture or not, the words, illustrations or symbols put directly onto postcards 'complete' the object and reframe the image printed on the surface of a card. As illustrated in the examples above, the 'Japan', 'Japanese' and 'Japonisme' subject matter is not limited to one stereotypical representation or interpretation. The consumer may attach all sorts of meanings which provide a unique message that adds personality to an everyday conversation, the visualisation of a shared private joke or an exotic gift sent along with birthday wishes.

This research suggests that Edwardian postcards are the ultimate process of appropriating images. The definition of the term 'image' differs depending on the disciplines and the fields of study as referenced in Introduction. An anthropologist, Hans Belting, attempted to bring the 'living body' back to the discussion of visual images during the 2000s (3). He defines 'image' as (1) 'a product of a given medium' such as 'photography, painting, or video' and (2) 'a product of our selves' such as 'dreams, imaginings, personal perceptions' and continues that it was 'the act of *fabrication* and the act of *perception*' that our living body associates with the images (3). In this argument, however, the tangible interaction with our living bodies is completely neglected from the discussion of body and image.

Instead, focusing on the material aspect of picture postcards and referencing material culture studies help present the third significant interaction between visual image and living bodies: the act of transformation, or perhaps, the act of violation. Daniel Miller explains 'consumption' as 'work done upon the object', which is to transform the object 'by its intimate association with a particular individual or social group, or with the relationship between these' (190, 191). Judy Attfield terms this process as 'the materialisation of identity' (148).[14] The Postcard is both an image and an object, connecting visual and material culture in most popular way. The images attached on cards were constantly revised in relation to the living bodies within the banal repetition of everyday lives, which is how the image of kimonos were appropriated by individuals, in this case, who were not often believed as the generators of Japonisme that were reproduced in the photographs.

Kimonos for Cross-Dressing, 1905

The final section of this book will be dedicated to the most radically subverted experience of kimonos enjoyed at the early twentieth century. The above shows the postcards depicting male-to-female cross-dressing in kimonos, which are held at the Wellcome

150 *Circulating Beyond*

Collection in London. The first one is posted on 4 December 1905 and shows two male cross-dressers dressed in thin printed cotton kimonos. With fans attached to their hair and winged eyeliner, they mimic the most notable characteristics of the 'three little maids' from *The Mikado* (Figure 5.7). The second example is posted on 9 December 1905 depicting a figure dressed in a full-length kimono, wearing a wig of a popular hairstyle of the 1900s and posing behind a screen (Figure 5.8). As discussed earlier, the postcard holds an outstanding agency to allow the handlers to violate and appropriate the image, which is also the case in the postcards discussed in this section. But, while the previous examples reproduced the well-used images of Japonisme, the scenes printed on Figures 5.7 and 5.8 themselves already violated the conventional social protocol of contemporary Britain. Thus, these postcards demonstrate multi-layered radical experiences of kimonos to both the wearers of kimonos in the photographs and the handlers of the postcards.

To begin with, let us discuss kimonos and the cross-dressing habits of Edwardian Britain. Cross-dressing was one of the most important sartorial phenomena in fashion history of the late Victorian and Edwardian periods. Cross-dressing means dressing up as the opposite sex, and it had several cultural and social meanings among Victorian people that differed between male and female impersonations.[15] Female-to-male cross-dressing was often used as social and political claim that intended to liberate women by demanding women's rights from earlier periods in Euro-American countries. Dianne Sachko Macleod introduced the Turkish trousers worn by aristocratic women in elite circles in the late Victorian period and argues that this 'cross-cultural cross-dressing' was an example that 'transformed the exotic "other" into a vehicle for gender change' (67). On the contrary, it could also be sometimes eroticised, especially on stages. There were, thus, two opposed images of male impersonation that formed a contradiction between the female reformers' claims and the male gaze.

In case of male-to-female cross-dressing, there was a tension between criminalised and 'safe' cross-dressing in this era. Female impersonation was often demonised by being associated with the homosexual acts that were made illegal in 1885.[16] In the second half of the nineteenth century, multiple sexually based crimes were widely reported in the media across Britain, including the arrest of Thomas Earnest Boulton (1847–1904) and Frederick William Park (1846–1881) in 1870; the police raid at a fancy dress ball in Manchester in 1880 that resulted in the arrests of 47 men, including female impersonators and finally, Oscar Wilde's trial in 1895, which accused Wilde for committing sodomy.

Although the cross-dressing in the streets was socially unacceptable and those who cross-dressed could be arrested, male-to-female cross-dressing was accepted and enjoyed as amusing entertainment on stage among the theatrical culture or in the special occasions such as fancy dress parties and the holiday dress-up events from the nineteenth century onwards. There were many extant photographs of famous female impersonators who were popular in theatres and music halls as well as of British citizens enjoying cross-dressing for special events.[17] The term 'drag' came to be used as 'feminine attire worn by a man' since 1870 according to the *Oxford English Dictionary*.[18] 'Drag' as a verb generally means 'to pull' or 'to draw', implying the association with the long trains of female dresses. Therefore, the cross-dressed performers in long and generally extravagant female dresses were often described as being 'in drag' since the late Victorian period.

The 'safe' male-to-female cross-dressing performed in theatres generally had two roles in Victorian and Edwardian entertainment. One of them is to mock the effeminate men or to laugh at them by stressing the 'ugliness' of the cross-dressed character.[19] According to Dominic Janes who studies Victorian queer dressing, the feminine fashion styles and delicacy of aesthetes and artists such as Wilde had been mocked in theatres and music

Figure 5.7 'Two Young Men in Drag Wearing Japanese Costumes', 1905. Photographic postcard. 13.7 × 8.6 cm. Wellcome Collection. 2043410i76. © Wellcome Collection, London.

Figure 5.8 'A Man in Drag', 1905. Photographic postcard. 14.2 × 8.8 cm. Wellcome Collection. 2044540i. © Wellcome Collection, London.

halls even before Wilde's trial, but the accusations of being a homosexual led to a boom in such lampoons (172). Male-to-female cross-dressing as a mockery of aesthetes or homosexuals contained both eroticism and disgust, denial and parody of something that was beyond the conventional gender ideals. Cross-dressing as parody reflects contemporary gender struggles.

The second role is to display the perfect and ideal femininity on stage, which came to be more popular in the twentieth century. One of the most successful female impersonators of the Edwardian era, Julian Eltinge (1881–1941), was not the object of laughter. He was a 'male actress' rather than a comedian, 'taking the lead in musical comedies using his pleasant light soprano voice to great effect' (Gardiner 37). There was nothing transgressive in their performances, but they were solely there as 'beautiful women'.

Some notable characteristics of both comedic and serious male-to-female cross-dressing that were also reflected in contemporary postcards. In either purpose, the most obvious is the representation of exaggerated feminine features via the reshaping of male bodies. In one postcard, Malcom Scott (1872–1929), a female impersonator who succeeded in theatres and music halls, parodied Camille Clifford of 'Gibson Girl' fame (Figure 5.9). Scott recreated Clifford's famous hourglass figure by reshaping his body into a voluptuous and clearly feminine one, possibly by using lacing and thick padding. Male-to-female cross-dressing in this era primarily existed as a representation of 'ideal' femininity, projecting an 'ideal' female body shape. The postcards of one of the most famous female impersonators of the Edwardian period, Julian Eltinge, disguised as a woman in

Figure 5.9 'Malcom Scott in character as a "Gibson Girl"', the 1910s. Photographic postcard. 13.7 × 8.5 cm. Wellcome Collection. 2044785i. © Wellcome Collection, London.

154   *Circulating Beyond*

a tight dress can also be easily found today.[20] His body was shaped into a stereotypically feminine silhouette that suggested what female body *should* be, rather than simply displaying a male body in female dress. Contemporary western female dresses required a certain body type, so many male cross-dressers moulded their body shapes when wearing dresses. The relationship between body and dress was, thus, not too overtly violated, as female dresses still framed 'female' bodies.

On Edwardian stage, the cross-dressing generally presented either 'male' or 'female' person; the deliberate blending of sexes was never attempted. In the world of art, however, the androgynous person of ambiguous gender was presented using Japanese elements by an artist from Brighton, Aubrey Beardsley, in the same year of Oscar Wilde's trial. Pursuing 'grotesque' expressions, Beardsley created several androgynous characters in his works. Among them, *The Mysterious Rose Garden* (1895) shows a figure with a moustache dressed in a floral-patterned kimono-like gown.[21] It is a well-known fact that Beardsley owned some Japanese *ukiyo-es*, and he was particularly interested in *shunga* [Japanese erotic *ukiyo-e* prints]. Elenora Sasso explained this figure in a kimono as 'a satanic Japanese figure of temptation' by comparing them with the figures depicted in Kitagawa Utamaro's *ukiyo-e* (51).[22] According to Sasso, the erotic expression of Utamaro's *ukiyo-e* was translated to gender ambiguity and its grotesqueness by Beardsley (51).

Chesa Wang shared a more in-depth view on Beardsley's interest in Japanese *ukiyo-es* in her article. Wang argued that it was *wakashu* [young Japanese boys who were 'both sexually ambidextrous and visually gender-ambiguous' (Wang)], who were often depicted in Japanese *shunga*, that particularly inspired Beardsley to create androgynous characters.[23] As Wang noted, it is unclear if Beardsley was aware of *wakashu* and their roles, it is likely that Beardsley came across them depicted in *shunga* for *wakashu* is one of the common characters in *shunga*. *Wakashu*, who commonly wears women's kimono, was often depicted as playing a submissive role in *shunga*, while Beardsley altered it to a 'satanic' character. Although this book will not explore this any further, it is important to note that gender ambiguity and the representation of androgyny were attempted through referencing Japanese *ukiyo-es* and the Japanese androgynous figures depicted in them. It is also important that this attempt was done rather safely done in Christian imagery.[24]

A historian, Grace E. Lavery, pointed out the 'queerness' of Japanese culture in her book chapter about the comic opera, *The Mikado*. She wrote, 'the strategic evasions both practiced and thematized by *The Mikado* [...] helped to install "Japan" as a placeholder object for queer men negotiating queer identities at the fin de siècle' (37). The queerness of Japan was either intentionally or unintentionally presented in Japonisme art and culture of the late Victorian period. What is extremely interesting and socially significant is that it was gender ambiguity and the queerness—rather than 'men' dressing up as women or *vice versa*—that was presented by using Japanese elements.

Gregory M. Pflugfelder discusses the relationship between the sartorial and tonsorial culture and gender from the early-modern to Meiji period in Japan, in which he proves that the sartorial codes of Edo Japan did not thoroughly rely on binary genders. According to Pflugfelder, 'Not only a sex/gender system but also an age/gender system occupies a central place in societal and cultural organization', referencing the acknowledged existence of male homosexuality as apparent in *wakashu* and *shudo* and the rather ambiguous dress codes of Japanese men of Edo-Japan (969). While the sartorial culture of Edo-Japan was not strictly ruled by the sexual dualism, it was in the Meiji period when the modernisation and the westernisation of Japan drew a strict line between men and women not only in their social roles but also in their attires:

> Instead, gender moved to the foreground in determining the individual's civic and societal obligations. More precisely, it was the genital distinction between male and female that came to outweigh other modes of defining gender, including the erotic triangle of "women, youths, and men" that Tokugawa popular culture had validated for more than two centuries' (970).

During the Meiji period, vast numbers of new rules on people's appearances were created, deciding how they should dress, what they can carry and what kind of hairstyles they can wear. The working men's uniforms were usually taken from the western precedents, adopting a new kind of masculinity that was represented by military uniforms and male suits, while Japanese women continued to wear kimonos. Among the rules set in Modern Japan, there was 'a Tokyo misdemeanour code of 1873, which prohibited males from attiring themselves as females, and females as males' (971).[25] In parallel to the change of masculinity in Japan, what people wore was also gendered in Meiji period, prior to which kimonos did not play many roles in representing 'genital distinction' or sexuality even though they were finely categorised depending on gender, age and social class. The material characteristic of a Japanese kimono, i.e. it is always shapeless to frame bodies inside as well as the semiotic existence, also liberated a kimono from the 'sex/gender system' as Pflugfelder argues.

The kimonos used for cross-dressing seen in Figures 5.7 and 5.8, therefore, suggest that the boundary between male and female bodies was blurred and made almost genderless. The persons in Figure 5.7 are dressed in thin cotton kimonos with floral printed patterns, which could be available from a few shillings in Britain in the early twentieth century. Looking closely, it is obvious that it was not through their bodies that presented that it was female-impersonation that these two were trying to present in the photograph. With 'feminine' features, such as the floral patterns, scattered flowers, little fans and makeup, their attires are completed as female impersonation. Kimonos merely frame their bodies without any sashes or belts, which imply that their kimonos are open and barely hide their male bodies.

In Figure 5.8, the person wears a wig in the fashionable 'Gibson Girl' style. The quality of both the screen and the kimono is not very luxurious; this kind of kimono could probably be purchased at the local shops or small department stores for one or two shillings and was likely made of cotton printed with roses. Because his kimono seems to have no linings and be made of thin printed cotton, it could not shape the body into a voluptuous form like Scott's. Even though only half of the model's body is visible in the photograph, his body is clearly not fully transformed into a 'female' body as expected from cross-dressers in contemporary society.

Unlike male cross-dressers in western dresses, the men in kimonos in the postcards mentioned above exemplify 'gender switching' while leaving the wearers' bodies as they originally are. While these men were feminised by the 'feminine' props surrounding them, their bodies reflected nothing about an altered gender. Cross-dressed kimonos evoked a genderless body by allowing un-transformed male bodies to participate in female impersonation. While femininity was presented in props, patterns and makeup, the kimonos themselves blurred the boundary between male and female bodies by simultaneously

156 *Circulating Beyond*

projecting both genders and neither all at once. Here, the kimonos offered a radically subverted sartorial experience to the three wearers.

Now, it is also important to consider the 'work' done to each card, focusing on the 'materialisation of identity' through the radical images of kimonos. As written above, the postcard boom of the early twentieth century produced numerous kinds of postcards. There were many kinds of manufacturers from a massive postcard company such as Raphael Tuck & Sons to a small photography studio. People could even have their own photographs printed on postcards for a reasonable price, which they could then send to their friends or use as self-promotion.[26] The two postcards discussed in this section could also be privately made, leaving the possibility that the senders are also the models in the photograph.

Figure 5.7 was sent to a 'Miss Leonard ("She of the smile")' who lived or worked at a place on Lancaster Road, Fallowfield in Manchester. The post mark is on 4 December 1905. Miss Leonard and the address written on the card were not found in the contemporary records, while there are large properties on Lancaster Road today. There is a short rhyme written on the postcard which reads:

To a girl who for a "time will"
Be, dissatisfied with "rhyme, till"
She recollects that "I'm still"
Aware of idiom "Smile Bill"
Though she may not think it true
yet believe what I now say to you
That like "Sunny Jim" it is of course
Why? because it won't come off
its Force (of habit)[27]

The rhyme is possibly a pun on then-famous wheat-based breakfast cereal called 'Force', first manufactured in the United States in 1901 (Montague-Jones). The character of the product, 'Sunny Jim', became popular on billboard posters in the 1900s in Britain and the United States.[28] The story behind 'Sunny Jim' is that the character was first called 'Jimmy Dumps' turned into 'Sunny Jim' after having 'Force' (Montague-Jones). This playful rhyme was likely sent to make the receiver smile by playing on the words taken from the popular advertisement. The two cross-dressers in kimonos on the front side of the card show a unique combination with the rhyme that encouraged the receiver to smile, which might correlate the cultural tradition of cross-dressing as a joke or comedy in Edwardian Britain. Furthermore, the rhyme also holds a flirty and mysterious atmosphere, also reminding us of the understanding of cross-dressing as dubious and bizarre in the contemporary society.

Figure 5.8 was sent to a 'Miss Hadland'. She might have been living or working at the address written on the card, Bickwell House, Sidmouth in Devon. The card was sent on 9 December 1905. In the contemporary records, nothing about 'Miss Hadland' that was associated with this address was found, while there seemed to be some properties named 'Bickwell House' in Sidmouth in the 1900s.[29] Its message reads:

When shall we meet again/your time is drawing near/I am expecting exchange when we meet/Please don't forget/ Yours L M[30]

This message is highly simple but slightly implicative. It is unlikely that the message written on this postcard intended any jokes and the sender rather sounds in a hurry, expecting something from 'Miss Hadland'. The message is brief and has a lot of hidden meanings that weren't directly expressed. Only the sender and the recipient could find out what was the 'exchange' that was expected to happen between them. The secretive air of the message written on this card adds a seductive implication to the photograph on the front. The reciprocity of the image and the message created a secret enclosed space for 'Miss Hadland' and 'LM'.

The front and the back of postcards are definitely correlated. Messages are usually rooted in their everyday lives. Images on the front, on the contrary, are the fiction that is penetrated to the daily communication, being deliberately chosen to create some certain atmospheres that could only be shared between the handlers. The distinctive relationship between images and messages allows an exclusive experience of kimonos that is immensely diverse and exoteric but exceedingly intimate and private.

This chapter showed how postcards allowed Japonisme to be experienced much more broadly in Britain in the early twentieth century. What was depicted on Edwardian postcards was visually already different from *cartes de visites* of the former period. Especially, the depiction of the non-Europeans, including the Japanese, became much diverse, showing both the representations that focus on their bodies and their culture. However, in addition to the difference in representations of the Japanese people seen in the mediums of the new century, the material characteristics of postcards also made this experience unique. As discussed earlier, postcards were so much more than just a thing to 'observe' as opposed to *carte de visites*. Victorian consumers of *cartes de visites* could acquire, touch and observe *cartes* and what was depicted. Some people may have written words on them but ostensibly *cartes* existed to be 'observed', not altered or modified. On the contrary, postcards were only fully complete when written on—the meaning of the image could be rewritten and revised by the sender. The editing process made them a highly personal, creative and constantly changing medium. Thus, even the postcards that depicted the replica of the clichéd scenes of Japonisme of the former period could allow consumers of the postcards to appropriate and modify them as they please.

The experience of kimonos through postcards in Edwardian Britain allowed the working-class people to appropriate Japonisme through the process of rewriting, revising and recreating meanings. Although the adoption of kimonos in Britain has a long history, about 85% of the population was generally ignored as there was no contact at all. However, kimonos began to circulate across Britain and ended up being adopted beyond just the act of wearing or 'observing' but as a diverse, private and intimate everyday means of communication.

Using kimonos for cross-dressing casually violated the social taboos of Edwardian Britain. The kimonos worn by the male-to-female cross-dressers on postcards subverted the customs of British female impersonation. They blurred the boundary between male and female bodies by creating a genderless body. Kimono made the wearers' bodies 'ambiguous', which could be deeply associated with the 'queerness' of Japan understood in Victorian Japonisme. While reshaping male bodies was always necessary to fill western female dresses, shapeless garments such as kimonos could complete female impersonation with their bodies remaining as they were. Therefore, male-to-female cross-dressing in kimonos was in a grey area between the cross-dressing that could be considered socially acceptable and unacceptable.

158 *Circulating Beyond*

The images of cross-dressers in kimonos create each singular space, each holding different meanings when being combined with the works done on postcards by the handlers. By corresponding to the original stereotypes of cross-dressing of the Edwardian Britain, the images on postcards can produce a mysterious, subverted and non-conventional air to invite the handlers to that special space. These experiences connected the ordinary and the fantasy, allowing the one and only experience of kimonos within the communications of the 'masses'.

Notes

1 The short fiction by Dorothy Marsh published in the May 1920 issue of *Quiver*, 'The Pink Kimono: A Story of Values and Love', shows silk kimonos as the symbol of wealth and class. See Savas 'Changes in the Representation of Kimono and Kimono-clad Women in British Popular Fiction in the Early Twentieth Century' 90–92.
2 The advertisement in the *Illustrated London News* on 13 October 1877 says that a packet of cards was sold from 6d to 1s. See the *Illustrated London News*, 13 October 1877 358. Another advertisement from the *Lancashire Evening Post* on 19 December 1899 writes that a dozen of cards was sold from 2s. See the *Lancashire Evening Post*, 19 December 1899 1.
3 The man called 'J. Henniker Heaton' declared that '[n]ow the postcard is the letter of the poor' in his letter to *The Times* published on 14 March 1896. See Heaton 5.
4 Gillen noted that postcards were often not employed by the 'very poorest', but it can at least be noted that postcards were also commonly used by the working-class people considering from the examples she examined. See Gillen 490.
5 A millwright lived in Dundee, Scotland, John Sturrock wrote in his diary on 24 September 1864 that he 'went to Roger's and stood for my carte de visite'. He wrote about *carte de visite* several times between 1864 and 1865. See Whatley 10, 19, 76, 80.
6 The full message can be read in an online database, Tuck DB Postcards. https://tuckdbpostcards.org/items/50435. Accessed 11 February 2023.
7 Frederick's name is on Rye Harbour War Memorials in the Holy Spirit Church in Rye Harbour, East Sussex.
8 Tea-gown' is one of the earliest and popular forms that adapted Japanese characteristics, for it was widely worn by women of upper- and upper-middle-class since the 1870s. For more information on tea gown, see Sasai.
9 Sasai writes that there were many children who dressed up as 'Japanese' at the fancy dress balls during the 1890s. See Sasai 240–246.
10 The full message can be read in an online database, Tuck DB Postcards. https://tuckdbpostcards.org/items/49875. Accessed 11 February 2023.
11 The full message can be read in an online database, Tuck DB Postcards. https://tuckdbpostcards.org/items/49887. Accessed 11 February 2023.
12 The full message can be read in an online database, Tuck DB Postcards. https://tuckdbpostcards.org/items/49886. Accessed 11 February 2023.
13 The full message can be read in an online database, Tuck DB Postcards. https://tuckdbpostcards.org/items/49878. Accessed 11 February 2023.
14 Attfield refers to textile and clothes in particular, while the vast kinds of objects including picture postcards also involve 'the dynamic act of consumption' that are in deep association with 'the constructing of identities'. See Attfield 124–126.
15 'Male impersonation' means women dressing up as men and 'male impersonator' means the person who dresses up as a man. 'Female impersonation' and 'female impersonator' therefore defines the opposite.
16 The Criminal Law Amendment Act in 1885 made 'gross indecency' a crime in the UK, which remained in English law until 1967.
17 A lot of these photographs are held at the Wellcome Collection, London.
18 'Drag' was first used in *Reynold's Newspaper* on 29 May 1870.
19 The play titled *Charley's Aunt*, which was first performed at the Theatre Royal in Bury St. Edmunds, Suffolk in 1892, is probably the most famous performance that is with a cross-dressed character. Charley's aunt was played by an English comedian William Sydney Penley (1851–1912).

20 Many of them can be found in Wellcome Collection in London.
21 The print is held at the Victoria and Albert Museum in London. The accession number for this work is E. 379–1899.
22 Sasso particularly points out the similarity to Utamaro's *Teahouse Maidens under a Wisteria Trellis* (1795). See Sasso 51.
23 Informed by Yui Hayakawa, University of Tsukuba.
24 Beardsley remarked that *The Mysterious Rose Garden* 'represent[ed] nothing more or less than the Annunciation' in an article titled 'Apostle of the Grotesque' in *The Sketch*, 10 April 1895. See 'An Apostle of the Grotesque' 562.
25 The 1873 code resulted many arrests in Tokyo during the 1870s. The ban of cross-dressing was no longer included in 1880 but the discriminatory ideas on cross-dressing stayed afterword. For more on the ban of cross-dressing in Meiji Japan, see Mitsuhashi or Sakazume.
26 According to the advert from the *Pearson's Weekly* on 9 March 1905, the place called 'Portrait Postcard Studio' in London made 6 cards for 1s and 6d.
27 The full message can be read in the Wellcome Collection. The reference number is 2043410i. https://wellcomecollection.org/works/qkvtzsne/items. Accessed 27 February 2023.
28 The Victoria and Anbert Museum holds a poster of 'Force', reproducing the character 'Sunny Jim'. The accession number for this work is E.56–1973.
29 According to the record of Sidmouth Town Council, a local architect, R. W. Sampson (1866–1950) built a house named 'Bickwell House' for his own occupation in 1903. But 'Miss Hadland' was not found in association with Sampson in the census record of 1901 and 1911. For the information of the houses built by Sampson in Sidmouth, see Sampson Houses Database – August 2014 at Sidmouth Town Council's website. https://www.sidmouth.gov.uk/images/Sampson_Houses_Database_Aug_2014.pdf. Accessed 27 February 2023.
30 The full message can be read in the Wellcome Collection. The reference number is 2044540i. https://wellcomecollection.org/works/bm7cbvev/items. Accessed 27 February 2023.

Works Cited

Anon. 'A History of the British Picture Postcard'. *Royal Mail*, https://www.royalmail.com/postcards. Accessed 8 February 2021.

Anon. 'An Apostle of the Grotesque'. *The Sketch*, 10 April 1895, pp. 561–562.

Anon. *Ashton Weekly Reporter, and Stalybridge and Dukinfield Chronicle*, 28 June 1862, p. 1.

Anon. *51st Report of the Postmaster General on the Post Office*. Eyre and Spottiswoode, 1905.

Anon. 'Our Eastern Ally: facts about Japan's Strength and Resources'. *The Penny Illustrated Paper*, 22 February 1902, p. 116.

Anon. *Richmond & Ripon Chronicle*, 1 December 1866, p. 8.

Anon. *The Lancashire Evening Post*, 19 December 1899, p. 1.

Anon, 'The World's First Postage Stamp'. *The British Library*, https://www.bl.uk/collection-items/the-worlds-first-postage-stamp. Accessed 8 February 2021.

Attfield, Judy. *Wild Things: The Material Culture of Everyday Life*. Berg, 2000.

Auslander, Leora. 'Beyond Words'. *The American Historical Review*, vol. 10, no. 4, 2005, pp. 1015–1045.

Barthes, Roland. *Camera Lucida: Reflections on Photography*. Hill & Wang, 1981.

Belting, Hans. *An Anthropology of Images: Picture, Medium, Body*. Translated by Thomas Dunlap, Princeton UP, 2011 [first published by Verlag Wilhelm Fink in German in 2001].

Benthien, Claudia. *Skin: On the Cultural Border between Self and the World*. Translated by Thomas Dunlap, Columbia UP, 2002 [first published by Rowohlt Taschenbuch Verlag GmbH in German in 1999].

Buckley, Cheryl and Hazel Clark. *Fashion and Everyday Life: London and New York*. Bloomsbury, 2017.

Colomb, John C. R. 'The Treaty with Japan'. *The Times*, 20 February 1902, p. 12.

Crary, Jonathan. *Techniques of the Observer: On Vision and Modernity in the Nineteenth Century*. MIT Press, 1992.

160 *Circulating Beyond*

Cure, Monica. *Picturing the Postcard: A New Media Crisis at the Turn of the Century*. U of Minnesota P, 2018.

Didi-Huberman, Georges. *Devant l'image: Question posée aux fins d'une histoire de l'art*. Les Éditions de minuit, 1990.

———. *Ouvrir Vénus: Nudité, rêve, cruauté*. Editions Gallimard, 1999.

Edwards, Elizabeth. 'Evolving Images: Photography, Race and Popular Darwinism'. *Endless Forms: Charles Darwin Natural Science and the Visual Arts*, edited by Diana Donald and Jane Munro, Yale UP, 2009, pp. 166–193.

Freedberg, David. *The Power of Images: Studies in the History and Theory of Response*. U of Chicago P, 1989.

Gagnier, Regenia. *Individualism, Decadence and Globalization: On the Relationship of Part to Whole, 1859–1920*. Palgrave Macmillan, 2010.

Gardiner, James. *Who's a Pretty Boy Then?: One Hundred & Fifty Years of Gay Life in Pictures*. Serpents Tail, 1997.

Gidoni-Goldstein, Ofra. 'Kimono and the Construction of Gendered and Cultural Identities'. *Ethnology*, vol. 38, no. 4, 1999, pp. 351–370.

Gilbert, Pamela K. *Victorian Skin: Surface, Self, History*. Cornell UP, 2019.

Gillen, Julia. 'Writing Edwardian Postcards'. *Journal of Sociolinguistics*, vol. 17, no. 4, 2013, pp. 488–521.

Heaton, Henniker J. 'The Twelve Tables of Postcard Law'. *The Times*, 14 March 1896, p. 5.

Heffer, Simon. *The Age of Decadence: Britain 1880–1914*. Windmill Books, 2017.

Henning, Michelle. 'The Subject as Object: Photography and the Human Body'. *Photography: A Critical Introduction*, 3rd Edition, edited by Liz Wells, Routledge, 2004, pp. 159–192.

Janes, Dominic. *Oscar Wilde Prefigured: Queer Fashioning and British Caricature, 1750–1900*. U of Chicago P, 2016.

Johnson, Donald Clay and Helen Bradley Foster, editors. *Dress Sense: Emotional and Sensory Experiences of the Body and Clothes*. Berg, 2007.

Kirk, Anna Marie. 'Japonisme and Femininity: A Study of Japanese Dress in British and French Art and Society, c. 1860–c. 1899'. *Costume*, vol. 42, 2008, pp. 111–129.

Kramer, Elizabeth. '"Not so Japan-Easy": The British Reception of Japanese Dress in the Late Nineteenth Century'. *Textile History*, vol. 44, no. 1, 2013, pp. 3–24.

Lavery, Grace E. *Quaint, Exquisite: Victorian Aesthetics and the Idea of Japan*. Princeton UP, 2019.

Macleod, Dianne Sachko. 'Cross-Cultural Cross-Dressing: Class, Gender and Modernist Sexual Identity'. *Orientalism Transposed: Impact of the Colonies on British Culture*, edited by Julie F. Codell and Dianne Sachko Macleod, Routledge, 1998, pp. 63–85.

Miles, Melissa and Jessica Neath. 'Staging Japanese Femininity: Cross-cultural Dressing in Australian Photography'. *Fashion Theory*, vol. 20, no. 5, 2016, pp. 545–573.

Miller, Daniel. *Material Culture and Mass Consumption*. Basil Blackwell, 1987.

———. 'Why Some Things Matter'. *Material Cultures: Why Some Things Matter*, edited by Daniel Miller, UCL Press, 1998, pp. 3–21.

Mitsuhashi, Junko 三橋順子. *Josou to nihon-jin* 女装と日本人 [*Female Impersonation and Japanese*]. Koudansha 講談社, 2008.

Montague-Jones, Guy. 'Force Cereal Axed after 112 years of Production'. *The Grocer*, 26 January 2013. https://www.thegrocer.co.uk/cereals/force-cereal-axed-after-112-years/235914.article. Accessed 27 February 2023.

Nordau, Max. *Degeneration* [translated from the second edition of the German work]. London, William Heinemann, 1895.

Pflugfelder, Gregory M. 'The Nation-State, the Age/Gender System, and the Reconstitution of Erotic Desire in Nineteenth-Century Japan'. *The Journal of Asian Studies*, vol. 71, no. 4, 2012, pp. 963–974.

Pretorius, Fransjohan. 'The Boer Wars'. *BBC History*, 29 March 2011, http://www.bbc.co.uk/history/british/victorians/boer_wars_01.shtml#six. Accessed 8 February 2021.

Saito, Yuriko. *Aesthetics of the Familiar: Everyday Life and World-Making*. Oxford UP, 2017.

———. *Everyday Aesthetics*. Oxford UP, 2007.

Sakazume, Satomi 坂詰智美. '"Ishiki kaii jyorei" no naka no gender' 「違式註違条例」のなかの ジェンダー ['Gender in Ishiki-kaii Ordinance']. *The Journal of Law and Political Science* 専修 法学論集, vol. 128, 2016, pp. 1–24.

Sasai, Kei 佐々井啓. *Victorian Dandy: Oscar Wilde no fukusyoku-kan to 'atarashi onna'* ヴィ クトリアン・ダンデイ：オスカー・ワイルドの服飾観と「新しい女」 [*Victorian Dandy: Oscar Wilde's Fashion Theory and the 'New Woman'*]. Keisou Shobou 勁草書房, 2015.

Sasso, Elenora. *The Pre-Raphaelites and Orientalism: Language and Cognition in Remediations of the East*. Edinburgh UP, 2018.

Savas, Akiko サワシュ晃子· '20 seiki syotou no eikoku ni okeru nihonsei yusyutsuyou kimono no ryutsu to nichiei gyousha no sougo kousyou ni tsuite 20 世紀初頭の英国における日本製輸出用 キモノの流通と日英業者の相互交渉にいて ['Japanese Kimonos for the British Market at the Beginning of the 20th Century']. *Journal of the Japan Society of Design*, vol. 65, 2014, pp. 15–29.

———. '20 seiki syotou no eikoku no taisyu shosetsu ni okeru kimono to kimono Sugata no josei hyoushou no henka' 20 世紀初頭の英国の大衆小説におけるキモノとキモノ姿の女性表 象の変化ーキモノブームという視点からー ['Changes in the Representation of Kimono and Kimono-clad Women in British Popular Fiction in the Early Twentieth Century']. *Studies in Japonisme*, vol.35, 2015, pp. 77–95.

———. 'Dilute to Taste: Kimonos for the British Market at the Beginning of the Twentieth Century'. *International Journal of Fashion Studies*, vol. 4, no.2, 2017, pp. 157–181.

Teulie, Gilles. 'Orientalism and the British Picture Postcard Industry: Popularizing the Empire in Victorian and Edwardian Homes'. *Cahiers victoriens et édouardiens*, vol. 89, Spring, 2019.

Tucker, Jennifer. *Nature Exposed: Photography as Eyewitness in Victorian Science*. John Hopkins UP, 2005.

Wang, Chesa. 'Aubrey Beardsley: Understanding Androgyny Through Shunga'. *Erudition Magazine*, 29 April 2021, https://www.eruditionmag.com/home/aubrey-beardsley-understanding-androgyny-through-shunga. Accessed 7 September 2021.

Whatley, Christopher A, eds. *The Diary of John Sturrock: Millwright, Dundee 1864–1865*. Tuckwell Press, 1996.

Wilson, Verity. 'Western Modes and Asian Clothes: Reflections on Borrowing Other People's Dress'. *Costume*, vol. 36, no. 1, 2013, pp. 139–157.

Conclusion

One mission of this book was to collect the elements, clues and figures—however, small, ordinary and, therefore, insignificant they may seem—that showed the paths and traces that Japan and the kimono as an image, material, concept and metaphor took in Britain during the late nineteenth and early twentieth century, which allowed us to recognise the overall picture of sartorial Japonisme that included the spaces and people in Britain and in Japan that had generally been excluded from the previous studies.

The reference to Japan in Britain began with fine arts in the second half of the 1860s and then permeated the mainstream fashion of upper and upper-middle-class women. Since 1885, kimonos and human bodies (both British and Japanese) could have been observed for around a shilling at the Japanese Native Village, and some Japanese-themed comic operas and musical comedies opened in West End theatres. Since the 1900s, the kimono—not just characteristics of it but its form and shape—began to be adopted more widely as an indoor gown. Kimono-shaped gowns became a cliché as indoor gowns for upper- and middle-class women. Furthermore, the Japanese kimono (and related gowns) was also uniquely adopted and enjoyed within popular cultures of fancy dress, cross-dressing and acrobat performances. Finally, bodies in kimonos were featured in the cheapest and easiest mode of communication of the early twentieth century: postcards. Thus, within a roughly fifty-year span from 1865 to 1914, the kimono changed its function from a decorative and fashionable object to a cheap means of everyday communication circulated across the country.

The kimono, not only as a dress but also as an idea, existed everywhere from the high society to the popular culture in which kimonos especially subverted, deviated or transcended the cultural clichés and the social norms. The experience of kimonos within popular culture showed the process of restructuring Japonisme while simultaneously making some radical influences on the cultures and society in Britain. The agency of kimonos was not only effective in taking British people away from their comfort zone by the kimono's exoticness, but the ideas regarding kimonos created and nurtured within Britain also had a power to create spaces for unusual, radical and shifting responses and reactions. Sartorial Japonisme did not only exist thoroughly for Fashion with the capital F or within the history of trade but was freely variegated and widely pervaded by the contemporary individual.

'Experience' was the key concept in the process of writing about the kimonos in Victorian and Edwardian Britain, which gave me a manifold perspective of a phenomenon, an object or an image. The experience of kimonos discussed in this book involved to wear, to choose, to buy, to paint, to interpret, to observe, to destroy, to conceive and to converse with kimonos. Experience, which means how we act, think, perceive and imagine in

DOI: 10.4324/9781003334255-7

cycles of tension and resolution, is relevant to any people anywhere; the physical contact or the possession of the subject is not the main concern in this argument. Examination of the experiences of kimonos cannot exclude micro-level considerations such as the various interactions and encounters with people. By taking an interdisciplinary approach, this study illustrated that the effects of kimonos also reached the working-class community in the early twentieth century, which was generally overlooked in the academic studies of Japonisme. In circulation, the power of kimonos was found on many different occasions in Britain from 1865 to 1914, showing that the kimono was not just a fashionable or exotic garment but provided various experiences to the various kinds of spaces and people of different backgrounds, classes and genders than generally imagined.

Sartorial Japonisme and the Experience of Kimonos should be considered a process to understand the relationship between the kimono and the living people. Kimonos were brought to Britain as part of a cross-cultural consumption, but the sartorial Japonisme as an entire phenomenon should rather be understood as an intercultural experience that drifted through society beyond all kinds of boundaries and interacted with the individual human beings. Thus, the stories shared in this book reminded us of the significance of realising the material's capacity to transform cultures, society and lives. Each example, event and outcome are not suggested here as quiescent facts but as part of protensive connections that dominate every individual until today.

Index

Note: *Italic* page numbers refer to figures and page numbers followed by "n" denote endnotes.

aesthetes 9, 60–61, 65, 67, 72–74, 87–88, 114, 150, 153
aestheticism 9, 53n12, 60, 62, 118
aesthetic circle 59
aesthetic dress 9, 26, 35, 53n12, 61, 66–68, 73
aesthetic movement 9, 60–61, 65–66, 95
agency 6, 10, 12n1, 100, 111–112, 150, 162; material agency 6–7
Aglaia 65–66, 67, 87
Ainu 121–125, 133, 134n9, 135n10, 135n12
Ainu Home 122–125, 133
Alma-Tadema, Laura 26
Alma-Tadema, Laurence 26, 65
ancient Greece 33, 60, 65–66, 74
Anderson, Arthur 46
Angel in the House 46
Anglo-Japanese Alliance 128, 134n8, 141
amateur theatricals 9–10, 93, 105–109, *106, 107*
Appadurai, Arjun 7
Arts and Crafts Movement 60, 66, 112
Ashelford, Jane 43, 61
Attfield, Judy 149, 158n14
Auslander, Leora 7

Baldry, Alfred Lys 25, 53n8
Bantock, Leedham 46
Barnett, Henrietta 118
Barnett, Samuel 118
Beardsley, Aubrey 32–36, *32, 34, 35*, 53n16, 53n18, 154, 159n24; *Salomé* 33–35, *35*, 54n18
Beato, Felix 113, 134n5
Belting, Hans 6, 149
Bing, Samuel 60, 89n19
Bird, Isabella 8, 44
Boer, Inge 94, 140
Boulton, Thomas Earnest 150
Bowley, Arthur L. 76, 126, 135n15
Boyce, George Price 20–21

Brassey, Anna 44
Browning, Robert 29
Buhicrisan, Tannaker 111–112, 114, 125, 134n2
Burne-Jones, Edward 60, 65
Burty, Philippe 3

Callot Soeurs 74
carte de visites 139–140, 142, 157, 158n5
Carte, Richard D'Oyly 37–38, 106
Cavafy, George John 23
Chant, Laura Ormiston 132
charity bazaar 10, 93
Clark, Kenneth 16, 53n1
corset 27, 61, 67, 71, 74, 87, 100
Corwin, Nancy A. 113, 134n4
Crary, Jonathan 139
cross-dresser 11, 150, 154–158
cross-dressing 94, 149–150, 153–158, 159n25, 162
The Critetion theatre 46
Cure, Monica 138–139

The Daly's theatre 40, 43, *43–45*, 49
Debenham & Freebody 94
Devonshire House Ball 100, 102–103
Dewey, John 1
Diamond Jubilee 100
Didi-Huberman, Georges 12n2, 16, 53n1
drag 150, *151, 152*, 158n18
drapery 16, 25–26, 53n9, 53n10, 66, 87, 144
dress history 2–3, 7, 117

East End 117–118, 121
East Enders 117–118, 133
Edwardes, George 40, 106
Edwards, Elizabeth 139–140, 142
Edwards, John Passmore 118
Eicher, Joanne 2
The Egyptian Hall 125, 135n13

166 *Index*

Eltinge, Julian 153
Emery, Elizabeth 4, 53n3
everyday experience 1–2, 5, 11
exoticness 15, 108–109, 113, 162

fancy dress 9–10, 93–100, 96, 99, 102, 108–
    109, 109n6, 147, 150, 162
fancy dress ball 10, 93–94, 100, 102, 108,
    147, 150, 158n9
female impersonation 11, 150, 155, 157,
    158n15
First World War 84, 140, 144
Flower, Cyril 25
Formosa Hamlet 122–125
Fortuny, Mariano 74, 75, 89n18, 89n19
Fragonard, Jean-Honoré 25, 53n9
Freedberg, David 6
Fry, Roger 87
The Fuji Family 128, 135n14
Fukai Akiko 5, 38, 67, 74, 76

The Gamage's 80
Gartlan, Luke 113, 134n5
The Geisha 5, 36, 40, 42–47, 43–45, 49, 51–
    52, 54n25, 105, 108, 126, 147
Gillen, Julia 139, 142, 158n4
Gilroy-Ware, Cora 9, 12n4, 90n27
Godwin, Edward William 26, 66–67
The Grand Japanese Bazaar 103–105,
    108–109
Grimshaw, John Atkinson 22, 27–28, 30,
    53n13

Hann, Rachel 97, 109n1
hakama 72–73, 122, 128, 130
happi 129
Harrods 80
Haweis, Mary Eliza 62, 88n2
Healthy and Artistic Dress Union 65–66, 67
Heffer, Simon 140
Henning, Michelle 140
himation 72
Hirota Takashi 78
Hollander, Anne 25
The Holloway Empire 128, 135n14
Holt, Ardern 94–95, 98, 109n2; *Fancy Dresses
    Described* 94, 98, 99, 100, 109n2
Hotta-Lister, Ayako 121
'human zoo' 111–112, 141
The Humphrey's Hall 112, 115–117

industrialisation 60, 66, 112
Ingres, Jean-Auguste-Dominique 29

Jackson, Anna 113
The Japan-British Exhibition 10, 111, 121–
    125, 133, 134n8, 134n9, 141
Japanese acrobat troupes 125, 127, 134n2

The Japanese Native Village 10, 36–37, 49,
    54n25, 103, 111–117, 122–123, 125,
    127, 133, 141, 162
Jay, Isabel 47

Kaiser, Susan 2
Kanayama Ryota 36–37
Kawazoe Yu 128
Kift, Dagmar 126
King Edward VII 121
King George V 80
kimono-shaped gown 5, 8, 10–11, 43–44, 47,
    54n22, 54n23, 68, 70, 76, 80, 85, 87,
    162
The Kiralfy brothers 121, 123
Kirk, Anna Marie 26
Komeima Yukiko 5, 36
Koyama Noboru 36–37, 103, 111, 125, 134n2
Kume Kazusa 3, 62, 88n5

Lacambre, Geneviève 15
The Ladies' Field 105, 106–107, 108
The Lady 62
Lavery, Grace E. 38, 54n19, 154
Lee, Josephine 36–37
Leyland, Frederick Richards 22, 53n5
Liberty 38, 43, 54n22, 64–70, 70–72, 73,
    89n11, 89n12, 89n13; Liberty, Arthur
    65, 87
Lind, Letty 42, 44–45
The Lukushima Japanese troupe 128
The Lysistrata 32; *The Lysistrata of
    Aristophanes* 33–35, 53n16

MacKenzie, John M. 4, 112
Macleod, Dianne Sachko 150
Madame Butterfly (Puccini) 51
Meiji government 111–112, 125, 134n8, 141
Meiji period 78, 131, 154–155
The Merry Japs 126, 135n18
migimae 69
Miller, Daniel 6–7, 149
Miller & Franklin 84, 89n24
The Mikado 5, 9, 36–40, 42, 44, 47, 51,
    54n19, 54n20, 68, 95, 105, 108, 111,
    113, 126, 133, 147, 150, 154
Minato Chihiro 25, 53n9
Mitchell, Rebecca N. 94, 102
Miyatake Kimio 123–125, 135n11, 135n12
Moore, Albert 26, 53n8, 53n10, 60, 66, 67
Morris, William 60, 65, 104

Nagasawa Ishizo 114–115, 134n6
Nead, Lynda 16
New English Art Club 28
'New Japan' 10, 124, 132, 134, 141
New Women 46, 95
Nicklas, Charlotte 7

obi, *obi*-belt 8, 16, 18, 27, 43, 54n21, 59, 62, 65, 72–74, 102, 128, 134n5, 146
'Old Japan' 10, 37, 39, 66, 113–114, 116–117, 133, 141
Ono Ayako 3
Olympia (Manet) 29

Paiwan ethnic group 124
Paiwan people 124–125, 133
Paquin, Jeanne 74
Park, Frederick William 150
Peacock Room (Whistler) 22
Pearce, Susan 7
Pettigrew, Harriet Selina 29
Pettigrew, Rose Amy 30, 53n14
Pflugfelder, Gregory M. 154–155
Philip, Rosalind Birnie 24
Pitcher, William Charles 38; 'Wilhelm' 38, 54n20
Poiret, Paul 74, 96
Pollen, Annebella 7
Pomeroy, Florence Wallace 61
Post-Impressionist Exhibition 87, 89n25
Pre-Raphaelite 21, 32, 60–61, 117
Princess Alexandra 96, 97

The Queen 8, 62, 63, 118, 119, 121
Queen Mary 80
Queen Victoria 96, 100, 102, 109n4

Raphael Tuck & Sons 11, *132*, 139–140, *141*, 142, *143–147*, 145, 156
rational dress 61; rational dress movement 61; Rational Dress Society 61–62, 88n2, 88n4
Rossetti, Dante Gabriel 16, 20–22, *20*, 24, 53n4, 61, 65, 88n3; *The Beloved ('The Bride')* 20–21, *20*
Rossetti, William Michael 119
Rothenstein, William 29, *29*, 33, 54n17
Roussel, Théodore *28*, 28–31, 35; *The Reading Girl* 28, *28*, 30, 35
Royal Academy 26, 28, 30, 60
Ruskin, John 60, 66, 88n1

Said, Edward 4, 11, 12n6, 93; *Orientalism* 4
Saito Yuriko 2
Salmon, Arthur John Balliol 122
Santoi, Marie 126–127, 135n18, 135n19
Sasai Kei 5, 36, 38, 43, 46, 62, 68
Sasso, Elenora 21, 32, 35, 93, 102, 154, 159n22
Sassoon, Louise Judith 100, *101*, 102, 109n6
Sato Tomoko 21, 28
Savas, Akiko 5, 36, 47, 67, 80
The Savoy theatre 36–38, 111, 113
Second Boer War 140
Scott, Malcolm 153, *153*, 155

Shiino Shibey 67; Shiino Shobey Silk Store 67, 69
shudo 154
shunga 33–34, 154
Simmel, Georg 7
Social Darwinism 112, 140–141
Stead, Alfred 119
The St. Martin's Hall 125
Summers, Leigh 61

Takashimaya 76–80, *78–79*, 87, 89n20, 89n21; Takashimaya Historical Archive 76, *78–79*
Taylor, Lou 2–3
tea gown 8–9, 11, 22, 38, 43, 47, 51, 59, 62, *63*, 64–65, *64*, 68–69, 73, 80, 87, 89n7, 98, 100, 114, 146, 158n8
Tempest, Marie 40–42, *43*
Terry, Ellen 26, *27*
'thing to wear' 15, 22, 30
Tissot, James-Jacques-Joseph 15–16, *17–19*, 18, 21, 24, 26–27, 30, 53n2, 53n3; *Japanese Girl Bathing (Japonaise au Bain)* 16, *17*, 18, 26; *Young Lady Holding Japanese Objects* 18, *18*; *Young Women Looking at Japanese Articles* 18, *19*
Tomkinson, Michael 107–108
Torii Kiyonaga 24, *24*; *Minami Juni-ko* 24
The Toynbee Hall 118

Uji Village 123
ukiyo-e 23–26, 33–34, 66, 154
Utagawa Hiroshige 26

variety theatre 111, 125–128, 132–134

Wahl, Kimberly 26, 53n12, 61, 68, 88n2, 88n3
wakashu 154
Walford, Ambrose B. 119, 134n7
Wang, Chesa 154
Watanabe Toshio 3, 16, 21, 28
Wentworth, Michael 16
West End 5, 8–9, 15, 36–37, 51–53, 95, 105, 107, 162
The White Chrysanthemum 9, 46–47, *48*, 50–52, *50*, 126
Whitechapel Art Gallery 10, 111, 117–121, 133
The Whiteley's 80
Whistler, James Abbott McNeil 3, 16, 22–26, *22–23*, *25*, 30, 53n12, 60
Wild, Benjamin 97, 100, 109n4
Wilde, Oscar 33–34, 37, 51, 67, 89n10, 104, 108, 117, 150, 153–154
Wilson, Verity 146
Wirgman, Charles 113

168 Index

Woolf, Virginia 87, 90n26; *Orlando: A Biography* 87, 90n26
Worth, Charles Frederick 74, 96

Yamaguchi Eriko 21, 25, 53n10, 60
Yasumoto Kamehachi III 122

Yokohama Photography 113–114, 134n5
Yokoyama Toshio 3

Zatlin, Linda Gertner 33
Ziomek, Kirsten L. 123–124, 135n10